Classical Algorithms in C++

With New Approaches to Sorting, Searching, and Selection

Nicholas Wilt

John Wiley & Sons, Inc.

New York • Chichester • Brisbane • Toronto • Singapore

Publisher: Katherine Schowalter

Editor: Phil Sutherland

Assistant Editor: Allison Roarty

Managing Editor: Maureen B. Drexel

Text Design & Composition: Integre Technical Publishing Co., Inc.

Library of Congress Cataloging-in-Publication Data:
Wilt, Nicholas, 1970–
    Classical algorithms in C++: with new approaches to sorting,
    searching, and selection / Nicholas Wilt.
        p.   cm.
    Includes index.
    ISBN 0-471-10985-1 (acid-free paper)
    1. C++ (Computer program language)   2. Computer algorithms.
    I. Title.
    QA76.73.C153W553   1995
    005.1'33—dc20   95-7673
                                                             CIP

Printed in the United States of America

10 9 8 7 6 5 4 3 2 1

Contents

Acknowledgments

Portions of this book first appeared in article form in *PC Techniques*, *The C Users Journal* and *Dr. Dobb's Journal*.

I would like to thank Amna Greaves for needling me into deriving a fast rendering algorithm for Menger's Sponge, the lovely construct on the cover.

I'd like to thank my reviewers, anonymous and otherwise, for their many constructive suggestions. Thanks especially to my brother Mike on this count. Any errors that slipped through are entirely the fault of the author, of course.

I'd also like to thank the staff at John Wiley & Sons for making the creation of the book as pleasurable an experience as could have been expected. Paul Farrell was instrumental in pushing for the Menger's Sponge rendering on the cover, and Allison Roarty exhibited commendable patience and tolerance when work on the book suffered after a cross-continental move.

Finally, as always, I would like to thank my dearest Robin for being there. Your help with the technical figures is appreciated, but not as much as our partnership in life.

Introduction

Sorting, searching, and selection are a family of computer algorithms that help computers make sense of the data we throw at them.

Sorting, or placing items in order, is one of the most fundamental tasks that computers perform. Some of the earliest algorithms implemented on digital computers were sorting algorithms.

Searching is the efficient storage and retrieval of information by a computer.

Selection is a weak form of sorting: Instead of sorting the entire data set, we only want to know which item is the ith in the sorted order of N items. The median, for example, is computed by selecting the $(N/2)$th element in the sorted order. Selection is often neglected in implementation-minded algorithms books, and I have never understood why. It is closely related to the sorting and searching algorithms.

The common element that binds sorting, searching, and selection is that they operate on *sortable* data. Any two data elements can be compared to determine which should precede the other in a sorted order. Integers can be compared directly, often with a single machine instruction: 5 precedes 12 in the sorted order. Strings can be compared alphabetically: "Alpha" precedes "Beta" in the sorted order. When sorting and selecting, comparisons help us decide which elements should precede the others in the sorted order. When searching, comparisons point us in the direction to find a particular element.

Hundreds of sorting algorithms have been described in the literature. Selection Sort, Insertion Sort, and Shell Sort are a few of the asymptotically slow ones; Merge Sort, Quicksort, and Heapsort are a few of the asymptotically fast ones. We don't have room to discuss every sorting algorithm, but several sorting algorithms that meet a variety of needs are described in Part I.

Searching, covered in Part II, often entails data structures, not algorithms. Only two algorithms for searching are described, Linear and Binary Search. The remainder of the discussion of searching is devoted to dynamic data structures that can be inserted into, queried, and deleted from. *Linked lists* are a good, simple alternative when optimal asymptotic performance is not required. *Skip lists* are a randomized augmentation of linked lists that have better performance. *Binary trees* provide excellent average-case performance and form a theoretical basis for more sophisticated data structures; *red-black trees*, a type of binary tree, guarantee good worst-case performance; and *splay trees* are adaptive so that oft-accessed items in the tree can be accessed faster.

Selection, like searching, can be performed statically or dynamically. Part III begins by describing several algorithms for special cases of selection: minimum, maximum, and both minimum and maximum. For the general selection problem, we describe two algorithms and one data structure for selection. The first selection algorithm is closely related to Quicksort, and, like Quicksort, is asymptotically slow in the worst case. The second algorithm has an optimal worst-case runtime, at the price of reduced average-case performance. And for selection on dynamic data sets, a data structure called the *order statistics tree* is described.

Computer algorithms hold a special allure. Every implementation-minded aficionado of computer science knows that efficient algorithms are more important to fast programs than clever implementation strategies. Hand-coding a sorting algorithm in assembler does not guarantee that it will run quickly for a large number of inputs. Implementing a sorting algorithm whose runtime grows slowly as the number of inputs grows is much more important. Algorithms that are efficient in practice are the focus of this book.

Implementation

All of the algorithms and data structures in this book have been implemented in template-based C++. Templates allow generic descriptions of algorithms and data structures to be implemented for any data type. Once a template has been written, it can be used with any C++ class or data type, such as int or long. Templates are a fairly recent innovation in the ever-evolving C++ programming language, and not all compilers support them; however, they are so useful that I could not justify avoiding them for the source code in this book. The source code has been tested with a variety of compilers, including Borland C++, Microsoft Visual C++, and the Power Macintosh C++ compiler.

The C++ programming language has been growing steadily in popularity since its inception for two reasons. First, it is based on C, a popular third-generation programming language. Second, it contains many modern programming constructs to aid in the development of large and robust programming projects. These include object-oriented programming concepts such as data abstraction, data hiding, inheritance, polymorphism, and parameterized data types, as well as more mundane ideas such as type safety and exception handling. Because the majority of C++ is converted C, often it does not take advantage of these newer features. C++ has only begun to attain its potential as a programming language. In this book I hope to address that drawback for some of the most venerable algorithms in computer science.

Implementation Notes

Sometimes several implementations of a certain algorithm are given. Recursive and iterative implementations of many algorithms are given; and between two partitioning schemes and several different ways to choose a partitioning element, at least eight permutations of Quicksort are possible. Rather than simply presenting a single way to solve a problem, it seems better to present a variety and discuss the tradeoffs. No single implementation is ideal for all applications.

Object-oriented purists will be offended at some of the tradeoffs taken in the C++ code presented here. C-style arrays, described with base pointers and counts, are used instead of an abstract "Array" class or class template. The source code is intended to be useful right out of the box, a constraint that would be compromised by imposing a nonstandard representation on the reader. As it stands, the source code should be easy to incorporate into existing C code recently ported to C++ and not difficult to incorporate into C++ code that uses abstract representations of arrays.

Contacting the Author

Please direct feedback and questions about the book and source code to me, Nicholas Wilt, at CompuServe [75210,2455]. From the Internet, you can reach me at 75210.2455@compuserve.com.

About the Cover

The cover depicts Menger's Sponge, a beautiful fractal construct described by Leonard M. Blumenthal and Karl Menger in *Studies in Geometry* (W. H. Freeman and Company, 1970). A Menger's Sponge can be constructed by dividing a cube into a set of $3 \times 3 \times 3$ cubes, then removing one subcube from each face and the center (seven cubes total). Each of the 20 remaining cubes can then be recursively subdivided in the same way. The process can be repeated indefinitely, resulting in finer and finer detail. The complexity of the Sponge increases exponentially as you increase the number of levels of subdivision.

Observant readers are probably looking at the cover and wondering what possible relationship it has with the material in the book. Menger's Sponge gracefully blends a regimented, orderly appearance with an inherently chaotic character: We can never know exactly what it looks like because there is no limit to the number of subdivisions required to construct one. So before making a picture of Menger's Sponge, we must decide on the complexity desired. In this way, the Sponge is a wonderful visual representation of the delicate balance between the order and chaos needed for efficient sorting, searching, and selection. The algorithms described herein have to impose order on the input data to work properly, but the less work they put into ordering the data, the faster they go. For example, Hoare's selection algorithm doesn't have to sort the input array completely to get its job done, so it does not; and therefore it runs much faster than the sort would. As when rendering the Sponge, we chose the level of complexity desired.

Rendering Algorithm

The Menger's Sponge shown on the cover has been subdivided four times and contains $20^4 = 160,000$ cubes. If the six sides of each cube were modeled using four polygons (a top piece, two side pieces, and a bottom piece), 3.84 million polygons would be needed to model this Sponge. Since it was rendered using a ray tracing algorithm, that would take a prohibitive amount of time. Even on a million-dollar SGI workstation, the time to render Menger's Sponge with polygons increases exponentially with its complexity.

Therefore, instead of modeling the Sponge with polygons, it was rendered procedurally using an algorithm based on voxel traversal. The voxel traversal algorithm was originally used for uniform spatial subdivision, a method to make ray tracing faster; however, it was easily adapted to render Menger's Sponge instead.

The ray intersection routine computes the lower and upper limits of the ray's intersections with the bounding box of the Sponge. It then steps through the Sponge using the voxel traversal algorithm, testing for intersection (if required) at each juncture. No matter how complex it is, the Sponge is very dense, and most rays find an intersection after only a few steps. Thus, the procedural algorithm is asymptotically much faster than trying to model the Sponge using polygons. (The runtime no longer increases exponentially with the Sponge's complexity.)

The resulting algorithm is extremely fast. While the Sponge is lit by two light sources, it still only took 25 minutes to render at 1024 × 1024 resolution on my 486DX2/66. The final rendering at 4096 × 4096 resolution took less than four hours. As an added bonus, the procedural algorithm eliminated many rendering artifacts that appeared when rendering the polygon-based model.

Conventions

Typeface Conventions

C++ keywords are given in bold (**static**). Source code, pseudocode and related functions and variables are set in Courier (`BuildHeap`).

Pseudocode Syntax

Many algorithms are described in pseudocode as well as implemented in C++. The pseudocode used for this book is somewhat different from that used in most algorithms texts, in that it is more C++-like.

- Arrays are numbered from 0. Most algorithms texts use a Pascal-like pseudocode that numbers arrays from 1. Having a conflict between the C++ source code and the pseudocode would be confusing.

- The dot operator . is used to denote access to a field in a data structure. This is analogous to the C++ operator, except that we don't really use the concept of a pointer in the pseudocode. Thus, the dot can be used for direct member access or access through a pointer without losing any clarity.

- Square brackets [] denote indexing into an array.

- The most significant departure from C++ is that assignment is denoted by ← (for example, Sum← 0) while equality and inequality are denoted by = and ≠.

Other than these key points, which may take some getting used to, the pseudocode should be very readable.

Notation

Some of the notation used in this book may be unfamiliar. A table of the notation used herein follows.

$\Omega(f(N))$ Denotes the asymptotic lower-bound runtime of an algorithm. See Chapter 2 for a description of the $\Omega(N \lg N)$ lower bound on comparison-based sorting.

$O(f(N))$ Denotes the asymptotic upper-bound (worst-case) runtime of an algorithm.
Example: Insertion Sort is $O(N^2)$, which means that it never takes more than some proportion of N^2 comparisons to sort N items.

$\Theta(f(N))$ Denotes the asymptotically tight bound on the runtime of an algorithm. The algorithm is both $\Omega(f(N))$ and $O(f(N))$. For example, Merge Sort is $\Theta(N \lg N)$: Its asymptotic worst-case runtime is the same as the fastest possible runtime.

$\lg x$ Denotes $\log_2 x$, the logarithm in base 2 of x.

$\ln x$ Denotes the natural logarithm of x.

$M \bmod N$ Denotes the remainder of M/N.

$\lceil x \rceil$ Ceiling
Denotes the smallest integer not less than x. For example, a binary heap that contains N elements has height $\lceil \lg N \rceil$.

$\lfloor x \rfloor$ Floor
Denotes the largest integer not greater than x.

CHAPTER 1

Algorithms and Asymptotic Notation

1.1 Introduction

An algorithm is like a recipe. It is a sequence of steps that accomplishes something useful. In the context of computer programming, algorithms compute a value or rearrange data in a useful way.

Algorithm designers are driven by three overriding concerns, to varying degrees:

- Correctness. If the algorithm does not do what it purports to do, it is useless.

- Efficiency. Computer algorithms should work quickly.

- Ease of implementation. Many algorithms have been invented but never implemented. Computer algorithms that are difficult to implement are of interest only to theoreticians. (Such algorithms are useful, however, since they may inspire more feasible algorithms.)

We won't get too mathematically rigorous when discussing algorithms' correctness. Rather, we'll concentrate more heavily on ways to ensure the correctness of the code implementing the algorithms. We'll spend more time worrying about algorithms' efficiency. Analyzing how much time an algorithm will take to run can range from trivial to tedious. While we will discuss simpler proofs of algorithms' runtime, we'll leave the more complicated ones to the references.

As for ease of implementation, we address only those algorithms that are feasible to implement. They aren't too complicated, and they all offer favorable tradeoffs in certain situations. Those tradeoffs will be discussed as appropriate.

We will use a variety of tools for describing algorithms in this book: prose with accompanying figures, C++ source code, and a Pascal-like pseudocode when the C++ overwhelms the essential details of the algorithm.

As an example, let's take a look at an algorithm for computing the maximum value of an array. First we'll give the pseudocode, which works on an array $A[0..N - 1]$.

```
1 Maximum(A, N)
2   x ← A[0]
3   for i ← 1 to N-1 do
4     if A[i] > x then
5       x ← A[i]
6   return x
```

When this pseudocode has been executed, it returns the maximum value of the array. In C++, this pseudocode can be implemented as a function template, as follows.

```
// Max function template
// Returns maximum of an array
template<class T>
T
Maximum(const T *base, int N)
{
    T ret = base[0];
    for (int i = 1; i < N; i++)
        if (base[i] > ret)
            ret = base[i];
    return ret;
}
```

Here it's a toss-up between the pseudocode and the C++ in terms of readability, provided you know C++ syntax for templates. In cases like this, you'd probably never see the pseudocode.

1.2 Asymptotic Notation

Asymptotic notation is a tool for describing the runtime of an algorithm. Algorithms' runtime depends on the amount of data they operate on; for example, Maximum depends on the number of elements in the array. Sorting algorithms' runtime depends on the number of items to be sorted. Usually this data can be characterized with a single variable N and the runtime can be described in terms of N. For example, Maximum operates on an N-element array. It examines each element in the N-element array, so it takes twice as long to perform Maximum on an array of 200 elements as an array of 100 elements. The runtime of Maximum is linear in N.

Because Maximum is linear, its runtime can be written in the form of the line equation $y = mx + b$:

$$\text{Runtime} = (t_{element})N + t_0 \qquad\qquad (1.1)$$

where N is the number of elements in the array, $t_{element}$ is the time required per element, and t_0 is the time required no matter how many elements are in the array (for example, the time to call and return from the function).

We're most interested in the runtime when N gets large, though. The true test of an algorithm is whether it can operate on large datasets in a reasonable amount of time. And as N gets large, t_0 gets insignificant. Only $t_{element}$ is relevant. To characterize the algorithm's runtime, all we need to know is how much time it takes to process an element.

So, how much time *does* it take to process an element? A few observations will show that this parameter isn't needed either. After all, Maximum will take about 100× less time on a modern desktop computer than on a ten-year-old one. And using a RISC workstation will take less time than using a personal computer. In fact, if we want to preserve a platform-independent description of the algorithm, we have to lose the coefficient altogether. It can be measured separately for each platform we are interested in, but the only useful description of the algorithm's *asymptotic runtime*—that is, the runtime as N gets very large—is a function of how the runtime grows with N.

So Equation 1.1 can be restated in almost as useful a way as follows: The runtime for Maximum grows linearly as N increases.

1.2.1 Notation

There are a number of notations for asymptotic runtime. The most useful is the "big-oh" notation. Using the "big-oh" notation, Maximum is $O(N)$ (read "order of N"). In general, $O(f(N))$ means that the runtime is proportional to $f(N)$ in the worst case. The algorithm can't possibly run slower than some proportion of $f(N)$. Usually we use "big-oh" notation when discussing the runtime of an algorithm.

Formally, $O(f(N))$ refers to a set of functions denoted as follows:

$$O(f(N)) = \left\{ \begin{array}{l} g(N)\text{: There exist positive constants } c \text{ and } N_0 \\ \text{such that } 0 \le g(N) \le cf(N) \text{ for all } N \ge N_0 \end{array} \right\}$$

This set notation means that if you can pick constants c and N_0 for some function $g(N)$ such that $0 \le f(N) \le cg(N)$, then $g(N)$ is a member of $O(f(N))$. Practically speaking, this set consists of functions that have been multiplied by a constant or that have lower-order components. For example, $g(N) = 2N \lg N$ is a member of $O(N \lg N)$ because you can pick $c = 3$, $N_0 = 1$ and the inequality holds. Similarly, $g(N) = N \lg N + N$ is $O(N \lg N)$ because you can pick $c = 2$, $N_0 = 3$ and the inequality holds.

Another asymptotic notation, $\Omega(f(N))$, gives the best-case runtime: It denotes that the algorithm can't possibly run faster than proportional to $f(N)$. For example, Maximum is $\Omega(N)$ because every element in the array has to be examined for the algorithm to work correctly.

Like $O(f(N))$, the notation $\Omega(f(N))$ refers to a set of functions, as follows.

$$\Omega(f(N)) = \left\{ \begin{array}{l} g(N)\text{: There exist positive constants } c \text{ and } N_0 \\ \text{such that } 0 \le cf(N) \le g(N) \text{ for all } N \ge N_0 \end{array} \right\}$$

Just as O-notation imposes an upper bound on a function to within a constant factor, Ω-notation imposes a lower bound.

When both conditions apply—an algorithm is both $O(f(N))$ and $\Omega(f(N))$—then another notation can be used: $\Theta(f(N))$. This denotes that the algorithm runs in time proportional to $f(N)$ in the worst case and that it cannot run faster. In a sense, the algorithm is optimal: To get an asymptotically faster algorithm, you have to change the rules somehow.

One way to change the rules is by making assumptions about the incoming data. For example, searching an array is $\Theta(N)$ if the array is unsorted; however, a much faster $\Theta(\lg N)$ algorithm can be used if the array is in sorted order.

1.2.2 Asymptotic Notation Examples

To get a feel for asymptotic notation, let's examine the asymptotic runtime for a few code fragments.

Example 1. Nested for Loops

What is the asymptotic runtime of the following code fragment?

```
1 ArrayMaximum(a, N)
2   MaxSoFar = -∞;
3   for i ← 0 to N-1 do
4     for j ← 0 to N-1 do
5       if (array[i][j] > MaxSoFar)
6         MaxSoFar = array[i][j]
7   return MaxSoFar
```

Our intuition tells us that no matter what N is, line 2 takes an insignificant amount of time. (See Example 2.) Line 3 gets executed N times, and each of those N times, line 4 gets executed N times as well. Lines 5 and 6 take a constant amount of time whenever they are executed. Because lines 2 and 3 are nested, lines 5 and 6 are executed N^2 times. As intuition would have it, the overall runtime of this code fragment is $O(N^2)$.

Example 2. Swapping Two Elements in an Array

The asymptotic runtime to swap two elements in an array does not depend on the number of elements. It may take two instructions on a CISC machine, or a few more on a RISC architecture. It may take milliseconds or microseconds depending on how fast the processor is and how large the data is. But no matter how slow or fast the swap operation is, it takes a constant amount of time in a given environment, independent of the number of elements in the array.

This operation is "constant time," or $O(1)$.

Example 3. Nested for Loops Revisited

What is the asymptotic runtime for the following code fragment?

```
1 SelectionSort(A, N)
2   for i ← 0 to N-2 do
3     MinSoFar ← i
4     for j ← i+1 to N-1
5       if A[j] < A[MinSoFar] then
6         MinSoFar ← j
7     Swap(A[i], A[MinSoFar])
```

At first glance, this code fragment looks a lot like Example 1. The difference is that line 4 begins the nested for loop at i, not 0. The inner loop executes lines 5 and 6 a total of $\sum_{i=0}^{N-1} N - i$ or

$$N^2 - \sum_{i=1}^{N} i = \frac{N(N-1)}{2}$$

times. This is about half as many operations as in Example 1, but it is still $O(N^2)$.

Example 4. Merge Sort

Here is a more involved analysis of an algorithm's worst-case runtime. Merge Sort works by recursively sorting the two halves of the input array, then merging the two subarrays into a single sorted array. A complete description of Merge Sort is given in Chapter 4.

Merge Sort's runtime can be described recursively, as follows.

$$T(N) = \begin{cases} 2T(N/2) + N, & N > 1 \\ 1, & N = 1 \end{cases}$$

The bottom expression reflects that it takes constant time to "sort" a one-element array. The expression $2T(N/2)$ is the time required for the two recursive calls. (This expression is technically $T(\lceil N/2 \rceil) + T(\lfloor N/2 \rfloor)$, but using the simpler expression simplifies our analysis without affecting the outcome of the proof.) N is the time required to merge the two subarrays.

The definition for $O(f(N))$ is the family of functions $g(N)$ such that some constants c and N_0 exist so that $0 \le g(N) \le cf(N)$ for all $N \ge N_0$. We can prove by induction that this definition holds for the recurrence for $f(N) = N \lg N$. We guess that $T(N)$ is $O(N \lg N)$. Substituting $N \lg(N/2)/2$ for $T(N/2)$, then, we have the following.

$$T(N) \leq 2c\left(\frac{N \lg(N/2)}{2}\right) + N$$
$$\leq c(N \lg N/2) + N$$
$$= cN \lg N - cN \lg 2 + N$$
$$= cN \lg N - cN + N$$
$$\leq cN \lg N$$

We now must establish that the inequality holds for some constants c and N_0. It holds for $c = 2$ and $N_0 = 2$, so Merge Sort does in fact run in $O(N \lg N)$ time.

1.2.3 Combining Runtimes

Algorithms often are combined to perform certain tasks. For example, you might want to sort each row of an $N \times N$ matrix. This nests two operations, the "each row" and the "sort":

For each of N rows:
 Sort the N elements in the row.

The top operation is $\Theta(N)$, since each element in the N-element array is being operated on. The second operation, as we will discuss in Part I, is $\Theta(N \lg N)$. To determine the asymptotic runtime of the entire operation, multiply these two expressions together. The preceding algorithm for sorting each row of an $N \times N$ matrix, then, is $\Theta(N^2 \lg N)$.

Another way to combine algorithms is by doing them in sequence. In this case, the overall runtime is dominated by the largest single runtime. For example, performing Merge Sort on an array (which takes $\Theta(N \lg N)$ time), then performing a Binary Search on that array (which takes $\Theta(\lg N)$ time) requires $\Theta(N \lg N)$ time overall; as N grows, the runtime of the Binary Search step becomes insignificant.

1.2.4 Comparing Runtimes

To determine whether the runtime of one algorithm is faster than that of another, compare the functions in the asymptotic notation as they go to infinity. Usually this is easy; N^2 is faster than N^3, for example. If the runtimes are more complicated, you can compare the functions $f(x)$ and $g(x)$ of two algorithms by dividing one by the other and examining how they behave as $N \to \infty$:

$$\lim_{N \to \infty} \frac{f(x)}{g(x)}$$

If the limit diverges as $N \to \infty$, then $f(x)$ grows faster than $g(x)$. If the limit approaches 0, then $g(x)$ grows faster than $f(x)$. If the limit approaches some constant, then the two functions grow equally fast.

Example 1. Root Versus Logarithm

Which is asymptotically more efficient, $\sqrt{N}$ or $\ln N$?

$$\lim_{N \to \infty} \frac{\sqrt{N}}{\ln N} = \lim_{N \to \infty} \frac{N^{1/2}}{\ln N}$$

L'Hôpital's Rule holds that

$$\lim_{x \to \infty} \frac{f(x)}{g(x)} = \lim_{x \to \infty} \frac{f'(x)}{g'(x)}$$

so we can rewrite the limit as follows:

$$\lim_{N \to \infty} \frac{\sqrt{N}}{\ln N} = \lim_{N \to \infty} \frac{\frac{1}{2}N^{-1/2}}{1/N}$$

Multiplying the numerator and denominator by N yields $\frac{1}{2}N^{1/2}$. Since this expression diverges as $N \to \infty$, $\sqrt{N}$ grows faster than $\ln N$.

If we had put $\ln N$ in the numerator instead of the denominator, the expression would have gone to 0, leading us to the same conclusion.

Example 2. Base of Logarithm

Which is asymptotically more efficient, a $\log_2 N$ algorithm or a $\log_{10} N$ algorithm?

Intuitively, it would seem that higher-base logarithms are more desirable, since they are smaller for large N. For example, $\log_2 1000 \approx 10$, while $\log_{10} 1000 = 3$. However, logarithm functions of different bases differ only by a constant, according to the following rule:

$$\log_a x = \frac{\log_b x}{\log_b a}$$

where a and b are the different bases. So asymptotically, logarithms of different bases grow at the same rate.

Logarithms of base 2 come up often in the study of algorithms, so in this book, we often use the notation "$\lg N$" to denote $\log_2 N$. But asymptotically, the base of the logarithm is not important.

1.2.5 Asymptotic Runtimes and Constant Factors

Asymptotic runtimes are very important. Even though an algorithm that is asymptotically slower may run faster for small N, usually it will lose ground quickly. For example, my preliminary timings of Insertion Sort showed a runtime of about $0.555N^2$ microseconds, where N is the number of elements being sorted. The naive Merge Sort implementation had a runtime of $5.90N \lg N$ microseconds. Here, the coefficients are referred to as "constant factors."

For small N, Insertion Sort is much faster than Merge Sort (more than twice as fast for $N = 20$). The two algorithms finish in a dead heat at $N = 63$. And as N grows large, Merge Sort is overwhelmingly faster. For example, for $N = 10000$, Insertion Sort runs in about 55 s, while Merge Sort runs in less than 0.8 s. Even if we hand-coded Insertion Sort in assembler, this would only decrease the constant factor of 0.555 microseconds, and Merge Sort's faster asymptotic runtime would catch up quickly.

Algorithmists are fond of referring to constant factors rather contemptuously. You could rewrite a routine in assembler to be ten times faster and academics would sniff, "It's only faster by a constant factor." And they'd be right, in a way: As we just saw with Merge Sort versus Insertion Sort, asymptotic efficiency can win over a constant factor very quickly. But if two commercial programs are identical except that one is ten times as fast, it is obvious which one would sell and which would get panned in the trade press. So sometimes constant factors matter.

And although asymptotic runtimes are important, sometimes the constant factor is so large that the algorithm is impractical.

If Merge Sort were faster than Insertion Sort only for $N > 10^{20}$, we might be less inclined to use it. While algorithms like that are interesting theoretically, we will not discuss any that are impractical to implement.

1.2.6 Further Reading

Here are some books that go into a great deal more depth on the art of analyzing algorithms.

Bentley, J. *Programming Pearls*. Reading, MA: Addison-Wesley, 1986.

> An excellent overview of practical programming techniques; not only algorithms analysis but techniques to ensure correct implementation.

Cormen, T., C. Leiserson, and R. Rivest. *Introduction to Algorithms*. Cambridge, MA: MIT Press, 1990.

> The best introduction to algorithms that I know of.

Graham, R., D. Knuth, and O. Patashnik. *Concrete Mathematics*. Reading, MA: Addison-Wesley, 1989.

> Discusses the mathematics needed for computer science in detail.

Sedgewick, R. *Algorithms in C++*. Reading, MA: Addison-Wesley, 1992.

> Introduces a huge number of algorithms with more coverage and less depth than Cormen, Leiserson, and Rivest.

1.3 Practical Algorithms Implementation

Bentley [BENT86] gives an excellent summary of techniques to help implement algorithms correctly. We will use many of the methods mentioned here, though not every method is used on every algorithm.

1.3.1 Assertions

In this book, the word *assertion* is used in two related ways. One is as a software engineering term, where separate debug and release versions of the software product are maintained. Maguire [MAGU93] gives a good overview of this technique. By maintaining an in-house debug version of the software, you have an opportunity to insert cross-checks to verify that the software is operating correctly. These cross-checks are called *assertions*. An assertion checks to see if a condition is true. If it is not, the assertion code complains loudly, terminates the program, or both. The intrusive behavior is deliberate: Developers have to address assertion failures as soon as they crop up, or the program will no longer work.

One good application for an assertion might involve cross-checking a subtle hand-coded assembly language routine against a more straightforward implementation in a high-level language. The assertion fails if they disagree. By maintaining the two implementations in parallel, they are much more likely to operate correctly. Of course, this type of compute-intensive assertion is why separate debug and release versions of the software are maintained. When the time comes to build a release version of the product for customers, the assembly language routine can be called by itself with some confidence that it will work correctly.

Anything that has to work before customers get the software is a good candidate for an assertion. Subroutines that require an even number of inputs, frequency transform routines that require that the number of inputs be a power of 2, and pointers that can be validated are all good candidates for assertions. The efficiency of the debug version is not important; the release version of the software, which is compiled without assertions, will be efficient.

In this book, the source code omits many possible assertions to make it more readable. However, it does include some important tools so readers can incorporate assertions into their own code. The CheckInvariant member function of the BinaryTree class template, for example, checks to make sure the binary tree is valid. RedBlackTree, which inherits from BinaryTree, refines CheckInvariant to make sure the red-black tree properties also hold for the data structure. CheckInvariant was an important tool for me while developing the binary tree code.

The other meaning for the word *assertion* comes from theoretical computer science. In this context, an assertion is a statement about the program that can be made at a certain point to help prove it correct. For example, an assertion can be placed in the Maximum algorithm to find the maximum value in an array, as follows.

```
1  Maximum(A, N)
2      x ← A[0]
3      for i ← 1 to N-1 do
4          if A[i] > x then
5              x ← A[i]
6          Assert: x ≥ A[0..i]
7      return x
```

Each iteration of the loop increases the number of elements that x is greater than. Since i is equal to N-1 at the termination of the loop, x ≥ A[0..N-1] when the routine returns. The assertion helps give a convincing proof of the correctness of Maximum.

1.3.2 Loops

The assertion used to prove Maximum correct is a special assertion called a *loop invariant*. Loops are common, and they deserve special attention when proving algorithms correct. The loop can be broken down into three steps:

1. Initialization. The loop invariant condition is established.
2. Preservation. The loop invariant is maintained until the termination condition for the loop is met.
3. Termination. The loop accomplishes its task on termination.

Arguing that the initialization and preservation steps are correct lets you use the loop invariant to show that the loop has accomplished its purpose on termination. Once the three steps have been shown to be correct, you separately argue that the loop terminates. Once this is done, the loop has been proven correct.

As an example, let's take another look at SelectionSort.

```
1  SelectionSort(A, N)
2      for i ← 0 to N-2 do
3          MinSoFar ← i
4          for j ← i+1 to N-1
5              if A[j] < A[MinSoFar] then
6                  MinSoFar ← j
7          Swap(A[i], A[MinSoFar])
```

We'll look at the inner loop first. The loop invariant is that
A[MinSoFar] ≤ A[i..j-1]. At the beginning of the loop, the loop
invariant holds because MinSoFar is equal to i and j is initialized
to i+1. When the loop is executed, lines 5 and 6 replace MinSoFar
if A[j] is less than A[MinSoFar]. j is then incremented and the
loop invariant still holds. When the loop terminates, j is equal to
N and the loop invariant (which still holds now that the loop has
terminated) states that A[MinSoFar] ≤ A[i..N-1]. So the inner
loop correctly computes the index of the minimum element in the
subarray ranging from i to the end of the array.

Now we can look at what the outer loop is doing. The loop
invariant for the outer loop is that A[k] < A[k+1] for 0 ≤ k ≤ i.
Every time the inner loop completes, this is obviously the case because the inner loop computes the minimum element of the subarray A[i..n-1] and swaps it with A[i]. Thus, when the outer loop
completes, i has traversed from 0 to $N - 2$ and the invariant states
that A[k] < A[k+1] for 0 ≤ k ≤ N - 1. In other words, the array
is sorted after Selection Sort completes.

Although I am sure you will be disappointed to hear this, this
is the first and last time we analyze loops in such exhaustive detail
in this book. But you may find it useful to apply this analysis to
other loops in the book, such as the loops in the iterative Merge Sort
implementation given in Chapter 4 or the iterative Binary Search
implementation in Chapter 7.

1.3.3 Subroutines

To prove that a piece of code containing a subroutine is correct, the
precondition and postcondition of the subroutine must be stated.
The precondition is the condition that must hold before the subroutine is called in order for it to behave properly. The postcondition is
the condition that holds after the subroutine has been called. Once
it has been proven that the subroutine arrives at the postcondition
if the precondition is true, the code can be proven correct without
further consideration of the subroutine's implementation.

A good example of an algorithm that contains a subroutine
is Quicksort, which calls Partition. Partition splits an array
A[0..N-1] into two subarrays and returns the index of the last element in the left-hand subarray, q. The postcondition for Partition
is that every element in the subarray A[0..q] is less than or equal

to every element in the subarray `A[q+1..N-1]`. `Quicksort` uses this postcondition to implement a fast sorting algorithm, described in Chapter 4.

1.3.4 Recursion

Recursion is a form of subroutine call; that a subroutine happens to be calling itself does not change the idea of precondition and postcondition. Some forms of recursion also can be thought of as loop constructs, since they can be described in terms of initialization, invariant, and termination stages. Although C++ directly supports functional recursion, it is generally to be avoided because it uses the machine stack in a nondeterministic way and running out of stack tends to break the program. So eliminating recursion is one of the exercises we undertake when developing a routine in this book.

A special form of recursion, *tail recursion*, is when exactly one recursive call occurs at the end of the routine. Tail-recursive routines can be trivially converted to loops. As an example, let's consider Euclid's algorithm for the greatest common divisor. The GCD of two integers is the largest integer that divides evenly into both. The GCD of 20 and 45, for example, is 5. Euclid described an algorithm for the GCD that exploits the identity.

$$\gcd(a, b) = \begin{cases} \gcd(b, a \bmod b), & b \neq 0 \\ a, & b = 0 \end{cases}$$

(The identity assumes $a \geq b$ without losing any generality.)

This algorithm can easily be implemented recursively, as follows.

```
int
gcd(int a, int b)
{
     if (a < b) Swap(a, b);
     if (b == 0)
          return a;
     return gcd(b, a%b);
}
```

Because this `gcd` implementation is tail-recursive, it can be expressed as a loop just as easily.

```
int
gcd(int a, int b)
{
    if (a < b) Swap(a, b);
    while (b != 0) {
        int nextb = a % b;
        a = b;
        b = nextb;
    }
    return a;
}
```

Note how the termination condition and variables in the recursive construct convert into a loop.

Binary Search, described in Chapter 7, is a good example of a tail-recursive routine. Quicksort, described in Chapter 4, is a good example of a recursive routine that is nontrivial to implement iteratively.

PART

Sorting

Sorting is one of the most pervasive algorithms in computer science. At any moment, a significant percentage of all the computer horsepower in the world is devoted to sorting. Not only is it an operation to be performed for its own sake, but it serves as a preprocessing step or subroutine to be used by other algorithms. Because of its universality, sorting is one of the most-studied problems in computer science.

This part of the book begins by discussing the implementation and complexity of sorting in Chapter 2. A simple, fast sorting algorithm called Insertion Sort is discussed in Chapter 3. Another simple sorting algorithm, Selection Sort, is discussed in Chapter 3, as is Shell Sort, a variation of Insertion Sort that is asymptotically faster. An efficient, venerable sorting algorithm called Merge Sort and the most practically useful of sorting algorithms, Quicksort, are discussed in Chapter 4, as is a priority queue data structure that can be transformed into an efficient algorithm called Heapsort. Chapter 5 concludes with a wrapup of the tradeoffs between the different algorithms discussed, an analysis of their runtimes, and discussions of further reading and future work.

Overview of Sorting

Before exploring sorting algorithms in detail, we should go over some issues that arise when implementing them. We will discuss terminology and implementation issues in Section 2.1. In Section 2.2, we will explore the complexity of the sorting problem and prove a lower bound on the runtime of comparison-based sorting techniques.

2.1 Issues in Sorting

The descriptions of sorting algorithms in this book have a great deal in common. All operate on arrays whose elements range from 0 to $N - 1$, where N is the number of elements being sorted. All of our sorting algorithms assume that the array elements can be accessed randomly in constant time, and all are implemented as function templates in C++ with the following definition:

```
template<class T>
void
SortingAlgorithm(T *base, int N)
{
  // Reorders base[0..N-1] so that
  // base[i-1] ≤ base[i] for all 1 ≤ i < N.
}
```

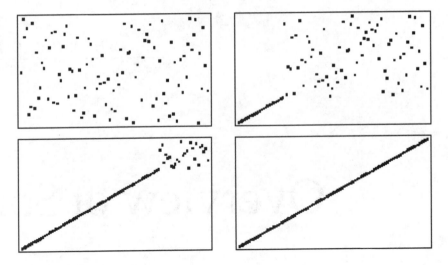

Figure 2.1.   Sorting an array.

The behavior of each sorting algorithm is depicted graphically in the same way. A scatter chart of the array elements shows how the sorting algorithm works to put the elements in order. The array elements go from left to right; the height of the dots in the scatter chart correspond to the value of the array element (higher elements have greater values). Figure 2.1 shows an array progressing from random to sorted order. These charts were generated with Microsoft Excel from diagnostic printouts generated by the algorithms. The charts were then exported to Encapsulated Postscript files so they could be placed in the book.

Other issues that arise when implementing sorting algorithms are discussed in the following sections.

2.1.1 Keys and Satellite Data

In most applications, there is more data in each element than is required to compare them. The data used to compare elements is called the *key*; the other data in the element is called *satellite data*. When we discuss comparing elements, we assume that the keys are used for the comparisons; when swapping and otherwise manipulating elements, the entire element is dealt with, satellite data and all.

2.1.2 Stability

A sorting algorithm is stable if it does not reorder elements with equal keys. Some sorting algorithms, such as Insertion Sort and Merge Sort, are easy to implement so they are stable; others, such as Quicksort, are virtually impossible. When possible, the sorting algorithms in this book are implemented in stable fashion. We will discuss the stability of each sorting implementation as appropriate.

2.1.3 Sentinels

The runtime of a sorting routine often can be improved by placing a sentinel at one end of the array. A sentinel is a special value placed at the head or tail of a data structure to keep the code correct while eliminating some code in the inner loop. For example, a comparison can be eliminated from the inner loop of Insertion Sort by placing a sentinel value of ∞ at the head of the array. Placing the sentinel there ensures that the loop will terminate correctly even though the comparison has been taken out.

There are many places in this book where sentinels could be put to use to make the code more efficient. We've avoided their use for two reasons. First, the value of ∞ is debatable. If signed 16-bit integers are being sorted, there is no value guaranteed to be greater than any other value unless you want to eliminate 32767 from the set of numbers you are willing to sort. That's not an acceptable compromise for a general-purpose implementation. Also, for user-defined classes, the library would require users to specify a value of ∞, since there's no way to ask a class what its particular ∞ is.

The second reason not to use sentinels is that the sorting routine is not in charge of allocating the array, so it would be up to clients of the sorting routine to allocate space for the sentinel. This is inconvenient for clients, since then they have to figure out how to reference elements beyond the sentinel when they're not calling the sorting routine.

In short, sentinels are application-specific. They can make routines faster or even simpler when used judiciously, but it is difficult or impossible to use them in general-purpose code.

2.1.4 External Sorting

External sorting techniques allow the computer to sort more elements than it can hold in random access memory. In particular, most external sorting techniques model the incoming data as if it were sequential in nature, as if it were on a tape. When computers were first invented, all sorting applications were external because the computers had so little memory. The data to sort was stored on cards or tapes. Fortunately, tapes have been supplanted as primary storage for computers, rendering external sorting techniques largely obsolete.

Why is external sorting obsolete when computers always can be asked to sort more data than they can hold in physical memory? The answer is that modern operating systems provide virtual memory. Virtual memory works by having the operating system keep only "required" portions of memory around. Frequently referenced memory is kept in physical RAM for fast access, while unused memory can be written out to a hard disk. Modern computers have the infrastructure needed to track which portions of memory are in frequent use and which can be sent to the hard disk safely. They also have the machinery required to quickly tell the operating system if a program has referenced memory that resides on the hard disk, so the system can load it back into physical memory.

Many modern operating systems, including Mach and Windows NT, go one step further. These systems feature mapped file I/O, which lets programs map files into their address space and access them as if they are in memory. The operating system uses the same memory management hardware to implement this feature as it does to implement the usual virtual memory scheme.

In short, most operating systems let computers pretend they have as much memory as they have space on their hard disk. There is a practical limit, of course; if a program references its data in a way that causes frequent page faults, then the system can grind to a halt as it swaps pages in and out of physical memory. (This behavior is called *thrashing*.) Should a system run out of disk space or begin thrashing, the limits of virtual memory have been reached and an external sorting technique may be needed.

Interested readers can refer to Knuth [KNUT73] for an exhaustive treatment of external sorting techniques.

2.1.5 Locality of Reference

Locality of reference is a measure of how unpredictably the sorting algorithm accesses memory. Sorting algorithms with good locality of reference access array elements that are near each other, so the operating system can keep them in physical memory together easily. Sorting algorithms that access memory in near-random fashion cause thrashing much sooner than sorting algorithms with good locality of reference. We'll discuss the locality of reference of each algorithm briefly, as appropriate.

2.2 Complexity of Sorting

How does a computer sort? We might start out by examining how people do. Given a set of index cards to alphabetize, people usually start at the beginning with one card. Then they look at the second card; if it's before the first, they place it before; otherwise they keep it after. Then two cards are sorted. The process continues with each unsorted card being placed in the proper position among the previously sorted cards. The process of deciding where to place the card is based on the alphabetical order: Cards in the sorted set must be compared alphabetically with the unsorted card in order to decide where to put it. Most algorithms discussed in this book use comparisons.

Whether we sort using comparisons is an important distinction, because we can establish a lower bound on the efficiency of a sorting algorithm that uses comparisons. It's easy to establish a lower bound of $\Omega(N)$ on sorting, because if fewer than N elements are considered the neglected elements may wind up out of order. But we can establish a stronger lower bound on comparison-based sorting, as follows.

What if, for the sake of argument, we count comparisons while ignoring all the other operations related to the sort? If we establish a lower bound on the number of comparisons alone required to sort, this is certainly valid as a lower bound for the process of sorting— we assume everything else is infinitely fast! To highlight the number of comparisons required to sort an array, let's formulate the problem in terms of a decision tree. Figure 2.2 depicts one of several decision trees to sort three elements.

The first comparison is at the top of the tree, and the correct comparisons to narrow the possibilities are shown at each decision in the tree. Notice that the comparisons in the figure are internal nodes in the tree, while permutations of the input are at the leaves. The leaves of the decision tree must contain all of the $N!$ possible permutations; if any permutation is neglected, that permutation cannot be sorted. So the decision tree contains $N!$ leaf nodes.

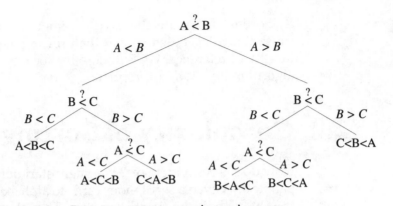

Figure 2.2.   Decision tree to sort three elements.

For a decision tree of height h, the number of comparisons required to sort is $O(h)$. Since a binary tree of height h has at most 2^h nodes, we can write the inequality:

$$2^h \geq n!$$

Taking logarithms, we obtain:

$$h \geq \lg(n!)$$

This establishes a lower bound on h, the worst-case number of comparisons required to sort the input. Asymptotically, $\lim_{n \to \infty} \lg(N!) = N \lg N$, so sorting using comparisons to order the data is $\Omega(N \lg N)$ for an array with N elements. Thus, the fastest possible runtime for a comparison-based sorting algorithm is $O(N \lg N)$.

Several sorting algorithms that use $O(N \lg N)$ comparisons, including Merge Sort and Heapsort, are described later. However, in Chapter 3, simple sorting algorithms that work well for small N will be described.

Asymptotically Slow Sorts

As we discussed in Chapter 1, asymptotic runtime is held in high regard by theorists who design algorithms. Thus, Merge Sort, an asymptotically fast sorting algorithm, is accorded a great deal more respect than Selection Sort. Asymptotic runtime only captures part of the picture, however: It describes how the runtime grows as the number of inputs approaches infinity. When sorting small arrays, a less asymptotically efficient algorithm is often faster, up to a certain number of inputs.

Asymptotically efficient algorithms have some other disadvantages. Both Merge Sort and Quicksort require auxiliary storage space, while Heapsort is by far the slowest of the three asymptotically fast algorithms discussed in Chapter 4. None of the asymptotically slow algorithms given in this chapter require auxiliary storage to work.

Insertion Sort, described in Section 3.1, sorts by moving each element into the position where it belongs in the array. For "almost-sorted" arrays where each element only has to be moved a constant number of times, its runtime appraoches $O(N)$.

Selection Sort, described in Section 3.2, sorts by repeatedly finding the minimum element of the array and placing it at the beginning. Since it only performs $O(N)$ swaps, its runtime approaches $O(N)$ for arrays composed of large, cumbersome elements that can be quickly compared but require a long time to move within the input array.

Section 3.3 describes Shell Sort, a variation of Insertion Sort that initially compares and swaps elements that are far away from each other in the input array. Shell Sort is asymptotically more efficient than Insertion Sort or Selection Sort, but not as fast as the $O(N \lg N)$ sorting algorithms described in Chapter 4.

3.1 Insertion Sort

Insertion Sort is the computer analog of the typical human's method of sorting. The array is initially divided into sorted and unsorted parts, with the first element of the array in the sorted part. In turn, each remaining element in the array is placed in the correct position of the sorted array. Pseudocode for Insertion Sort can be written as follows.

```
1    InsertionSort(base, N)
2        for i←2 to N-1 do
3            for j←i to 2 do
4                if base[j] < base[j-1] then
5                    Swap(base[j], base[j-1])
6            Assert: base[1..i] is sorted.
```

Line 5 gives an assertion that helps prove Insertion Sort correct. Each iteration of the loop in line 2 increases the size of the sorted subarray at the beginning of the array. When the loop terminates, the loop invariant holds for every element in the array.

We can improve the runtime of InsertionSort by picking up the element being moved into a temporary variable, as follows.

```
1    InsertionSort(base, N)
2        for i←2 to N do
3            T←base[i]
4            j←i
5            while j>1 and base[j-1]>T do
6                base[j]←base[j-1]
7                j←j-1
8        base[j]←T
9        Assert: base[1..i] is sorted.
```

This routine pulls base[i], the element to place into order, into a temporary variable. It then shifts elements into the hole vacated by T until it has opened up the hole where it fits in the sorted order. By avoiding repeated Swap operations, this routine runs much faster than the first formulation.

We could improve the runtime further by placing a sentinel at the head of the array. Placing a sentinel with the value ∞ at base[0] lets us eliminate the comparison j>1 in line 5 of the pseudocode just given. Since there's not much to that loop, eliminating one comparison could have a perceptible impact on the runtime.

3.1.1 Stability

The implementation of Insertion Sort described here is stable. (It does not reorder elements that are equal.) The while loop in the second implementation of Insertion Sort terminates if an equal element is found, so the element is not shuffled any farther down than preceding elements with equal keys.

3.1.2 Runtime

For an N-element array, insertions are performed (up to $N - 1$, to be exact). While a person typically can insert an index card into a file in constant time, a computer needs $O(N)$ time to shuffle the other items out of the way for the item to be inserted. So Insertion Sort is $O(N^2)$ overall.

Figure 3.1 shows Insertion Sort operating on a 150-element array.

Insertion Sort is useful in practice for two reasons. First, it is good at sorting small arrays because it has a small constant factor. More sophisticated methods of sorting, such as Quicksort, generally take longer to sort a small number of elements than Insertion Sort. Second, Insertion Sort runs in linear time for almost-sorted arrays. Because each out-of-order element only needs to be moved down a little to be placed in order, the step of insertion actually runs in constant time.

Listing 3.1 gives an efficient implementation of Insertion Sort after Bentley [BENT86]. In the source code included with the book, the InsertionSort function template is in <insort.h>.

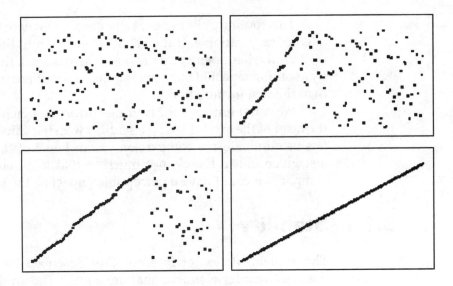

Figure 3.1.   Insertion Sort in action.

Listing 3.1.   `InsertionSort` function template.

```
// ================================================================
// InsertionSort function template.
//
//      Sorts an N-element array using the Insertion Sort.
//
// Parameters:
//      T *base         Base of the array to search.
//      const int N     Number of elements in the array.
//
// Return value: None.
//
// Requires:
//      operator== and operator< must be defined on the class T.
//
// Runtime:
//      O(N^2) for an N-element array.
//      O(N) for sorted and almost-sorted arrays.
// ================================================================
template<class T>
void
InsertionSort(T *base, int n)
{
    int i, j;
```

```
// Loop invariant:
// all elements [0..i-1] are in sorted order.
// Each element in the array is moved into the sorted
// portion in turn.
for (i = 1; i < n; i++) {
    // If the element to be moved into the sorted portion
    // of the array is out of order...
    if (base[i] < base[i-1]) {

        // Pull it out of the array
        T t = base[i];

        // Shuffle the elements in the sorted portion
        // of the array to make room for base[i].

        for (j = i; j && t < base[j-1]; j--)
            base[j] = base[j-1];

        // Insert the new sorted element.
        base[j] = t;
    }
  }
}
```

3.2 Selection Sort

Selection Sort works by incrementally building the sorted array in order from the first element to the last one. First, it finds the minimum element in the array and swaps it with the first element. Now the smallest element is where it belongs in the sorted order. Next Selection Sort finds the minimum element in the remaining elements and swaps it with the second element. After repeating this process N times for an N-element array, the array has been sorted. Pseudocode for Selection Sort is as follows.

```
1   SelectionSort(base, N)
2       for i←0 to N-1 do
3           MinIndex←index of Minimum(base[i..N])
4           Swap(base[i], base[MinIndex])
5           Assert: base[0..i] is in sorted order.
```

Line 5 contains the same assertion used to show that Insertion Sort is correct. Like Insertion Sort, Selection Sort incrementally builds the sorted array from left to right. However, Selection Sort potentially does not move the data as much as Insertion Sort, since each element is moved to its final spot in the array at most one time.

Selection Sort performs comparisons and N swaps so, like Insertion Sort, it has a worst-case runtime of $O(N^2)$.

Figure 3.2 depicts Selection Sort operating on a 150-element array.

Many sorting algorithms have been developed that are asymptotically faster, and one of these algorithms is often a better choice for general-purpose sorting applications. However, because Selection Sort only performs swaps, it is well suited to applications where the comparisons are cheap but the swaps are expensive.

Listing 3.2 shows the `SelectionSort` function template, which implements Selection Sort in C++. In the source code included with the book, this function template is given in `<selsort.h>`.

The implementation of Selection Sort given here is stable. The scan for the minimum element proceeds from left to right, and the min-so-far element is replaced only by elements that are strictly less than it. The leftmost of equal elements is always selected as the minimum, resulting in a stable sort.

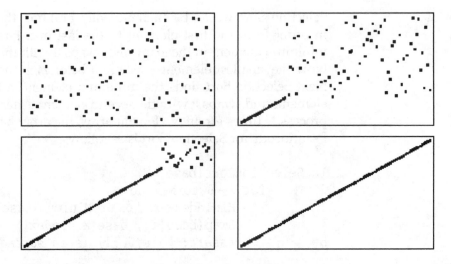

Figure 3.2.   Selection Sort in action.

Listing 3.2. `SelectionSort` function template.

```
// ================================================================
// SelectionSort function template.
//
//      Sorts an N-element array using the Selection Sort
//      algorithm.
//
// Parameters:
//      T *base          Base of the array to sort.
//      int N            Number of elements in the array.
//
// Return value: None.
//
// Requires:
//      operator< must be defined on the class T.
//
// Runtime:
//      O(N^2).
// ================================================================

template<class T>
void
SelectionSort(T *base, int N)
{
    // Working from beginning of array, swap each element with
    // the minimum of the remaining elements.  This renders
    // the array sorted from front to back.
    for (int i = 0; i < N; i++) {
        int mini = i;
        for (int j = i+1; j < N; j++) {
            if (base[j] < base[mini])
                mini = j;
        }
        Swap(base[i], base[mini]);
    }
}
```

3.3 Shell Sort

Shell describes a sorting technique that is similar to Insertion Sort, but it is asymptotically faster because it works with elements that are farther apart [SHEL59]. Comparing and reordering elements that are far apart combats one of the obvious flaws of Insertion Sort:

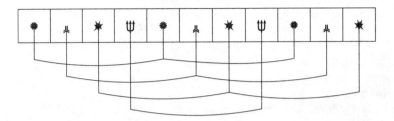

Figure 3.3.   Interleaved subarrays for Shell Sort.

If a small element starts out at the end of the input array, it takes $O(N)$ time to move that one element into position.

Shell Sort works by performing Insertion Sort on interleaved subarrays in the input array. Each subarray consists of elements that are some constant h apart. Figure 3.3 depicts these interleaved subarrays in an 11-element array. In the figure, $h = 4$, so the first, fifth, and ninth elements are in one group; the second, sixth, and tenth elements are in another; and so on. Figure 3.3 delineates the groups: Elements that are in the same subarray are wired together. Shell Sort begins with large h, so sorting the subarrays consists of placing elements that are far apart into sorted order. Then h is decreased, and much of the work of sorting the new, closer-together subarrays has already been done. Finally, h works its way down to 1, when adjacent elements are compared and reordered to yield the sorted output array.

Listing 3.3 gives a C++ implementation of Shell Sort after Sedgewick [SEDG92]. In the source code included with the book, this function template is given in <shellsrt.h>. Figure 3.4 shows how Shell Sort progresses on an array of 150 elements.

Knuth [KNUT73] refers to Shell Sort as a *diminishing increment sort*, since any sequence of decreasing h will result in a correctly sorted array. Different sequences result in different runtimes. For example, if the sequence $h = 2, h = 1$ is used, the algorithm runs in $O(N^2)$ time. The sequence $h_s = 2^s - 1, 1 \le s \le \lfloor \lg N \rfloor$ results in a runtime of $O(N^{3/2})$.

Thus, choosing the increments to use is something of a black art. We use an increment sequence recommended by Sedgewick [SEDG92]: ... 40, 13, 4, 1. The sequence is generated by evaluating the sequence $h_{i+1} = 3h_i + 1$ in reverse order, starting at the lowest value of h_i that is greater than $N/9$.

Listing 3.3.   `ShellSort` function template.

```
// =================================================================
// ShellSort function template.
//
//       Sorts an N-element array using the Shell Sort algorithm.
//
// Parameters:
//       T *base           Base of the array to search.
//       int N             Number of elements in the array.
//
// Return value: None.
//
// Requires:
//       operator== and operator< must be defined on the class T.
//
// Runtime:
//       No strong bounds on Shell Sort's runtime have been
//       proven.
// =================================================================
template<class T>
void
ShellSort(T *base, int N)
{
    for (int h = 1; h <= N/9; h = 3*h+1)
        ;
    while (h) {
        for (int i = h; i < N; i += 1) {
            T temp = base[i];

            for (int j = i; j > h - 1 && temp < base[j-h]; j -= h)
                base[j] = base[j-h];

            // Insert the new sorted element.
            base[j] = temp;
        }
        h /= 3;
    }
}
```

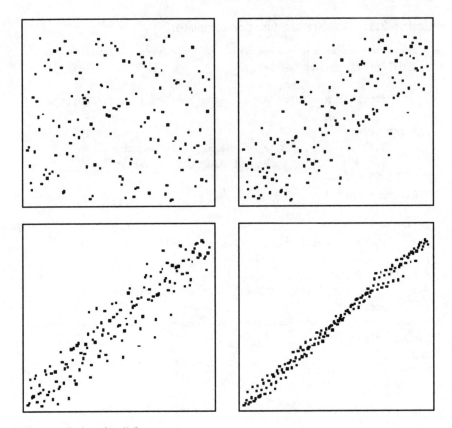

Figure 3.4. Shell Sort in action.

The runtime of this Shell Sort implementation is exceptionally difficult to analyze. In fact, exact bounds on its runtime have not been proven as of this writing. Two conjectures are $O(N \lg^2 N)$ and $O(N^{1.25})$.

Shell Sort comfortably occupies the void between the asymptotically slow Insertion Sort and Selection Sort algorithms, which are unsuitable for large N, and the asymptotically fast Merge Sort, Quicksort, and Heapsort algorithms, which may have constant factors that are too high or require too much auxiliary memory to be appropriate for some sorting applications. Because Shell Sort does not have optimal asymptotic performance and does not exhibit good locality of reference, another sorting technique would probably be best for large or external sorting applications.

3.3.1 Stability and Locality of Reference

It is hard to imagine a Shell Sort implementation that is stable, since elements in different interleaved subarrays can be reordered without any consideration for each other.

Shell Sort exhibits the worst locality of reference of any sorting technique in this book, since it accesses the array at intervals that the paging algorithm for an operating system would find hard to predict. In fact, according to Shell, the ready availability of large amounts of computer memory was one reason he designed Shell Sort. (Most sorting algorithms that predate his own were designed for external sorting.)

CHAPTER 4

Asymptotically Fast Sorts

As input arrays grow in size, the time required to sort them does also. For large arrays, any one of the $O(N \lg N)$ sorting algorithms described in this chapter will blow the doors off the less asymptotically efficient algorithms given in Chapter 3. The tradeoffs to consider when choosing one of the algorithms described here involve auxiliary space and runtime. Merge Sort, described in Section 4.1, requires $O(N)$ auxiliary space to sort an N-element array. Quicksort, described in Section 4.2, requires a significant effort to implement iteratively and can also take up to $O(N)$ auxiliary space; it is also generally the fastest known sorting algorithm for large arrays. Finally, Section 4.3 describes Heapsort, which does not require auxiliary space or a recursive implementation. Unfortunately, Heapsort is also the slowest of the three. These tradeoffs will be discussed in more detail in each section and in the Sorting Wrapup given in Chapter 5.

4.1 Merge Sort

Merge Sort is a highly efficient algorithm for sorting that Knuth attributes to John von Neumann [KNUT73]. In fact, it may have been one of the first algorithms ever implemented on a digital computer.

Although other algorithms with faster average runtimes have become more popular, Merge Sort remains important because of its excellent locality of reference.

Merge Sort works like this:

1. Recursively sort the first half of the array.
2. Recursively sort the second half of the array.
3. Merge the two subarrays into a single sorted array.

After steps 1 and 2 have executed, the array has been divided into two sorted subarrays. These subarrays are then merged by comparing the first two elements and placing the smaller one first. The process is repeated until all the elements of the two subarrays have been merged into a single, sorted array. Chapter 1 contains a proof that the total runtime for Merge Sort is $O(N \lg N)$.

Informally, steps 1 and 2 are executed $O(\lg N)$ times, and the Merge step requires $O(N)$ time, so the total runtime for Merge Sort is $O(N \lg N)$.

Since the lower bound on comparison based sorts is $\Omega(N \lg N)$, Merge Sort is an optimal comparison-based sort.

There is a catch to Merge Sort, however: It does not sort in place. The Merge step requires $O(N)$ space for an N-element array— you need someplace to put the merging elements, and neither of the subarrays being merged is suitable. Listing 4.1 gives `Merge`, a C++ function template to merge two sorted subarrays into a sorted temporary array. Listing 4.2 gives `MergeSortHelper` and `MergeSortRecursive`, function templates that work together to perform Merge Sort on an input array. `MergeSortRecursive` allocates the temporary space required by Merge Sort, then calls the recursive `MergeSortHelper` function template. `MergeSortHelper` uses the `Merge` function template to merge subarrays until the input

Listing 4.1.   Merge function template.

```
// ------------------------------------------------------------
// Merge function template
//      Merges two adjacent, sorted subarrays into a single
//          sorted subarray.
//
// base: base of the subarray that the subarrays start at.
// mid: the index into the lower subarray.
```

```
// N: the maximum index into the subarray.
//
// Example call:
//
// Say we have an array arr = {1, 2, 3, 4, 7, 9, 6, 8} and we
// want to merge the two 2-element subarrays at the end into one.
// Then we call:
//      temp = new int[4];
//      Merge(arr + 4, 2, 4, temp);
//
// This will reorder the final four elements in the array in
// sorted order: {1, 2, 3, 4, 6, 7, 8, 9}.

// It is no coincidence that 2, the number of elements in each
// subarray, is half of 4, the number of elements in the total
// subarray.  Equal-sized subarrays need only be merged O(lgN)
// times to sort the array, and each merge operation is O(N),
// so an optimal O(NlgN) sorting time is achieved.
// -----------------------------------------------------------

template<class T>
void
Merge(T *base, int mid, int N, T *temp)
{
    int inx = 0, inx1, inx2;

    for (inx1 = 0, inx2 = mid;
         inx1 < mid && inx2 < N;
         inx += 1) {
        if (base[inx1] < base[inx2])
            temp[inx] = base[inx1++];
        else
            temp[inx] = base[inx2++];
    }

    while (inx1 < mid)
 temp[inx++] = base[inx1++];
    while (inx2 < N)
 temp[inx++] = base[inx2++];

    // Copy merged array back to the source array.
    for (inx = 0; inx < N; inx++)
 base[inx] = temp[inx];
}
```

Listing 4.2. Merge Sort Recursive function template.

```
// --------------------------------------------------------------
// MergeSortHelper function template
//
//      This recursive function sorts an array using the Merge
//      Sort algorithm.  It is called by MergeSortRecursive.
//      MergeSortRecursive allocates the temp array needed to
//      perform the merges, then calls this function, then
//      deallocates the temp array.
//
// Parameters:
//
//      T *base         Array to sort.
//      int N           Number of elements in array.
//      T *temp         Temporary to use to merge subarrays.
//
// Return value: None
//
// Runtime:
//      O(NlgN) for an N-element array.
//
// --------------------------------------------------------------
template<class T>
void
MergeSortHelper(T *base, int N, T *temp)
{
    if (N < 2)
        return;
    int mid = N/2;
    MergeSortHelper(base, mid, temp);
    MergeSortHelper(base + mid, N - mid, temp);
    Merge(base, mid, N, temp);
}


// --------------------------------------------------------------
// MergeSortRecursive function template
//
//      This function calls MergeSortHelper to merge-sort
//      an array.
//
// Parameters:
//
//      T *base         Array to sort.
//      int N           Number of elements in array.
```

```
//
// Return value: None
//
// Runtime:
//      O(NlgN) for an N-element array.
//
// --------------------------------------------------------------
template<class T>
void
MergeSortRecursive(T *base, int N)
{
    T *temp = new T[N];
    MergeSortHelper(base, N, temp);
    delete[] temp;
}
```

array has been sorted. In the source code included with the book, these function templates are given in <merge.h>.

Figure 4.1 shows MergeSortHelper working to sort an input array.

If we closely examine how MergeSortHelper works, we can derive an iterative implementation. First it recurses on the front half of the array. Then it recurses on the front half of that subarray, and so on until it considers the front two-element subarray. The two recursive calls return immediately, since one-element arrays are automatically in sorted order; then the routine merges the two one-element subarrays. (This amounts to comparing the two elements and swapping if they are out of order.) When the routine returns, it has sorted a two-element array; the calling routine then recursively sorts the next two-element array, and so on until the array consists of $N/2$ sorted, two-element subarrays.

After sorting the last two-element subarray, MergeSort-Recursive returns to a higher level of the recursion. This higher level merges two-element subarrays into four-element subarrays. Depending on the size of the original input array, the actual number of elements in the subarrays varies a little, but the idea is that *the number of elements being merged doubles after each level of recursion completes.* The idea of repeatedly doubling the size of the sorted subarrays until the entire array is sorted can be expressed iteratively as easily as it was expressed recursively.

The MergeSort function template given in Listing 4.3 performs Merge Sort iteratively. In the source code included with the book, MergeSort is given in <merge.h>.

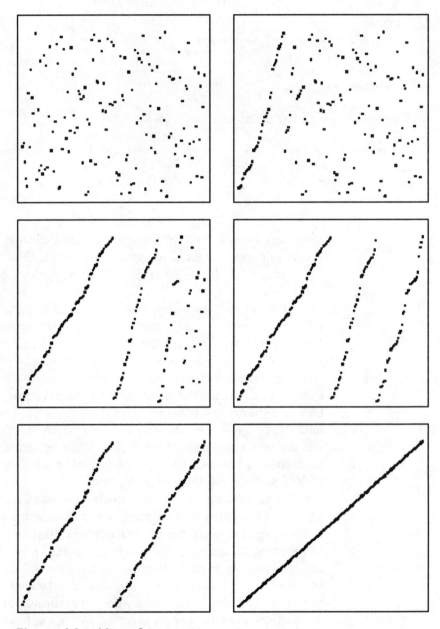

Figure 4.1. Merge Sort in action.

Listing 4.3. Merge Sort function template.

```
// -------------------------------------------------------------
//
// MergeSort function template
//
//      This function implements Merge Sort iteratively.
//
// Parameters:
//
//      T *base          Base of the array to sort.
//      int N            Number of elements in the array.
//
// Return value: None
//
// Runtime:
//      O(NlgN) for an N-element array.
//
// -------------------------------------------------------------

template<class T>
void
MergeSort(T *base, int N)
{
    int i, j, n;
    T *temp = new T[N];

    // Outer loop:
    //    i is the number of elements in each of the
    //       two subarrays being merged.  It doubles
    //       on each iteration, so the outer loop
    //       is executed O(lgN) times.
    //    n is i*2, the total number of elements in
    //       the target subarray.  We keep track of
    //       n for the sake of efficiency.
    for (i = 1, n = 2; n < 2*N; i *= 2, n *= 2) {
        // Inner loop: j executes the O(N) merge
        // step on each n-element subarray.
        for (j = 0; j < N; j += n) {
            if (j + i < N) {
                // This conditional is to take care
                // of the non-power-of-two-element
                // subarray at the end of the array.
```

(continued)

```
        int N2 = (j + n < N) ? n : N - j;
        Merge(base + j, i, N2, temp);
    }
  }
    }
    delete[] temp;
}
```

Although the iterative version of Merge Sort has the same asymptotic runtime as the recursive version, it does behave differently. Rather than merging two subarrays of size $N/2$, it merges subarrays that contain $2^{\lceil \lg N \rceil - 1}$ and $N - 2^{\lceil \lg N \rceil - 1}$ elements. For example, the highest level of recursion on a 100-element array merges 64- and 36-element subarrays. In contrast, MergeSortRecursive merges two 50-element subarrays. Figure 4.2 shows the iterative MergeSort function template operate on an array. (Contrast it with Figure 4.1.)

4.1.1 Stability

If we take care with the Merge function template, we can implement Merge Sort stably. The key is to ensure that Merge places elements from the left-hand subarray before elements from the right-hand subarray if they are equal. The Merge function template given in Listing 4.1 does this; as long as Merge is called with the subarrays in the correct order, all of the Merge Sort implementations given here are stable.

4.1.2 Locality of Reference

Variations of Merge Sort are popular for external sorting applications, and it is easy to see why: It has excellent locality of reference. Merge Sort only has three hot spots where nearby array elements are accessed. The heads of the two subarrays being merged, plus the head of the temporary array, are the only locations that are accessed intensively during Merge Sort. Furthermore, many of the accesses to the subarrays are close to one another (as when the two- and four-element subarrays are being merged). This locality of reference works in Merge Sort's favor when sorting more data than the computer can hold in RAM.

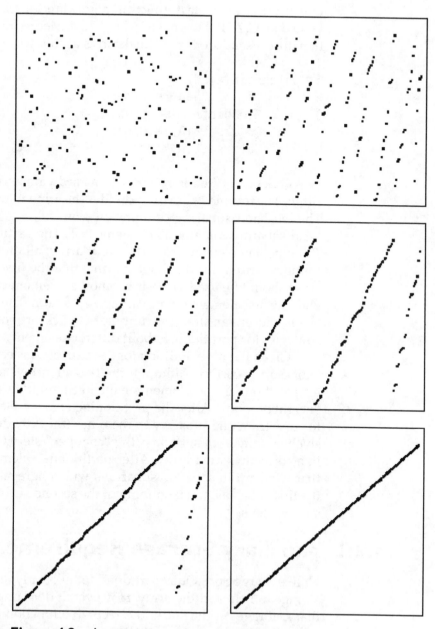

Figure 4.2. Iterative MergeSort in action.

4.2 Quicksort

Quicksort is a very fast, practical algorithm for sorting. It was invented by C. A. R. Hoare [HOAR62]. Like Merge Sort, it is recursive in nature. Pseudocode for Quicksort is as follows.

```
1  Quicksort(A, N)
2      if N<2 then return
3      Midpoint←Partition(A, N)
4      Quicksort(A, Midpoint)
5      Quicksort(A+Midpoint, N-Midpoint)
```

Quicksort often is referred to as a divide-and-conquer algorithm. The routine `Partition` divides the array into two subarrays. The left-hand subarray contains all elements $\leq T$ and the right-hand subarray contains all elements $\geq T$. The partitioning element T can be any element from the input array; all of the partitioning routines written for this book assume that the first element in the array should be used. If desired, another element can be swapped with the first element before calling `Partition`. The partitioning element chosen can affect the runtime of Quicksort, so we will discuss strategies for partitioning about different elements.

Given the postcondition for `Partition`, it is easy to show that Quicksort is correct. Although the two subarrays are unsorted after partitioning, the elements have been shuffled into the correct "neighborhood": After the partitioning step, no element will have to cross from one subarray to the other (the "divide" step). Recursively sorting each subarray (the "conquer" step) therefore results in a correctly sorted array. After partitioning, elements equal to T that wind up in separate subarrays will congregate at the end of the first subarray and beginning of the second subarray during the sorting steps.

4.2.1 Auxiliary Storage Requirements

Unlike Merge Sort, Quicksort does not explicitly allocate auxiliary storage to help sort the array. However, it does implicitly use auxiliary storage on the stack; the recursive function calls effectively store the algorithm state on the machine stack for later reference. In the worst case, a naive version of Quicksort can use up to $O(N)$ space on the stack while running. (We will describe this worst case while discussing the worst-case runtime of Quicksort.) If a really large array is being sorted, you may overflow the machine stack while Quicksort is running. The alternative is to implement Quicksort using an explicit stack (for instance, using the StackLList class template given in Chapter 8). We've used the machine stack in the implementations for this book.

4.2.2 Partitioning the Array

Listing 4.4 gives Partition, a C++ function template for partitioning. Partition assumes that the first element in the input array is T, the element to partition around. In the source code included with the book, Partition is given in <part.h>.

Listing 4.4. Partition function template.

```
// -----------------------------------------------------------
// Partition function template.
//
//      Shuffles elements in an array around the first element T
//      so that all elements <=T precede T in the array, and
//      all elements >T come after T in the array.
//
// Parameters:
//      T *base            Base of the array.
//      int n              Number of elements in the array.
//
// Return value: int
//      Returns the new index of T after partitioning.
//
// Runtime:
//      O(N) for an N-element array.
//
// -----------------------------------------------------------

// The usual partitioning routine.  Works toward the middle
// from the beginning and end of the array.
template<class T>
int
Partition(T *base, int n)
{
```

```
    T part = base[0];
    int i, j;

    i = -1;
    j = n;
    while (i < j) {
        do j -= 1; while (part < base[j]);
        do i += 1; while (base[i] < part);
        if (i < j)
            Swap(base[i], base[j]);
    }
    return j+1;
}
```

Partition works from both ends of the array. "Left" and "right" indices are started just outside the array bounds at -1 and N, respectively. Each index is moved toward the center until it points at an array element that does not belong in that partition of the array. For the left index, an element that is $> T$ does not belong in the left-hand partition; for the right index, an element that is $< T$ does not belong in the right-hand partition. After the indices have been moved until they both point at out-of-order elements, the elements are swapped. This one operation restores the partition on both sides so the process of moving the indices can continue. Figure 4.3 shows Partition working on an input array.

When the indices cross one another, the partition is established: Partition has shuffled the elements of the input array so that the left-hand subarray contains all elements $\leq$ base[0] and the right-hand subarray contains all elements $\geq$ base[0]. Partition returns the index of the last element in the left-hand subarray.

For completeness, we will describe a simpler partitioning scheme invented by Lomuto. Instead of moving two indices toward each other until they meet, one index is kept still while the other advances from left to right. If an element that belongs in the left-hand partition is found by the advancing index, the first index is incremented and the two elements are swapped. This grows the left partition by one element.

Listing 4.5 gives a C++ implementation of LomutoPartition. In the source code included with the book, LomutoPartition is given in <part.h>. LomutoPartition's interface is the same as Partition: It takes the same parameters and returns the index of the last element in the left-hand subarray.

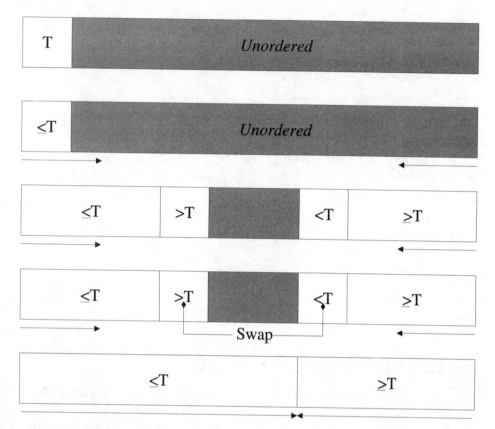

Figure 4.3. Partition.

Listing 4.5. LomutoPartition function template.

```
// ------------------------------------------------------------
// LomutoPartition function template.
//
//      This function also partitions an array about the first
//      element, but it works from only one end of the array
//      instead of working from both ends simultaneously.
//
// Parameters:
//      T *base          Base of the array.
//      int n            Number of elements in the array.
//
// Return value: int
//      Returns the new index of T after partitioning.
//
```

(continued)

```
// Runtime:
//      O(N) for an N-element array.
//
// ----------------------------------------------------------

template<class T>
int
LomutoPartition(T *base, int n)
{
    T part = base[0];
    int m = -1;

    for (int i = 0; i < n; i++) {
        if (base[i] < part) {
            m += 1;
            Swap(base[m], base[i]);
        }
    }
    return m+1;
}
```

4.2.3 Quicksort Runtime

If we assume that the middle partitioning element is chosen for each level of recursion, we can describe the runtime of Quicksort as $T(N) = N + 2T(N/2)$. The factor N is the time to partition the array; the other factor is the runtime to sort the two subarrays. As we showed in Example 4 (Section 1.2.2), the solution to this recursion is $N \lg N$, so Quicksort is expected to take $O(N \lg N)$ on average.

If the array is partitioned about the minimum each time, the subarrays will be $N - 1$ elements and 1 element, rather than both being about $N/2$ elements. If the subarrays are this disparate in size every time for a given run of Quicksort, it runs in $O(N^2)$ time. Thus, while Quicksort usually runs efficiently, it can run slowly depending on the implementation and the input.

It is when this worst-case runtime is elicited that the worst-case stack behavior of the algorithm surfaces: A recursive call is made for every element in the array. If a large array is being sorted, this will almost certainly blow the machine stack.

Listing 4.6 gives `QuickSortRecursive`, a function template that implements a naive version of Quicksort. Since `Partition` assumes that the first element of the subarray is the one to partition around, this implementation of Quicksort runs in $O(N^2)$ time on

Listing 4.6. `QuickSortRecursive` function template.

```
// =============================================================
// QuickSortRecursive function template.
//
//      Sorts an N-element array using a naive QuickSort
//      algorithm.
//
// Parameters:
//      T *base         Base of the array to sort.
//      int N           Number of elements in the array.
//
// Return value: None.
//
// Requires:
//      operator< must be defined on the class T.
//
// Runtime:
//      Expected O(NlgN) for an N-element array.
//      O(N^2) in the worst case.
// =============================================================

template<class T>
void
QuickSortRecursive(T *base, int n)
{
    if (n > 1) {
        int part = Partition(base, n);
        QuickSortRecursive(base, part);
        QuickSortRecursive(base + part, n - part);
    }
}
```

already-sorted input arrays. Figure 4.4 shows this version of Quick-sort running on an input array.

In the source code included with the book, `QuickSort-Recursive` and all the other function templates related to Quicksort are given in <qsort.h>.

4.2.4 Random Partitioning

Choosing the partitioning element randomly almost guarantees that the worst-case $O(N^2)$ behavior won't be seen. For the algorithm to evince its worst-case runtime despite randomizing the partition-

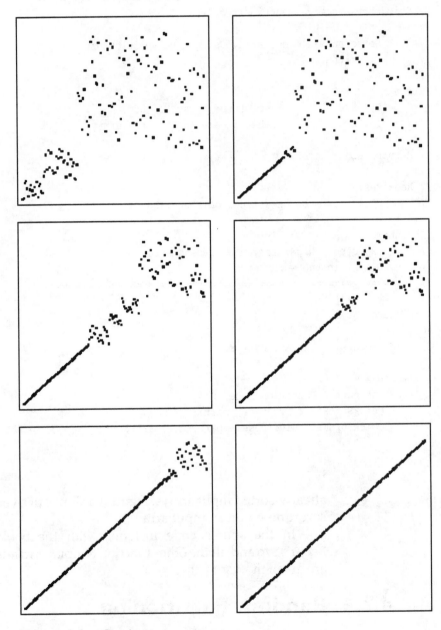

Figure 4.4. Quicksort in action.

ing element, it would have to pick the maximum element in the subarray N times in a row. The probability of this happening is vanishingly small.

Choosing a random partitioning element moves the responsibility for random inputs from the caller to the algorithm, where it belongs. Instead of having the caller worry about whether the input will elicit the algorithm's worst-case performance, the algorithm launches a "preemptive strike" against the input to guarantee that it will appear random during the run.

4.2.5 Median of Three

Another popular partitioning scheme, the "median of three," consists of using the median of the first, middle, and last elements as the partitioning element. Since this requires only a few comparisons, it barely impacts the runtime, and it makes it much more likely that a good partitioning element will be used. Listing 4.7 gives two function templates that implement Quicksort using the median-of-three partitioning scheme. MedianOfThree takes an input array and swaps the first element with the median of the first, middle, and last elements. This prepares the input array to be partitioned by either Partition or LomutoPartition. QuickSortMedianOfThree calls MedianOfThree to perform this operation before partitioning each subarray.

Listing 4.7. QuickSortMedianOfThree function template.

```
// ================================================================
// MedianOfThree function template.
//
//      Compares the first, middle and last elements in an
//      input array and swaps the median of the three with
//      the first element.  This prepares the array to be
//      partitioned by one of the algorithms in <part.h>.
//
// Parameters:
//      T *base         Base of the array to operate on.
//      int N           Number of elements in the array.
//
```

(continued)

```
// Return value: None.
//
// Requires:
//      operator< must be defined on the class T.
//
// Runtime:
//      O(1).
// ============================================================

template<class T>
void
MedianOfThree(T *base, int N)
{
    if (N >= 3) {
        // Swap first element with median of the first,
        // middle and last elements in the array.

        T *beg = base;
        T *mid = base + (N / 2);
        T *end = base + (N - 1);

        if (*beg < *mid) {
            if (*mid < *end) {
                // *mid is median
                Swap(*beg, *mid);
            }
            else {
                if (*beg < *end) {
                    // *end is median
                    Swap(*beg, *end);
                }
                else {
                    // No swap, *beg is already median
                }
            }
        }
        else {
            if (*mid < *end) {
                if (*beg < *end) {
                    // No swap, *beg is already median
                }
                else {
                    // *end is median
                    Swap(*beg, *end);
```

```
                }
            }
            else {
                // beg, mid, end are in reverse order,
                // so mid is median
                Swap(*beg, *mid);
            }
        }
    }
}


// ===============================================================
// QuickSortMedianOfThree function template.
//
//      Sorts an input array using the Quicksort algorithm.
//      Uses the median-of-three partitioning scheme to make it
//      harder to elicit worst-case, quadratic performance.
//
// Parameters:
//      T *base          Base of the array to sort.
//      int N            Number of elements in the array.
//
// Return value: None.
//
// Requires:
//      operator< must be defined on the class T.
//
// Runtime:
//      Expected O(NlgN) for an N-element array.
//      O(N^2) in the worst case.
// ===============================================================
template<class T>
void
QuickSortMedianOfThree(T *base, int N)
{
    if (N > 1) {
        MedianOfThree(base, N);
        int part = Partition(base, N);
        QuickSortMedianOfThree(base, part);
        QuickSortMedianOfThree(base + part, N - part);
    }
}
```

4.2.6 Small Subarrays

Quicksort can be made more efficient by not invoking the full Quicksort machinery for small subarrays. If the array to be sorted is
smaller than, say, 10 elements, we can use an algorithm that is
asymptotically less efficient but faster for small arrays. Insertion
Sort is such an algorithm. Then adding a line such as:

```
if (N < 10)
    InsertionSort(base, N);
```

will make the sort routine run faster. (Note: The 10 used is just
an example. In practice, the best cutoff value will vary from one
implementation to another.)

   In fact, as Sedgewick [SEDG92] points out, we can leave small
subarrays entirely unsorted until just before returning. Insertion
Sort is approximately $O(N)$ for "almost-sorted" arrays. After using
Quicksort to render the array "almost-sorted," we know Insertion
Sort will run quickly to finish off the job.

4.2.7 Replacing Recursion with Iteration

Quicksort ends with a recursive call. Tail recursion always can be
replaced by a loop with an equivalent initialization, invariant and
termination condition. Eliminating tail recursion usually results in
code that is almost as easy to read and almost always more efficient.
Also, by operating on the larger of the two subarrays in-line and
tail-recursing on the smaller one, the worst-case stack usage of the
algorithm can be reduced from $O(N)$ to $O(\lg N)$.

   Listing 4.8 gives a Quicksort implementation that uses the
median-of-three partitioning scheme, does not sort small subarrays, replaces the tail-recursive call with a loop, and uses Insertion
Sort on the final output from Quicksort. Since the cutoff value just
described varies from implementation to implementation, a macro
called QUICKSORT_CUTOFF is used to implement it. If left undefined
during the compilation phase, QuickSort will use a default value of
10; otherwise the value defined by the programmer before including
<qsort.h> will be used.

   Of the Quicksort implementations given here, the implementation in Listing 4.8 is generally the fastest. Figure 4.5 shows its
progress while sorting a large input array up to the point where
Insertion Sort is called.

Listing 4.8.   QuickSort function template.

```
// ================================================================
// QuickSortHelper function template.
//
//      QuickSort: this is the fastest implementation of
//      the algorithm in this class library.  It uses
//      median-of-three partitioning and eliminates tail
//      recursion for the second recursive call.  It also
//      cuts off the recursion at QUICKSORT_CUTOFF elements
//      per subarray and calls InsertionSort after partially
//      sorting the array using the QuickSort algorithm.
//      Since Insertion Sort approaches O(N) runtime for
//      almost-sorted arrays, cutting off the recursion early
//      and having Insertion Sort finish the job goes faster.
//      The optimal value for QUICKSORT_CUTOFF may vary, which
//      is why it can be overloaded by the compiler.  The
//      default value is 10.
//
// Parameters:
//      T *base          Base of the array to sort.
//      int N            Number of elements in the array.
//
// Return value: None.
//
// Requires:
//      operator< must be defined on the class T.
//
// Runtime:
//      Expected O(NlgN) for an N-element array.
//      O(N^2) in the worst case.
// ================================================================

#ifndef QUICKSORT_CUTOFF
#define QUICKSORT_CUTOFF 10
#endif

template<class T>
void
QuickSortHelper(T *base, int N)
{
    if (N > QUICKSORT_CUTOFF) {
        int left = 0;
        while (N > 1) {
```

(continued)

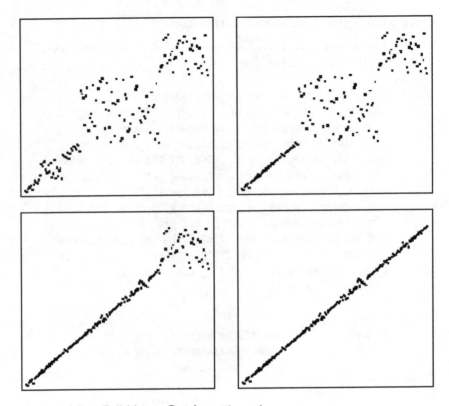

Figure 4.5.   Full-blown Quicksort in action.

```
        MedianOfThree(base + left, N);
        int part = Partition(base + left, N);
        QuickSortHelper(base + left, part);
        left += part;
        N -= part;
      }
    }
}

template<class T>
void
QuickSort(T *base, int N)
{
    QuickSortHelper(base, N);
    InsertionSort(base, N);
}
```

4.2.8 Stability and Locality of Reference

Quicksort is extremely difficult to implement stably [SEDG92]. None of the implementations given here are stable; for an asymptotically fast sorting algorithm that is also stable, refer to Merge Sort (Section 4.1).

Quicksort also exhibits poor locality of reference; between median-of-three partitioning and the approaching indices used to partition the subarrays, it generates many more hot spots in the data than most other sorting algorithms. These hot spots must be kept in memory by the operating system for good performance. For this reason, Quicksort should be restricted to internal sorting applications.

4.3 Binary Heaps and Heapsort

Williams [WILL64] describes the binary heap, a data structure that can be used to implement efficient priority queues and a worst-case $\Theta(N \lg N)$ sorting algorithm. The pool of memory that allocation routines use is also called a "heap"; binary heaps are a type of data structure that must not be confused with the memory allocation heap.

Our discussion of binary heaps follows those of Bentley [BENT86] and Cormen et al. [CORM90]. The three binary heap properties are as follows:

1. The heap is composed of nodes. Each node contains a key, which is used to order the node with respect to other nodes.
2. Every node in the heap has a key less than its children's keys. Property 2 is often called the *heap property*.
3. The heap does not contain any holes.

Property 1 lays out the format of the binary heap. Property 2 makes it possible to quickly find the minimum node in the data structure: Because every node has a smaller key than those of its children, the root node contains the minimum. Finally, as we shall see, Property 3 guarantees that binary heaps are efficient.

Figure 4.6 shows a binary heap. Note how the properties are manifested in the figure. In the following sections, we'll show how these properties make the following operations possible:

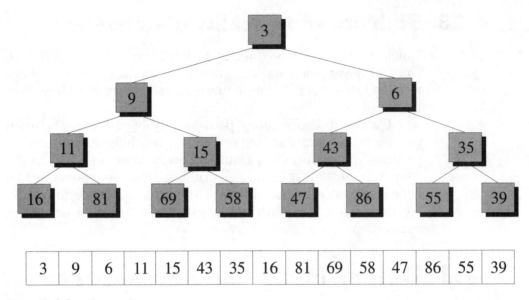

3	9	6	11	15	43	35	16	81	69	58	47	86	55	39

Figure 4.6.   Binary heap.

- **Insert:** Insert a node into the priority queue in $\Theta(\lg N)$ time.

- **Min:** Examine the minimum node in $\Theta(1)$ time.

- **ExtractMin:** Extract the minimum node in $\Theta(\lg N)$ time.

These are the core operations of a *priority queue*. Priority queues are useful in many applications. Whenever a multitasking operating system does a task switch, for example, a priority queue can be used to determine which process has the highest priority and should be given the CPU. Processes are inserted into the priority queue, and the next process to get the CPU depends on its priority, not the order the processes were inserted into the queue. Heaps provide an excellent solution to this and related problems.

Note that except for the minimum, heaps aren't especially good at finding a particular element. Searching for a particular node is so inefficient—$O(N)$ for an N-element heap—that it's rarely implemented. Neither is deletion, since deleting a particular node involves searching for it. These operations aren't implemented for this book. If the data structure has to support more operations than those just listed, a data structure for searching may be in order. A number of appropriate data structures are described in Part II.

Another note: Just given the preceding information, we can derive a $\Theta(N \lg N)$ sorting algorithm using heaps. First we insert the N elements into the heap; since each insertion requires $\Theta(\lg N)$ time, the total time to perform N insertions is $\Theta(N \lg N)$. Next we extract the minimum N times and place the extracted elements into the output array in sorted order. This operation also requires $\Theta(N \lg N)$ time. Since these two $\Theta(N \lg N)$ operations are performed one after the other, the asymptotic runtime of the whole operation is $\Theta(N \lg N)$. Unlike Quicksort, which degrades to $O(N^2)$ for unfavorable inputs, Heapsort is $\Theta(N \lg N)$ in the worst case. It's more efficient to code Heapsort inline than to implement it in terms of the heap data structure, so we'll put off further discussion until Section 4.3.6.

4.3.1 Representation

Since a binary heap does not contain any holes, it can be represented by a simple array. The root element of the array is in element 0. The left child of the ith element in the array is given by $2i + 1$; the right child is given by $2i + 2$.

Figure 4.6 includes the array that represents the binary heap.

Since heaps can be represented by arrays, often it is useful to impose the heap properties on a given array. Bentley [BENT86] describes an operation called SiftDown that can be used to do exactly this.

SiftDown is given an index into the array. This element roots the subtree for which the heap properties must be established. First SiftDown compares the element's children. If both children are greater than the element, SiftDown is done: The heap property is established. Otherwise, the element must be swapped with its lesser child and the process repeated for its new location. Pseudocode for SiftDown is as follows.

```
1   SiftDown (A, N, i)
2       while (i < N - 1) do
3           LeftChild←2*i+1
4           RightChild←2*i+2
5           Child←LeftChild
6           if (RightChild < N) then
7               Compare children
8               if (A[RightChild] < A[LeftChild]) then
```

```
9           Child←RightChild
10      if (A[i] < A[Child]) then
11          break
12      Swap(A[i], A[Child])
13      i←Child
```

The code for SiftDown is somewhat complicated by boundary conditions. Before comparing the children to each other or their parent, SiftDown must ensure the child nodes are actually in the heap. That is why RightChild is compared to N before permitting the comparison between A[LeftChild] and A[RightChild].

SiftDown can be used to establish the heap property on an entire array as follows.

```
1  BuildHeap(A, N)
2       for i←(N-1)/2 downto 0 do
3           SiftDown(A, N, i)
```

BuildHeap works from the bottom of the heap upward, starting with elements whose children are in the bottom row and working its way toward the beginning of the array. Because the elements in the bottom row of the heap can be considered tiny heaps containing one element, BuildHeap calls SiftDown only on elements whose children are heaps. Figure 4.7 shows BuildHeap at work. The shaded nodes conform to the heap properties. The small heaps at the base are expanded toward the root using SiftDown until they encompass the entire array.

SiftDown performs a constant number of operations at each level of the heap, so it is $\Theta(\lg N)$ for an N-element heap. This would imply an overall runtime of $O(N \lg N)$. Most of the heaps being operated on are small, however, and it can be shown that BuildHeap is actually $\Theta(N)$ [CORM90].

4.3.2 Insertion

Inserting a node into a binary heap involves two steps. First the new node is placed at the end of the array. Since the parent of this new node doesn't necessarily have a smaller key than the new node, Property 2 of binary heaps is probably no longer true. So the second step is restoring the heap property using an operation that Bentley calls SiftUp [BENT86]. Pseudocode for SiftUp is as follows.

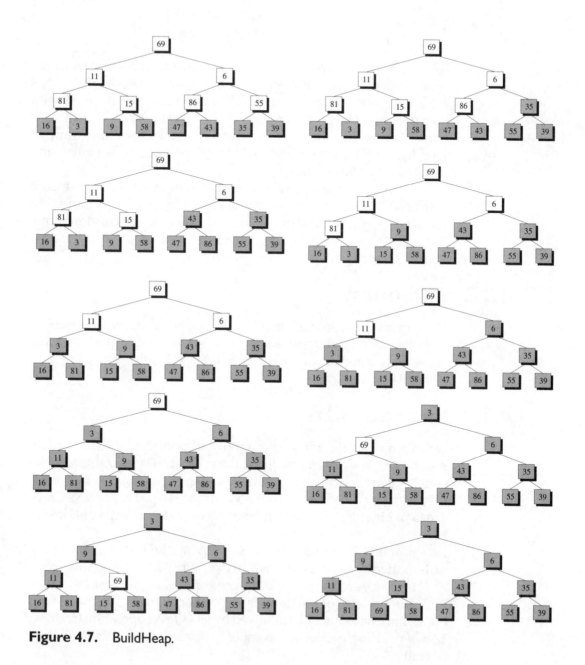

Figure 4.7. BuildHeap.

```
1   SiftUp(A, i)
2        while (i > 0 and A[i] < A[Parent[i]]) do
3               Swap(A[i], A[Parent[i]])
4               i←Parent[i]
```

SiftUp works by "sifting" the newly added node toward the root of the heap until Property 2 is restored. As long as the node's parent is greater than the node, the node must be swapped with its parent and the process repeated. SiftUp stops when the node's parent is less than the node, or when the node has been swapped with the root. Figure 4.8 shows SiftUp operating on a node being inserted into a binary heap.

SiftUp performs $\lceil \lg N \rceil - 1$ comparisons in the worst case, so it is $\Theta(\lg N)$. Inserting a node into the binary heap consists of placing the new node at the end of the heap, which requires constant time, then performing SiftUp. Thus, the total time required to insert a node is also $\Theta(\lg N)$.

4.3.3 Minimum

Since every node in the heap has a smaller key than either child, the root node is guaranteed to contain the minimum. Using the array representation described in Section 4.3.1, the minimum is in element 0 of the array.

4.3.4 ExtractMin

Examining the minimum is very well, but priority queues specialize in *extracting* the minimum. Since the minimum is guaranteed to be element 0 in the array, removing it runs in constant time. However, this leaves a "hole" at the root node of the heap. This breaks Property 3 of binary heaps, which guarantees that the heap contains no holes.

Property 3 can be satisfied by moving the last element to the just-vacated root element, then performing SiftDown on the root. SiftDown reestablishes the heap property using at most two comparisons per level of the heap. Since ExtractMin consists of an $\Theta(1)$ operation (the extraction) followed by an $\Theta(\lg N)$ operation (restoration of the heap properties using SiftDown), it runs in $\Theta(\lg N)$ time overall.

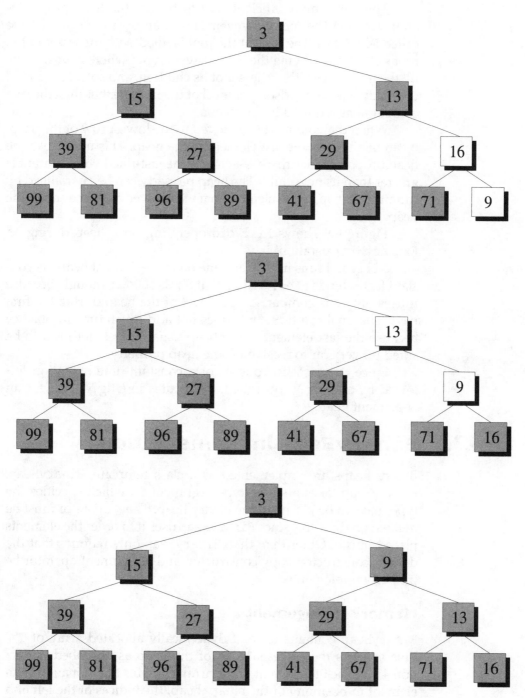

Figure 4.8. Binary heap insertion.

There is a more efficient way to restore the heap properties after vacating the root, however. This is an operation that I have called FillVoid: The void at the root is filled with the lesser of the root's children. Moving the child leaves a void where it was, so we fill the new void with the lesser of its children, and so on. FillVoid uses only one comparison per level of the heap, rather than the two comparisons required by SiftDown.

When the void has been moved to the lowest row of the heap, it can be filled by the last element in the heap. This may break the heap property, since there is a chance the just-filled void's parent is greater than its new child. The heap property can be guaranteed by running SiftUp on the element that was moved from the end of the heap.

Figure 4.9 shows FillVoid operating on a heap during an ExtractMin operation.

FillVoid runs in $\Theta(\lg N)$ time on an N-element heap. Its constant factor tends to be less than that for SiftDown, though, because it uses only one comparison per level of the heap during the first pass. The final call to SiftUp does not add much time in practice because the last element in the heap usually does not need to be sifted up very far to reestablish the heap property.

Since ExtractMin consists of a constant-time operation followed by an $\Theta(\lg N)$ operation, it executes in $\Theta(\lg N)$ time for an N-element heap.

4.3.5 BinaryHeap Implementation

Binary heaps are implemented as a class template, BinaryHeap. BinaryHeap takes a single type argument, T, which specifies the type that can be placed in the binary heap. The < operator must be defined on this type, since BinaryHeap uses it to order the elements placed into it. Other than that, BinaryHeap only requires that the default constructor, copy constructor, and assignment operator be properly implemented.

Memory Management

BinaryHeap contains elms, a dynamically allocated array of T's. This array is the representation of the heap as described in Section 4.3.1. The 0th element of the array contains the root and for an element in position i of the binary heap, the indices of the left and right children are $2i + 1$ and $2i + 2$.

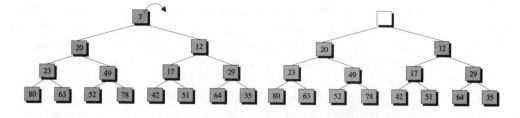

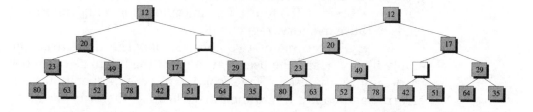

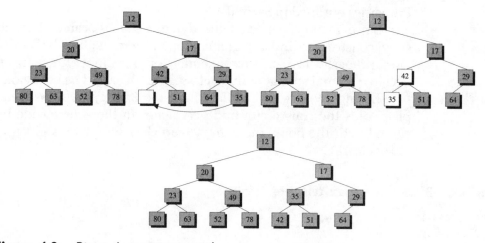

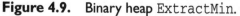

Figure 4.9. Binary heap `ExtractMin`.

Since the heap contains a dynamically allocated array, we could wind up reallocating the array many times over the course of a heap's life. After all, the array has to grow every time a new node is inserted, and some space is being wasted by an unused element if a node is removed.

In practice, it doesn't make sense to do any more dynamic memory operations than necessary. `BinaryHeap` minimizes dynamic memory operations by allocating extra elements at the end of the array. The current number of nodes in the heap is denoted N; the number of nodes actually contained is called Max. If Max==N before an insertion, then more room is needed at the end of the array. Max is doubled, a new array is allocated, and the contents are copied over.

No matter how few elements are in the heap, BinaryHeap never deallocates the array. This is because if the priority queue has grown large once in its lifetime, chances are it will grow just as big in the future. Besides, too much dynamic allocation and deallocation tends to cause memory fragmentation.

BinaryHeap contains two constructors. The first creates an empty binary heap. The user may suggest the initial Max number. (A default of 4 is used.) The second BinaryHeap operation takes an array and copies it into the binary heap. It then runs Heapify to order the array elements so they conform to the Binary Heap Properties outlined in Section 4.3.

Since BinaryHeap contains dynamically allocated data, its copy constructor and assignment operator must be defined to work properly. Its destructor, like most of its member functions, is declared **virtual** so that derived classes can overload its behavior.

Listing 4.9 gives the definition of the BinaryHeap class template, plus the constructor and destructor. In the source code included with the book, the BinaryHeap class template is given in <binheap.h>.

Listing 4.9. BinaryHeap class template definition.

```
template<class T>
class BinaryHeap {
public:
    // Constructors and destructor.
    BinaryHeap(int _max = 4);
    BinaryHeap(const T *arr, int n);
    BinaryHeap(const BinaryHeap&);
    BinaryHeap& operator=(const BinaryHeap&);
    virtual ~BinaryHeap();

    // Core operations for binary heaps.
    void Insert(const T& x);    // Insert a value
    T Min() const;              // Examine the minimum
    T ExtractMin();             // Extract the minimum
    int Num() const;            // Number of elements in heap
```

```
protected:
    T *elms;
    int N;
    int Max;

    // Impose the heap property on the array.
    void BuildHeap();

    // Sift up the given element until its parent is less than it.
    virtual void SiftUp(int i);

    // Sift down the given element until its children are both
    // greater than it.
    virtual void SiftDown(int i);

    // The parameter of this function gives the index of an empty
    // node in the heap.  The function moves this void toward the
    // bottom of the heap by repeatedly filling it with the lesser
    // of its children until it does not have any children.
    // The void is then filled with the last element in the heap,
    // and that element is sifted up to finalize the heap property.
    virtual void FillVoid(int i);

};

template <class T>
BinaryHeap<T>::BinaryHeap(int max)
{
    elms = new T[max];
    N = 0;
    Max = max;
}

template<class T>
BinaryHeap<T>::BinaryHeap(const T *arr, int n)
{
    elms = new T[Max = N = n];
    for (int i = 0; i < N; i++)
        elms[i] = arr[i];
    BuildHeap();
}

template<class T>
void
```

(continued)

```
BinaryHeap<T>::BuildHeap()
{
    for (int i = (N-1) / 2; i >= 0; i--)
        SiftDown(i);
}


// Copy constructor
template <class T>
BinaryHeap<T>::BinaryHeap(const BinaryHeap<T>& x)
{
    elms = new T[N = x.N];
    for (int i = 0; i < N; i++)
        elms[i] = x.elms[i];
    Max = N;
}


// Copy operator
template <class T>
BinaryHeap<T>&
BinaryHeap<T>::operator=(const BinaryHeap<T>& x)
{
    if (elms)
        delete[] elms;
    N = x.N;
    Max = x.Max;
    elms = new T[Max];
    for (int i = 0; i < x.N; i++)
        elms[i] = x.elms[i];
    return *this;
}


template<class T>
BinaryHeap<T>::~BinaryHeap()
{
    delete[] elms;
}
```

Core Operations

The Insert member function inserts a new element into the heap.
It does not return any value, but if there is a problem allocating
memory, it will throw a xalloc exception. Insert calls the SiftUp
member function described in the next section.

ExtractMin extracts the minimum element from the binary heap and returns it. It calls the FillVoid member function described in the next section.

Min returns a pointer to the minimum element in the heap. It returns an actual pointer, rather than a copy of the minimum, so that the client of the class can examine or manipulate the element in the heap as needed.

Num returns the number of elements in the binary heap.

Insert, Min, ExtractMin and Num are implemented as described in Sections 4.3.2, 4.3.3, and 4.3.4. They are listed in Listing 4.10.

Listing 4.10. Insert, Min, ExtractMin and Num member functions.

```
template<class T>
void
BinaryHeap<T>::Insert(const T& x)
{
    if (++N >= Max) {
        T *temp = new T[Max <<= 1];
        for (int i = 0; i < N-1; i++)
            temp[i] = elms[i];
        delete[] elms;
        elms = temp;
    }
    elms[N-1] = x;
    SiftUp(N-1);
}

template<class T>
T
BinaryHeap<T>::Min() const
{
    return elms[0];
}

template<class T>
T
BinaryHeap<T>::ExtractMin()
{
```

(continued)

```
    T ret = elms[0];          // Here's the return value
    if (N > 1) { // Now restore the heap property
        FillVoid(0);                // Move the void to lowest row
                                    // then fill it and restore heap
                                    // property.
    }
    N -= 1;                   // Decrement number of elms.
    return ret;
}

template<class T>
int
BinaryHeap<T>::Num() const
{
    return N;
}
```

SiftDown, SiftUp, and FillVoid

SiftDown, SiftUp, and FillVoid are implemented as **protected** member functions. Clients of BinaryHeap should never need to call these functions directly, so **public** access is not appropriate. The source code, given in Listing 4.11, closely follows the descriptions as given in Sections 4.3.1 through 4.3.4.

Listing 4.11. SiftUp, SiftDown and FillVoid member functions.

```
template <class T>
void
BinaryHeap<T>::SiftUp(int i)
{
    while (i) {
        int p = (i-1) >> 1;
        if (elms[p] < elms[i])
            break;
        Swap(elms[i], elms[p]);
        i = p;
    }
}

template <class T>
void
BinaryHeap<T>::SiftDown(int i)
{
```

```
    int c;

    while ( (c = i+i+1) < N) {
        if ((c+1 < N) && (elms[c+1] < elms[c]))
            c += 1;
        if (elms[i] < elms[c])
            break;
        Swap(elms[i], elms[c]);
        i = c;
    }
}

template<class T>
void
BinaryHeap<T>::FillVoid(int i)
{
    int c;

    while ( (c = i+i+1) < N) {
        if ((c+1 < N) && (elms[c+1] < elms[c]))
            c += 1;
        elms[i] = elms[c];
        i = c;
    }
    // The void, pointed to by i, has now been
    // moved to the lowest row in the heap.
    // In order to keep Binary Heap Property 3
    // true, we must fill this gap and restore
    // the heap property from there using SiftUp.
    if (i < N-1) {
        elms[i] = elms[N-1];
        SiftUp(i);
    }
}
```

SiftUp, SiftDown, and FillVoid are called by BuildHeap, Insert, and ExtractMin to restore the properties of the binary heap as needed.

4.3.6 Heapsort

In Section 4.3, we mentioned how heaps could be used to implement a sorting algorithm. In terms of our heap data structure, it would be implemented as follows.

```
1  Heapsort(A, N)
2       BinaryHeap heap(A, N);
3       for i←0 to N-1 do
4            A[i] = heap.ExtractMin();
```

The problem with this approach is that the heap takes up just as much space as the array being sorted. Requiring $O(N)$ space to sort N elements is nothing new (see the discussion of Merge Sort), but in the case of Heapsort it is unnecessary. We can sort the array in place if we conveniently treat parts of it as *heap* and other parts as *sorted*.

We can start by performing BuildHeap on the array, with the sense of the comparisons reversed so that the root node contains the maximum element in the array rather than the minimum. Then we can incrementally construct the sorted array from back to front by swapping the maximum element in the *heap* part of the array to the beginning of the *sorted* part of the array. This grows the *sorted* part of the array toward the beginning of the array by one element, but breaks the heap property in the *heap* part of the array. So we run SiftDown on the heap subarray to restore its heap property.

Figure 4.10 depicts Heapsort at work.

In pseudocode, the operation looks like this.

```
1  Heapsort(A, N)
2       BuildHeap(A, N)
3       for i←N-1 downto 1 do
4            Swap(A[0], A[i])
5            SiftDown(A, i-1)
```

This can be written in-line, without references to BuildHeap or SiftDown. Listing 4.12 gives a template-based implementation of Heapsort. In the source code included with the book, the HeapSort function template is given in <heapsort.h>.

Heapsort is the only sorting algorithm described in this book that runs in *worst-case* $\Theta(N \lg N)$ time and requires only $O(1)$ auxiliary storage. Merge Sort has a worst-case runtime of $\Theta(N \lg N)$ but requires $O(N)$ auxiliary storage. Quicksort runs in worst-case time of $O(N^2)$ and requires $O(N)$ auxiliary storage on the machine stack in the worst case.

A good implementation of Quicksort is usually faster than Heapsort in practice, but Heapsort does not have the unfavorable

First, the array is "heapified" so that every node is greater than its children.

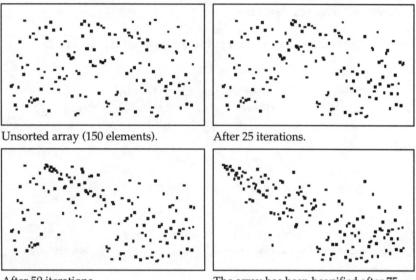

Unsorted array (150 elements).   After 25 iterations.

After 50 iterations.   The array has been heapified after 75 iterations.

The root node of the heap is the maximum. We can swap the maximum with the last element in the array, then sift the new root node down to its proper position. The sorted array is thus built from back to front.

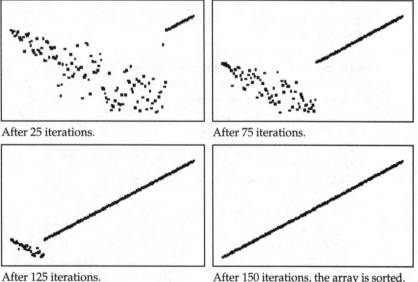

After 25 iterations.   After 75 iterations.

After 125 iterations.   After 150 iterations, the array is sorted.

Figure 4.10.   Heapsort in action.

Listing 4.12.   HeapSort function template.

```
// ================================================================
// HeapSort function template.
//
//        Sorts an N-element array using the HeapSort algorithm.
//
// Parameters:
//        T *base          Base of the array to sort.
//        int N            Number of elements in the array.
//
// Return value: None.
//
// Requires:
//        operator< must be defined on the class T.
//
// Runtime:
//        Worst-case O(NlgN) for an N-element array.
// ================================================================

template<class T>
void
HeapSort(T *base, int N)
{
    int i;

    // Impose the heap property on the array.
    // This step is O(N).
    //
    // Note: The usual sense of comparisons, which results
    // in the minimum elements being placed at the root,
    // has been reversed for HeapSort.
    for (i = (N-1)/2; i >= 0; i--) {
        int j = i;
        int c;
        while ( (c = j+j+1) < N) {
            if ((c+1 < N) && (base[c] < base[c+1]))
                c += 1;
            if (base[c] < base[j])
                break;
            Swap(base[j], base[c]);
            j = c;
        }
    }
```

```
// Now repeatedly swap the maximum with the last element
// in the array.  This takes the maximum out of the
// picture (it is now where it belongs), but breaks the
// heap property at the root.  So the root must be
// sifted down to reestablish the heap property.
// This step is O(NlgN).
for (i = N - 1; i > 0; i--) {
    int j = 0;
    int c;
    Swap(base[0], base[i]);

    while ((c = 2*j+1) < i) {
        if (((c+1) < i) && (base[c] < base[c+1]))
            c += 1;
        if (base[c] < base[j])
            break;
        Swap(base[j], base[c]);
        j = c;
    }
}
}
```

worst-case runtimes and auxiliary storage requirements imposed by Quicksort. If auxiliary storage is at a premium but an $O(N^2)$ algorithm isn't acceptable, Heapsort is an excellent choice.

4.3.7 Future Work

Some applications for priority queues require not only efficient Insert, Min, and ExtractMin operations but also operations called MergeHeap and DecreaseKey. MergeHeap merges two heaps into one. DecreaseKey decreases the key of a specified element in the heap without removing it. These operations are especially useful for implementing graph algorithms, which operate on mathematical graphs composed of vertices with edges connecting them. Any introductory algorithms text covers a plethora of graph algorithms; see Cormen et al. [CORM90] for an exceptionally thorough discussion.

MergeHeap and DecreaseKey are easy to implement for binary heaps. MergeHeap is done by copying the two heaps' arrays into a single, larger array, then calling BuildHeap. This operation is $O(N)$ where N is the total number of elements. DecreaseKey is just a call to `SiftUp`, which is $O(\lg N)$. Heap data structures have been invented that support these operations more efficiently.

Binomial heaps, described by Vuillemin [VUIL88], support the `MergeHeap` operation in just $O(\lg N)$ time. Binomial heaps still take $O(\lg N)$ time for `DecreaseKey`, however. Fredman and Tarjan [FRED88] describe another heap data structure, the Fibonacci heap, which supports `MergeHeap` and `DecreaseKey` in amortized $O(1)$ time.

Sorting Wrapup

Here we review the sorting algorithms described in this part of the book. Section 5.1 describes the tradeoffs of speed and space between the different algorithms, and gives accurate timing results for each sorting implementation. Section 5.2 discusses sorting without comparisons, a technique that can bring the lower bound of sorting algorithms from $\Omega(N \lg N)$ to $\Omega(N)$. Finally, Section 5.3 discusses the sorting literature and mentions a number of algorithms that were not implemented for this book.

5.1 Tradeoffs

We've described a number of sorting algorithms for a reason: There is no optimal sorting algorithm. If there were, fewer sorting algorithms might have been invented! Table 5.1 gives an overview of the sorting algorithms, their runtimes, and the amount of auxiliary space they require to complete. This table can be used to help decide which algorithm is best for a certain application.

5.1.1 Timing

Modern microprocessors, including the Pentium, Alpha, and PowerPC, contain extremely accurate hardware timers. Many of them are linked to the system clock, harking back to the MIX architecture described by Knuth [KNUT73], but even more applicable to the real

Table 5.1.   Overview of Sorting Algorithms

Algorithm	Stable	Expected Runtime	Worst-case Runtime	Auxiliary space
Insertion Sort	Yes	$O(N^2)$	$O(N^2)$	$O(1)$
Selection Sort	Yes	$O(N^2)$	$O(N^2)$	$O(1)$
Shell Sort	No	Unknown	Unknown	$O(1)$
Merge Sort	Yes	$O(N \lg N)$	$O(N \lg N)$	$O(N)$
Quicksort	No	$O(N \lg N)$	$O(N^2)$	$O(N)$
Heapsort	No	$O(N \lg N)$	$O(N \lg N)$	$O(1)$

Notes

- Insertion Sort generally has a lower constant factor than the others, so for small numbers of elements it is usually the fastest.
- Selection Sort performs many comparisons but very few swaps. For cumbersome data, it may be the best choice.
- Merge Sort has an optimal $\Theta(N \lg N)$ runtime but requires $O(N)$ auxiliary space.
- Quicksort uses $O(N)$ stack space in the worst case but only $O(\lg N)$ in the average case.
- Of the efficient algorithms, Quicksort is usually the fastest.
- Although Heapsort uses $O(1)$ auxiliary space and still has a runtime of $\Theta(N \lg N)$, it is usually slower than Merge Sort and Quicksort.

world. For Table 5.2, the timing tests were built under the Alpha version of Windows NT. The Alpha includes a "real-time process cycle counter" (RPCC) that counts clock cycles; on the 21064A/233 that I ran the benchmarks on, the RPCC had the same resolution as the 233 MHz processor clock.

Table 5.2.   Sorting Algorithm Runtimes

Algorithm	Runtime (clocks)
Insertion Sort	$1.93N^2$
Selection Sort	$4.84N^2$
Shell Sort	$38.1 N \lg^2 N$
Recursive Merge Sort	$38.2N \lg N$
Iterative Merge Sort	$44.4N \lg N$
Recursive Quicksort	$20.2N \lg N$
Quicksort (median-of-three)	$20.2N \lg N$
Full-blown Quicksort (cutoff $= 10$)	$17.8N \lg N$
Heapsort	$65.4N \lg N$

Each sorting algorithm was tested with a variety of input array sizes (from 10 to 100,000) to characterize the performance. The data being sorted was randomized, and several times were taken and averaged for each item count. No virtual memory was used in the test, so these results will be less useful for readers who require locality of reference.

The constant of proportionality was computed by fitting to the asymptotic runtime of the algorithm. The resulting expression describes the runtime extremely accurately.

The asymptotic runtime of our Shell Sort implementation is unknown, but the $N \lg^2 N$ curve fit the data slightly better than the $N^{1.25}$ curve.

The runtimes given in Table 5.2 are in clock cycles; the Alpha took about 1.93(100) = 1930 clock cycles to sort ten elements using Insertion Sort. The clock rate on the Alpha the tests were run on was 233 MHz, so the elapsed time is about 8.3 microseconds.

The relative constants of proportionality given in the table are more dependent on the algorithms than the actual implementations. (Insertion Sort is likely to be faster than recursive Quicksort on small arrays regardless of the type of computer.) In any case, it should be easy for readers to experiment to determine which sorting algorithm given is the best for their application.

There are several interesting points to make here.

- Recursive Merge Sort is slightly faster than the iterative implementation, which surprised me; usually iterative implementations of algorithms are faster.

- Quicksort is the fastest sort by far, but a nonrecursive implementation is fairly hard to come by (the stack has to be simulated) and its performance may degrade to $O(N^2)$.

- The recursive Quicksort implementation responded well to the randomized data used in the timing test; the median-of-three partitioning scheme is better for real applications, despite a slightly larger constant factor. Recursive Quicksort degrades to quadratic performance on sorted arrays, for example.

- Heapsort, the only algorithm that is guaranteed to run in $O(N \lg N)$ time and $O(1)$ auxiliary space, has the largest constant of proportionality.

- The results are not documented here, but I've obtained similar results on a Power Macintosh using its high-resolution timer. (The PowerPC 601 also has a cycle-counting register, though with slightly lower resolution than the one on the Alpha.)

5.2 Sorting Without Comparisons

We showed in Chapter 2 that sorting requires $\Omega(N \lg N)$ comparisons. However, we do not always have to compare elements to sort them. For example, if the elements can be characterized by small integers in the range $[0, k]$, then we can use an $O(N)$ sorting algorithm called Counting Sort. Counting Sort begins by constructing a histogram of the input. The histogram is an array $[0..k]$ of integers initialized to 0. For each element in the input, the corresponding histogram element is incremented. After the entire input has been scanned, the histogram contains an array of counts: Element 0 of the histogram contains the number of 0s that were in the input, element 1 contains the number of 1s, and so on. So once the histogram is computed, you can traverse it in order and, for each element in the histogram, send that many elements to the output.

If k is constant, the above sorting algorithm is $O(N)$. One good example of a problem that is easily solved with this algorithm is a grayscale image with 8-bit pixels. Each element of data only has $2^8 = 256$ possible values, and images typically have hundreds of thousands of pixels. It is much more efficient to histogram such data sets than to reorder them based on comparisons.

(In practice, histograms are not used to sort pixels per se; however, grayscale images still provide a good example of data sets where the number of elements overwhelms the number of values that the elements can attain. We provide more practical examples of uses for histograms in our discussion of selection algorithms.)

Other linear-time sorting algorithms include Radix Sort and Bucket Sort.

5.3 Literature

We've discussed all of the most important sorting algorithms, but there are some gaps in our coverage. For a more mathematically rigorous presentation, the reader can turn to an introductory text on algorithms, such as Cormen, et al. [CORM90] or Sedgewick [SEDG92].

Knuth cowrote an extensive bibliography with Rivest [RIVE72] and wrote a definitive and rigorous treatment of sorting [KNUT73]. The latter work includes an in-depth treatment of external sorting, which received short shrift here.

Bentley gives excellent descriptions of Insertion Sort, Quicksort, and Heapsort [BENT86]. Sedgewick developed an exhaustive treatment of Quicksort [SEDG78].

Searching

Searching consists of storing and retrieving data. The applications vary: One program may just want to store the data quickly, then retrieve it in any order. Another may want to maintain a set of items that can be accessed quickly in random order. Yet another may want to maintain a set of items that can be enumerated in order on demand. This part of the book discusses these and other searching problems and many of the data structures that have been invented to address them.

CHAPTER 6

Overview of Searching

Searching applications come in a variety of shapes and sizes. The simplest searching application is to maintain an unordered list of items so the items can be referred to later. In this case, fast insertion into the data structure is essential, and there is no need to keep the items in order. A simple array or unordered linked list is ideal for this type of application.

Sometimes a list of items is constructed once, then queried many times over its lifetime. In this case, constructing the data structure can take a long time, but the queries must run as fast as possible. A variant of Binary Search is an excellent way to address this type of application.

Sometimes the items in the data structure must be kept in order and be able to be inserted, deleted, and queried at any moment. Binary trees, red-black trees, splay trees, and skip lists all support these operations efficiently. They are optimized for different cases. Binary trees work well if items are inserted and deleted randomly, but their performance degrades if data is inserted in sorted order. Red-black trees avoid this worst-case behavior, but at a cost in the average case. Splay trees are optimized for localized access: Queried elements are propagated toward the root of the tree for faster access. Finally, skip lists are a probabilistic alternative to tree-based data structures that require less memory.

Sometimes users can give hints to the data structure as to where to begin searching, thereby decreasing the runtime. The hint is called a "finger" (analogous to pointing a finger at where to begin searching). Fingers and their potential applications are discussed for data structures that support them.

Many of the issues that arise in sorting also arise in searching.

6.1 Keys and Satellite Data

Search data structures rely on comparisons to order the data, so we again have the distinction between the key and the satellite data in each item. The key is used to perform the comparisons, while the satellite data passively accompanies each key wherever it occupies the data structure.

6.2 Equal Keys

Like sorting applications, where stability is an issue, searching applications have problems when elements with equal keys are inserted into a data structure. In this book, nothing prevents clients of the data structures from inserting two elements with the same key. In turn, no guarantee is made that querying that key will behave predictably. The data structure might give back the last element inserted that has that key, or it might not. Modifying the class templates so they replace elements with equal keys rather than adding new ones is a simple exercise, which I have left to the reader.

If it's important that elements be distinct, take steps to ensure that elements with equal keys are not inserted.

6.3 External Searching

The data structures described in this book operate in memory. Many data structures have been invented for database applications, where the data being searched resides on a disk. These data structures strive to minimize the number of disk accesses required to retrieve a record. None of these data structures are discussed in this book. (Interested readers should refer to one of the references, which cover databases and persistent objects more thoroughly than we have room for here.)

6.4 Dictionaries

A "dictionary" is any dynamic data structure that supports efficient insertion, deletion, and query operations. A number of different class templates that support these operations are implemented in this book in as consistent a way as possible. The operations that are defined on all dictionary classes are as follows.

```
void Insert(const T&);
```

This operation inserts an item into the dictionary.

```
void Delete(const T&);
```

This operation queries and deletes the given item from the dictionary.

```
T *Query(const T&);
```

This operation queries the given item in the dictionary and, if found, returns a pointer to it. If the item is not found, the function returns 0.

For many searching applications, Insert, Delete, and Query are all you need. If so, you would choose the data structure based on the pattern of insertions, deletions, and queries expected. For example, if these operations are likely to be performed randomly, an unadorned binary tree is probably sufficient. However, if the application involves a lot of queries that exhibit locality of reference, splay trees probably would be better. We will discuss the performance of the various data structures later in the book.

6.4.1 Dictionary Iterators

Iterators into a dictionary keep track of a location in the dictionary. They can be used to query the dictionary and also to traverse it in forward and backward order. Three iterator implementations are provided: one for an unordered linked list class, one for binary trees and their variants, and one for skip lists. Iterator implementations share a great deal, however, and the fundamental operations for iterators include the following.

Creation   Gives a dictionary to operate on and possibly a "finger" telling where to start pointing. In general, iterators start out pointing at the first element (smallest in the sorted order) by default.

The constructor has an opportunity to mark the data structure so it cannot be modified while an iterator is examining it. Otherwise, the element pointed to by an iterator could be deleted right out from under it.

Destruction Detaches the iterator from the data structure. If the data structure was marked to indicate that the iterator was attached to it, this mark can be removed by the destructor.

Dereference Provides access to the item currently pointed to by the iterator.

Next   Causes the iterator to point itself at the next item in the data structure. For ordered data structures, this item is usually the next one in the sorted order.

Previous   Causes the iterator to point itself at the previous element in the data structure. Not all data structures support this operation.

Many implementation issues arise with iterators. Implementing them as embedded classes is an attractive alternative, since doing so keeps from polluting the global namespace; however, every compiler I know of requires that the member functions of embedded classes in class templates be implemented in-line. This compromises readability to some extent. Another alternative is to declare the constructor for the iterator class **private** and declare the class to iterate on a **friend** of the iterator class. The class template to iterate on can then provide a member function to create an instance of the iterator.

Which implementation strategy is better is debatable, and the class templates for searching provided with this book actually take both approaches. The binary tree iterator class is implemented as an embedded class, while the skip list iterator class is a **friend** with a **private** constructor. I am interested in readers' thoughts on which approach is better and why. In the meantime, this high-level discussion merely gives an overview of the services an iterator class is expected to provide. The specific iterator implementations are discussed in more detail under the implementation of each data structure.

CHAPTER 7

Searching Arrays

The array is the simplest data structure, and we will explore some algorithms designed to work on arrays before we move on to more complicated data structures. Linear Search, described in Section 7.1, exhaustively compares each element in the array to the query element; it can take up to $O(N)$ time to find the query element.

Section 7.2 examines Binary Search and its variants. These algorithms require that the input array be sorted, but they run much faster as a result. First we will describe recursive and iterative implementations of Binary Search. Then Section 7.2.1 will describe how to eliminate the loop from Binary Search if the number of elements in the input array is known at compile time. Finally, Section 7.2.2 will describe a variant called Interpolation Search that works well if the caller can estimate where in the array the query element will be found.

7.1 Linear Search

Linear search is an algorithm that searches an array for a given element. It is optimal if the data being searched hasn't been structured somehow to make finding the elements contained in it easier. The algorithm is straightforward: Consider each element and, if it is equal to the key, return it; otherwise go on to the next element. As anyone who has searched for eyeglasses can attest, the algorithm may very well consider every element in the array before finding the right one, so it runs in linear time ($O(N)$) per its name. A function template for linear search is given in Listing 7.1. In the source code included with the book, this function template is given in `<lsearch.h>`.

As we have already seen in Section 4.3, structuring an array properly can lead to substantial increases in performance—in that case, when extracting the minimum element in the array. The next chapter discusses how sorting the array can substantially increase searching performance.

Listing 7.1.   LinearSearch function template.

```
// ===============================================================
// LinearSearch function template.
//
//      Searches an N-element array for a given query element.
//      The elements can be unsorted.
//
// Parameters:
//      T *base         Base of the array to search.
//      int N           Number of elements in the array.
//      const T& q      Query element.  The first array element
//                      equal to this query element will be
//                      returned.
// Return value: T *
//      A pointer to the first array element equal to the query
//      element, or 0 if no element equal to the query is found.
//
// Requires:
//      operator== must be defined on the class T.
//
// Runtime:
//      O(N) for an N-element array.
// ===============================================================
template<class T>
T *
LinearSearch(T *base, int N, const T& q)
{
    for (int i = 0; i < N; i += 1, base += 1)
        if (*base == q)
            return base;
    return 0;
}
```

7.2 Binary Search

Binary search assumes that the data being searched has already been sorted. If this is the case, then the key can be found in $\Theta(\lg N)$ time. The algorithm works like this.

1. Compare the middle element of the search array with the key. If there is only one element, return it if they are equal or return NOT-FOUND if they are not.
2. If the key is smaller than the middle element, recursively search the left-hand subarray. Otherwise recursively search the right-hand subarray.

Pseudocode for the algorithm is as follows.

```
1   BinarySearch(Base, N, Query)
2       if N ( 1 then return NOT-FOUND
3       Middle←N/2
4       if (Base[Middle]<Query) then
5           Search right-hand subarray
6           return BinarySearch(Base+Middle+1,
7                                   N-Middle-1, Query)
8       else if (Base[Middle]>Query) then
9           Search left-hand subarray
10          return BinarySearch(Base, Middle, Query)
11      Base[Middle] is equal to the query element
12      return Base[Middle]
```

Each comparison performed by the algorithm eliminates half of the remaining elements in the array from consideration, until only one element remains. Binary Search requires at most $\lfloor \lg N \rfloor + 1$ comparisons to search N elements (30 comparisons to search a billion-element array!). Binary Search is optimal: No algorithm can use asymptotically fewer comparisons to search a sorted array [KNUT73].

Figure 7.1 shows Binary Search in action on an example array.

Listing 7.2 gives BinarySearchRecursive, a recursive implementation of the algorithm. In the source code included with the book, this function template (and the other function templates described in this chapter) is given in <bsearch.h>.

Query: 86 (successful)

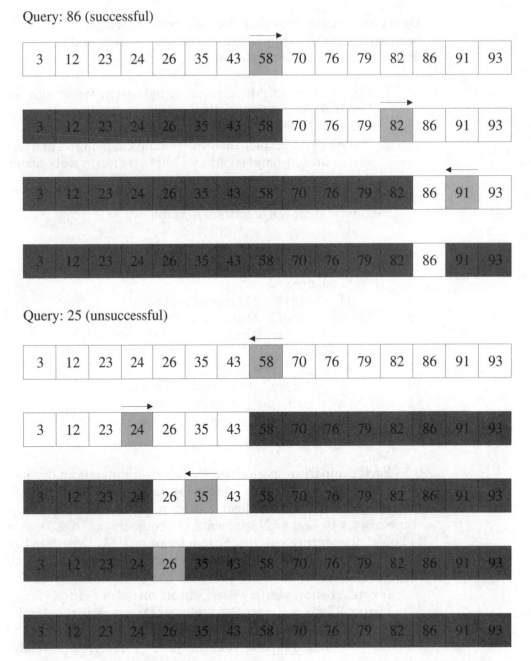

Query: 25 (unsuccessful)

Figure 7.1. Binary search in action.

Listing 7.2. `BinarySearchRecursive` function template.

```
// ================================================================
// BinarySearchRecursive function template.
//
//      Searches an N-element array for a given query element.
//      The elements must be sorted.
//
// Parameters:
//      T *base         Base of the array to search.
//      int N           Number of elements in the array.
//      const T& q      Query element.  The first array element
//                      found equal to this query element will
//                      be returned.
// Return value: T *
//      A pointer to an array element equal to the query element
//      or 0 if no element equal to the query is found.
//
// Requires:
//      operator== and operator< must be defined on the class T.
//
// Runtime:
//      O(lgN) for an N-element array.
// ================================================================
template<class T>
T *
BinarySearchRecursive(T *base, int N, const T& q)
{
    // If no elements in array, return not-found.
    if (N < 1)
        return 0;

    int mid = N/2;
    if (base[mid] < q) {
        base += mid + 1;
        N -= mid + 1;
    }
    else {
        if (base[mid] == q)
            return base + mid;
        N = mid;
    }
    return BinarySearchRecursive(base, N, q);
}
```

As an aside, I'd like to point out that the BinarySearch-Recursive function template is tail-recursive. As discussed in Chapter 1, tail-recursive functions can *always* be converted to iterative ones. Listing 7.3 gives an iterative version of BinarySearch.

Listing 7.3. BinarySearch function template.

```
// ===============================================================
// BinarySearch function template.
//
//      Searches an N-element array for a given query element.
//      The elements must be sorted.
//
// Parameters:
//      T *base         Base of the array to search.
//      int N           Number of elements in the array.
//      const T& q      Query element.  The first array element
//                      found equal to this query element will
//                      be returned.
// Return value: T *
//      A pointer to an array element equal to the query element
//      or 0 if no element equal to the query is found.
//
// Requires:
//      operator== and operator< must be defined on the class T.
//
// Runtime:
//      O(lgN) for an N-element array.
// ===============================================================
template<class T>
T *
BinarySearch(T *base, int N, const T& q)
{
    while (N >= 1) {
        int mid = N/2;
        if (base[mid] < q) {
            base += mid + 1;
            N -= mid + 1;
        }
        else {
            if (base[mid] == q)
                return base + mid;
            N = mid;
        }
    }
```

```
        }
    return 0;
}
```

7.2.1 Inlining Binary Search

Bentley [BENT86] describes a way to optimize the straightforward Binary Search implementation given here by inlining the code. We'll only outline the idea and give a representative example; the inlining can be modified to work for any fixed N.

To start, consider what happens with Binary Search when the number of elements in the input array is a power of 2, say, 64. Binary Search starts by examining the 32nd element in the array. If the element is greater than the query element, Binary Search recurses on the left-hand subarray; otherwise it recurses on the right-hand subarray. If the left-hand subarray is chosen, there are 31 elements and the 16th element is examined; otherwise there are 32 elements and the 16th element is examined. Notice that the index of the middle element is always a power of 2. The only issue is what the base of the subarray should be—should it stay the same for the left-hand subarray, or move to the middle for the right-hand subarray?

Listing 7.4 gives `BinarySearch16`, a function template that performs Binary Search on an array that contains 16 elements. The variable `left` points just to the left of the subarray's base. Because the loop has been unrolled, `BinarySearch16` is likely faster than calling `BinarySearch` on a 16-element array.

Listing 7.4. `BinarySearch16` function template.

```
// =================================================================
// BinarySearch16 function template.
//
//      Searches a 16-element array for a given query element.
//      The elements must be sorted.
//
// Parameters:
//      T *base         Base of the array to search.
//      const T& q      Query element.  The first array element
//                      found equal to this query element will
//                      be returned.
// Return value: T *
//      A pointer to an array element equal to the query element
//      or 0 if no element equal to the query is found.
```

(continued)

```
//
// Requires:
//        operator!= and operator< must be defined on the class T.
//
// Runtime:
//        O(1).  Uses at most 5 comparisons.
// ================================================================
template<class T>
T *
BinarySearch16(T *base, const T& q)
{
    T *left = base - 1;
    if (left[8] < q) left += 8;
    if (left[4] < q) left += 4;
    if (left[2] < q) left += 2;
    if (left[1] < q) left += 1;
    left += 1;
    if (left - base >= 16 || *left != q)
        return 0;
    return left;
}
```

On further thought, the number of elements in the input array need not be a power of 2. If N is not a power of 2, just use the first comparison to decide whether to consider the first or last $2^{\lfloor \lg N \rfloor}$ elements (for example, for a 30-element array, check the 16th element and consider the first or last 16 elements). After one comparison, the array being searched has N a power of 2 and the algorithm works fine. As an example, the BinarySearch1000 function template is given in Listing 7.5.

Listing 7.5.   BinarySearch1000 function template.

```
// ================================================================
// BinarySearch1000 function template.
//
//        Searches a 1000-element array for a given query element.
//        The elements must be sorted.
//
// Parameters:
//        T *base          Base of the array to search.
//        const T& q       Query element.  The first array element
//                         found equal to this query element will
//                         be returned.
```

```
// Return value: T *
//      A pointer to an array element equal to the query element
//      or 0 if no element equal to the query is found.
//
// Requires:
//      operator!= and operator< must be defined on the class T.
//
// Runtime:
//      O(1).  Uses at most 11 comparisons.
// ================================================================
template<class T>
T *
BinarySearch1000(T *base, const T& q)
{
    T *left = base - 1;
    if (left[512] < q) left = base + 1000 + 1 - 512;
    if (left[256] < q) left += 256;
    if (left[128] < q) left += 128;
    if (left[ 64] < q) left +=  64;
    if (left[ 32] < q) left +=  32;
    if (left[ 16] < q) left +=  16;
    if (left[  8] < q) left +=   8;
    if (left[  4] < q) left +=   4;
    if (left[  2] < q) left +=   2;
    if (left[  1] < q) left +=   1;
    left += 1;
    if (left - base >= 1000 || *left != q)
        return 0;
    return left;
}
```

7.2.2 Interpolation Search

Binary Search is an excellent algorithm, but we can sometimes do better by estimating where in the array the element will fall. Instead of just bisecting the array into two subarrays of equal size, why not choose a more optimal division point? If the query element is expected to fall in the first quarter of the array, we can replace the line

```
int mid = N / 2;
```

with something like

```
int mid = (int) (0.25 * N);
```

This variation of Binary Search, due to Peterson [PETE57], is called
Interpolation Search. If the guess is fairly accurate and the array
elements are random, Interpolation Search has an expected runtime
of $O(\lg \lg N)$. If the guess is extremely poor, however, it can degrade
to $O(N)$, the same runtime as Linear Search.

Listing 7.6 gives a function template that implements Interpolation Search. To avoid floating-point arithmetic, the estimate is an
integer in the range $[0..N-1]$, the index of the expected location of
the query element.

Listing 7.6.   `InterpolationSearch` function template.

```
// ================================================================
// InterpolationSearch function template.
//
//      Searches an N-element array for a given query element.
//      The elements must be sorted.  The caller must give
//      a guess as to where the query element falls in the
//      interval.
//
// Parameters:
//      T *base         Base of the array to search.
//      int N           Number of elements in the array.
//      const T& q      Query element.  The first array element
//                      found equal to this query element will
//                      be returned.
//      int i           Estimate of element's position in array.
//
// Return value: T *
//      A pointer to an array element equal to the query element
//      or 0 if no element equal to the query is found.
//
// Requires:
//      operator== and operator< must be defined on the class T.
//
// Runtime:
//      O(lglgN) for an N-element array, assuming random data.
// ================================================================
template<class T>
T *
InterpolationSearch(T *base, int N, const T& q, int i)
{
```

```
    int left = 0;
    int right = N;

    while (left < right) {
        int mid = left + (right - left) * (long) i / N;
        if (base[mid] == q)
            return base + mid;
        if (q < base[mid])
            right = mid;
        else
            left = mid + 1;
    }
    return 0;
}
```

7.2.3 Conclusion

Binary Search is everything we could ask of an algorithm: simple, optimal, and relatively easy to implement. It forms the basis of many more complicated algorithms. An intimate understanding of Binary Search is important for anyone interested in computer programming.

Using Linear Search would be faster if only one search is going to be performed, since the $\Theta(N \lg N)$ time to sort the array overwhelms the savings afforded by Binary Search. The work of sorting the array has to be repaid by many binary searches. Binary Search is a great algorithm if you can precompute the sorted data set and search it many times. For more dynamic data sets, where the set of data changes between searches, efficient data structures such as binary trees have been invented. Such data structures are the focus of the rest of our discussion on searching.

Linear Lists

Linear lists are the first data structures for searching that we will discuss. They are well-suited to applications when the elements need to be kept track of, but not sorted or queried. Linear lists do not support efficient queries of arbitrary elements: No matter how the list is arranged, searching for an arbitrary element requires $O(N)$. If efficient queries are required, any of the other data structures for searching discussed in this book will be better suited than linear lists.

Unlike the other data structures discussed, linear lists do not lend themselves to generic implementation in C++. The applications are too varied, and the different types of linked lists are difficult to express in a class hierarchy. Different types of linear lists are good at different things, so it is necessary to examine the application requirements and come up with a suitable tradeoff among speed, complexity, and memory requirements.

Instead of implementing all the different types of linear lists, we will discuss the important permutations of the data structure and give some simple implementations that illustrate the major concepts. Section 8.1 discusses one of the most useful types of linear list, the linked list. The remainder of the chapter concentrates on lists whose ordering depends on the order of the operations performed rather than the keys of the elements inserted. Sections 8.2 and 8.3 discuss stacks and queues, both common and extremely useful data structures. Section 8.4 discusses deques, a linear list data structure that is more powerful (and more complicated to implement) than either stacks or queues. Section 8.5 gives implementations of a number of linear lists, including stack, queue, and deque implementations, and a simple list implementation. Finally, Section 8.6 discusses applications of linear lists in variety of contexts.

8.1 Linked Lists

Often programmers may wish to store a set of items for later reference, in no particular order. One way to store these items is in an array. An index into the array keeps track of the next element to be filled in. This index is incremented whenever an element is inserted.

There are a number of problems with this array-based scheme. The major one is that the array has to be allocated ahead of time. Preallocating the array is trivial if the programmer knows the maximum number of items that will be inserted into the array. Otherwise it becomes necessary to keep track of the number of items in the array and reallocate it when necessary.

Another problem with the array-based scheme is that preallocating the array wastes some elements. Linked lists require more memory per node, because they use pointers to string the data structure together. However, they never take up more memory than is necessary.

8.1.1 Singly-linked Lists

Figure 8.1 depicts the simplest type of linked list, the singly-linked list. The list contains a head pointer that points to the first node in the list. Each node contains Next, a pointer to the next node, and the last node in the list contains NULL. (In C++, the guaranteed-invalid pointer value is 0; we will be using the NULL notation from C to denote this concept.)

An empty list has a head pointer equal to NULL.

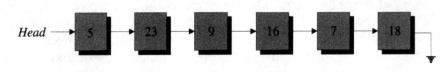

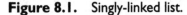

Figure 8.1.   Singly-linked list.

Traversal

Traversing the list consists of setting a pointer to the head node, then successively examining the nodes until the NULL pointer is encountered.

```
1  TraverseList(List)
2       ScanList←List.Head
3       while ScanList ≠ NULL do
4            Visit node pointed to by ScanList
5            ScanList←ScanList.Next
```

Insertion

Insertion into a singly-linked list can be done in $O(1)$ time by prepending the new node to the head of the list. The newly added node then becomes the new head of the list. The following pseudocode routine, SinglyLinkedInsert, implements this operation.

```
1  SinglyLinkedInsert(List, x)
2       Node *NewNode←new Node
3       NewNode.Contents←x
4       NewNode.Next←List.Head
5       List.Head←NewNode
```

Figure 8.2 depicts this implementation of linked list insertion.

If you want to preserve the list in sorted order, the insertion can be done in $O(N)$ time, as follows.

```
1  SinglySortedInsert(List, x)
2       Create the new node
3       Node *NewNode←new Node(x)
4       Scan for the proper place to insert node
```

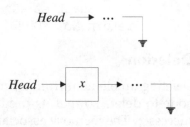
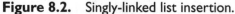

Figure 8.2. Singly-linked list insertion.

```
5          Node *Lead←List.Head
6          Node *Foll←NULL
7          while Lead ≠ NULL and Lead.Contents < x do
8                  Foll←Lead
9                  Lead←Lead.Next
10         if Foll = NULL then
11                 Prepend new node to head of list
12                 NewNode.Next←List.Head
13                 List.Head←NewNode
14         else
15                 Insert new node between Foll and Lead
16                 NewNode.Next←Lead
17                 Foll.Next←NewNode
```

Unless the memory requirement of an extra pointer per node is too much, using a tree-based data structure is usually better. Trees can be traversed in sorted order in $O(N)$ time (or expected $O(N)$ time), and they only require $O(N \lg N)$ time to construct, compared to the $O(N^2)$ time required to construct the sorted linked list.

Querying

Linked lists support queries in $O(N)$ time. Even when the linked list is in sorted order, it requires linear time to perform a query. Queries are performed with a slightly modified implementation of TraverseList.

```
1   SinglyLinkedQuery(List, x)
2       ScanList←List.Head
3       while ScanList ≠ NULL do
4           if ScanList.Contents = x then
5                   ScanList points at the element
6                   return ScanList
7           ScanList←ScanList.Next
8       return NOT-FOUND
```

Deletion

Deleting an element from a linked list is done by clipping out the node to delete so that its predecessor's Next pointer points at its successor. The memory associated with the node can then be freed.

In a singly-linked list, deletion requires $O(N)$ time because it takes this long to search for the predecessor node so its Next pointer can be modified. The resulting deletion routine follows.

```
1   SinglyLinkedDelete(List, x)
2        Lead←List.Head
3        Foll←NULL
4        while Lead ≠ NULL and Lead.Contents ≠ x do
5             Foll←Lead
6             Lead←Lead.Next
7        if Lead.Contents = x then
8             if Foll = NULL then
9                  Remove from head of list
10                 List.Head←Lead.Next
11            else
12            Remove from middle of list
13            Foll.Next←Lead.Next
14       delete Lead
```

Figure 8.3 depicts the deletion of a node from a singly-linked list.

Sometimes all that is needed is that each node in the list be considered and removed from the list, in no particular order. In this case, the head node can be removed in constant time.

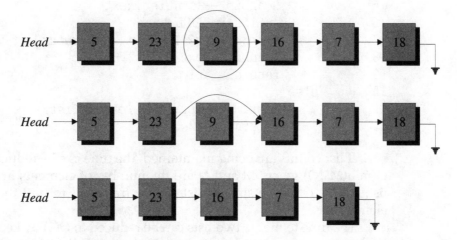

Figure 8.3. Singly-linked list deletion.

Reversal

A linked list can be reversed in $O(N)$ time as follows.

```
1   ReverseList(List)
2        Lead←List.Head
3        Foll←NULL
4        while Lead ≠ NULL do
5             Next←Lead.Next
6             Lead.Next←Foll
7             Foll←Lead
8             Lead←Next
```

The runtime to reverse a linked list can be reduced to $O(1)$ by using a doubly-linked list. Doubly-linked lists are described in Section 8.1.2.

Merging

Singly-linked lists can be merged in $O(N)$ time. The time is taken up by scanning to the end of one list so that the head of the other list can be appended. Pseudocode for this operation is as follows.

```
1   SinglyLinkedMerge(List1, List2)
2        ScanList←List1.Head
3        while ScanList ≠ NULL and
4             ScanList.Next ≠ NULL do
5             ScanList←ScanList.Next
6        if ScanList ≠ NULL then
7             Append List2 to List1 and return it
8             ScanList.Next←List2.Head
9             return List1
10       else
11            List1 is empty, so return List2
12            return List2
```

If list counts are being maintained, the time can be reduced to $O(\min(M, N))$ where M and N are the number of elements in each list. In this case, the smaller list can be traversed to find the last element.

The time to merge two lists can be reduced to $O(1)$ by keeping track of a pointer to the last element in the linked list (Tail).

List Counts

If desired, the number of elements in a linked list can be maintained along with the head pointer. While the list count requires only a few bytes per list and minimal time to maintain, it may have too much memory overhead for applications with many linked lists.

Tail Pointers

Sometimes a singly-linked list is constructed to be traversed once, from head to tail. If the nodes have to be considered in the order they were inserted, maintaining a pointer to the tail of the list as well as the head may make sense. In this case, nodes can be appended to the tail of the list in $O(1)$ time, and the list does not need to be reversed for the nodes to be considered in the correct order.

As pointed out earlier, a tail pointer also can be used to append two singly-linked lists.

8.1.2 Doubly-linked Lists

Figure 8.4 depicts another type of linked list, the doubly-linked list. The list contains head and tail pointers, which point at the first and last nodes in the list. Each node contains two pointers to the previous and next nodes in the list.

Doubly-linked lists let you append nodes to the head or tail of the list, search the list in either direction, and delete a node in $O(1)$ time because the node contains a pointer to its predecessor. (With a singly-linked list, the list must be searched from the head to find the predecessor.) This increased efficiency is not free, of course. Each node in the list contains two pointers, so a doubly-linked list requires more memory. And because both Previous and Next nodes have to be maintained, the code to implement a doubly-linked list is more complex.

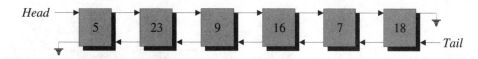

Figure 8.4.   Doubly-linked list.

Insertion

The next pseudocode routine inserts a node at the tail of the doubly-linked list. To insert at the head, swap references to Previous and Next and replace references to Tail with Head.

```
1   DoublyLinkedAppendToTail(List, x)
2        NewNode←new Node
3        NewNode.Contents←x
4        NewNode.Previous←List.Tail
5        NewNode.Next←NULL
6        List.Tail←NewNode
7        NewNode.Previous is the old tail of the list
8        if NewNode.Previous = Null then
9             List.Head←NewNode
10       else
11            NewNode.Previous.Next←NewNode
```

Figure 8.5 depicts DoublyLinkedAppendToTail in action.

Deletion

Deletion from a doubly-linked list can be performed in constant time, provided the node to delete is known. If a query has to be performed to find the node, you might as well use a singly-linked list. The following pseudocode routine for deletion assumes that the node is given.

```
1   DoublyLinkedDelete(List, Node)
2        Previous←Node.Previous
3        Next←Node.Next
```

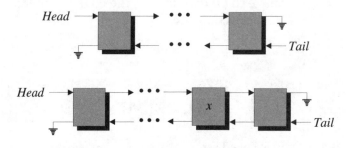

Figure 8.5.   Doubly-linked list insertion (at tail).

```
4       if Previous ≠ NULL then
5            Previous.Next←Next
6       else
7            List.Head←Next
8       if Next←NULL then
9            Next.Previous←Previous
10      else
11           List.Tail←Previous
12      delete Node
```

Figure 8.6 depicts DoublyLinkedDelete in action.

Reversal

By rethinking our representation of a node in a doubly-linked list, we can simplify the implementation and also implement reversal in constant time. Instead of storing a pair of pointers explicitly named Next and Previous, we can store a two-element array of pointers called Adjacent. Whenever we operate on the node, we specify a Boolean variable Direction that tells how to treat the pointers. If Direction can be 0 or 1, we can think of Adjacent[Direction] as "Next" and Adjacent[1-Direction] as "Previous." Even mentioning "Next" and "Previous" is a matter of convenience, since the linked list has lost the sense of direction imposed by the explicit Next and Previous pointers discussed up to now.

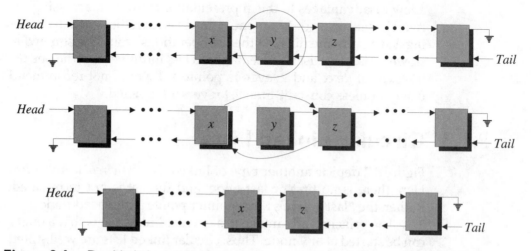

Figure 8.6. Doubly-linked deletion.

The head and tail pointers in the list data structure also need to be replaced by a two-element array End. We can then think of End[Direction] as the "head" of the list, while End[1-Direction] is the "tail" of the list.

Direction is a parameter of the list, so implementations of routines for insertion and deletion have access to it. Here is a rewrite of DoublyLinkedDelete that uses Direction.

```
1   DoublyLinkedDelete(List, Node)
2        Previous←Node.Adjacent[1-List.Direction]
3        Next←Node.Adjacent[List.Direction]
4        if Previous ≠ NULL then
5                Previous.Adjacent[List.Direction]←Next
6        else
7                List.End[List.Direction]←Next
8        if Next ≠ NULL then
9                Next.End[1-List.Direction]←Previous
10       else
11               List.End[1-List.Direction]←Previous
12       delete Node
```

Once we have reworked the representation of the doubly-linked list in this way, the list can be quickly reversed by replacing Direction by 1-Direction. Only two entry points are needed to implement insertion and deletion at the list ends as well. There are a few disadvantages to this representation, however; accessing the two-element array of Adjacent pointers is less efficient than accessing a structure member, so the list operations would be somewhat slower. Also, this list representation is less intuitive than the one using explicit Next and Previous pointers. I would not recommend using it unless constant-time list reversal is needed.

8.1.3 Circular Linked Lists

Figure 8.7 depicts another type of linked list, the *circular linked list*. Here there is no first or last node, and the list is not terminated. Rather, the "last" node's Next pointer points at the head node.

The principal advantage to a circular linked list is that a query can be started at any node. Thus, circular linked lists are well suited to applications where the search should start at a certain point for

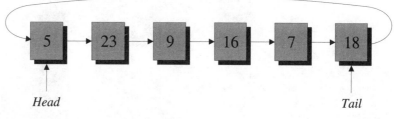

Figure 8.7. Circular linked list.

some reason. (The pointer telling where to begin to search is called a *finger*.) A good example of such an application, the Clock page replacement algorithm, is described at the end of this chapter.

8.2 **Stacks**

Certain special types of linear list impose an order on the elements that is based on the order of insertion and removal rather than the elements' keys. The first and most common and useful of these is a LIFO ("last-in-first-out") data structure called the *stack*. Stacks support two basic operations:

Push: Places an element at the top of the stack.

Pop: Removes the element at the top of the stack.

Stacks are easy to implement using either arrays or linked lists. For arrays, the array is preallocated and an index pointing at the stack top is kept. To push an element, the index is incremented and the new element is placed at the new location of the stack top. To pop an element, the element at the stack top is returned and the index is decremented. Figure 8.8 depicts a stack based on an array.

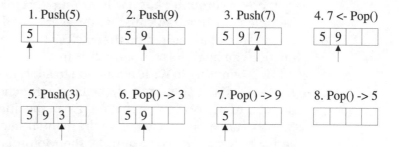

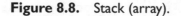

Figure 8.8. Stack (array).

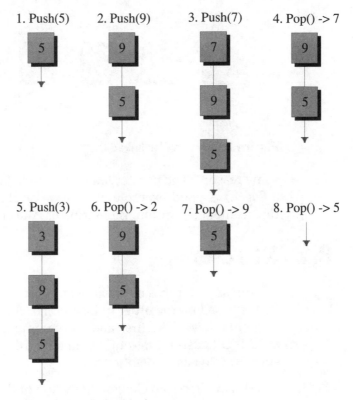

Figure 8.9. Stack (linked list).

Using a linked list, **Push** and **Pop** also can be implemented easily. **Push** allocates a new node and places it at the head of the linked list. **Pop** returns the element at the head of the list, then removes the node from the head. Figure 8.9 depicts a stack based on a linked list.

Stacks are a pervasive data structure in computer science. Every modern computer has hardware support for a "machine stack" to implement function calls. (Parameters, local variables, and return addresses are stored on the stack so that the state of the calling function can be restored upon returning.)

It is tempting to write a function to allocate space from the machine stack itself. (If provided, the library function is usually called `alloca`.) Many computers have built-in facilities for restoring the stack that are more efficient than the manual stack implementations we have discussed. For example, the Motorola 680x0 uses an instruction called `UNLK` to restore the stack just before returning from a function. Any space that was allocated from the machine stack is implicitly freed by this single instruction at the same time as the local variables.

There are some significant disadvantages to allocating memory from the machine stack, however. For one thing, the machine stack is much more limited than the heap manager used for dynamic memory allocation. The machine stack generally has a set limit that cannot be exceeded; if too much space is allocated from it, the program will crash. (This is why iterative implementations of algorithms are more desirable than recursive ones.) Also, for some machines that use register-based schemes to implement function calls, it may not be possible to allocate memory from the machine stack.

Thus, many applications for which stacks are necessary (Quicksort, for example) are best implemented using an array- or linked list-based stack.

8.3 Queues

Queues are similar to stacks, except that the item removed is the least-recently inserted item rather than the most-recently inserted item. Queues are called a "first-in-first-out" (FIFO) data structure for this reason: The first item added to the queue is also the first item removed. The two operations are called:

Add: Places an element at the head of the queue.

Remove: Removes the element from the tail of the queue.

Like stacks, queues are easy to implement using either an array or a linked list. For the array implementation, indices pointing at the head and tail elements are maintained. These indices move toward one another as items are inserted or removed from the queue. The indices can wrap around the maximum number of elements in the array. If they wrap around each other, the queue has overflowed. A queue implementation can track whether this is about to happen and reallocate the array. Figure 8.10 depicts a queue based on an array.

To implement a queue using a linked list, the list may be singly-linked or doubly-linked. If the list is singly-linked, adding an element can be implemented in $O(1)$ time, but removing an element requires $O(N)$ time. Figure 8.11 depicts a queue based on a doubly-linked list.

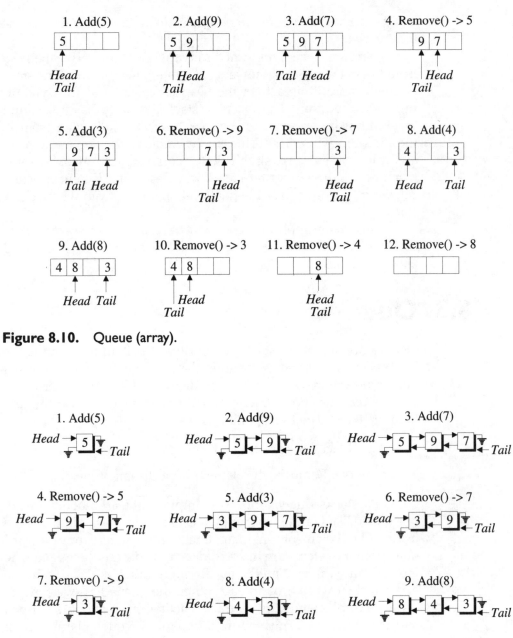

Figure 8.10.   Queue (array).

Figure 8.11.   Queue (linked list).

8.4 Deques

Deques (pronounced "decks") are linear list data structures more powerful than either stacks or queues. Stacks allow insertion and removal of elements only at one end, while queues allow insertion at one end and removal at the other. In contrast, deques permit insertion and removal at either end of the list.

An array implementation of a deque, like that of a queue, would keep track of head and tail indices into the array. These would simply wrap around the maximum number of elements in the array, as necessary; as with queues, a robust implementation would have to check whether the indices were about to cross, overflowing the data structure. Such an array-based implementation could perform all deque operations in constant time.

If a list representation is desired, a deque is best implemented using a doubly-linked list. That way, all the deque operations can be supported in constant time.

8.5 Other Issues

8.5.1 Iterators and Manipulators

When it comes to traversing and modifying a data structure such as a linked list, it is often appropriate to utilize *encapsulation*, one of the hallmarks of object-oriented programming. Rarely is it wise to lay open the inner workings of a data structure; treating it as a black box allows the implementation to change without causing undue trouble to clients of the class.

Iterators are classes designed to traverse a data structure without modifying it. Typically they are paired with the data structure they traverse. For example, a linked-list class template might include an embedded `Iterator` class that is used to traverse instances of the linked list.

The primitive operations typically defined on an iterator are as follows.

- **Valid:** Return whether the iterator currently points at a valid element.

- **Dereference:** Return the element currently pointed to.

- **Goto Next:** Go on to the next element in the data structure.

- **Rewind:** Go back to the head of the data structure.

There could be minor variations on this theme, such as "go to predecessor" and "go to successor" methods, if these were supported by the data structure.

Manipulators are designed to traverse and modify a data structure. Typically they implement the same operations as iterators, plus the following.

- **Insert:** Insert a new node at the current location.

- **Delete:** Delete the node currently pointed to.

Manipulators only really make sense when a modification can be made locally without affecting the entire data structure. More sophisticated data structures, such as the balanced binary trees described in Chapter 11, typically have to reorder themselves globally when a node is inserted or deleted. In this case, no manipulator class is given. Nodes have to be deleted by asking the data structure to do it.

The exact interfaces to an iterator or manipulator class will vary with the requirements of the data structure; see the next section for a discussion of the iterator and manipulator provided with the `SimpleList` class template.

8.5.2 Fingers

A finger is a pointer to tell where to begin searching a data structure. Fingers are especially appropriate for linked lists, since a judicious clue may be all that's needed to reduce the expected runtime of a query from $\Theta(N)$ to $\Theta(1)$.

8.5.3 Fixed-size Allocation

The nodes of a linked list are all the same size, provided the contents of each node are of uniform size. Implementing a fixed-length memory allocator has some distinct advantages over the more general facilities provided by the **new** operator. Fixed-length memory allocators are simpler to implement, faster, and less prone to fragmentation. If nodes are allocated and deallocated frequently, overloading the flexible heap management facilities provided by the C++ compiler with a fixed-length allocator may make sense.

8.6 Implementation

We can't possibly have implemented every permutation of linear list discussed in this chapter, but we have implemented a number of them. The SimpleList class template is designed to meet a wide variety of needs when programmers wish to store elements in no particular order for later reference. SimpleList provides iterator and manipulator classes to examine the list contents, as well. Despite the implications of the name SimpleList, the remaining class templates, DequeLList , QueueLList, and StackLList, are much simpler than SimpleList because their interfaces are simpler. SimpleList guards against creating manipulators to modify a list that is already being iterated on, for example. The other class templates do not provide iterators or manipulators, so there is no need for this type of safeguard.

With luck, these four class templates are at least a start on any application the reader may have in mind for linear lists.

8.6.1 SimpleList: Singly-linked List

The SimpleList class template implements a simple singly-linked linked list intended only as a placeholder for objects. It supports the following operations.

Operation	Runtime
Insertion at head	$\Theta(1)$
List count	$\Theta(1)$
Removal of head	$\Theta(1)$
Traversal	$\Theta(N)$
Extraction of a given element	$\Theta(N)$

Listing 8.1 gives <list.h>, the header file that implements SimpleList. Three related class templates are actually implemented. SimpleList is the linked list class. SimpleListIterator and SimpleListManipulator are the iterator and manipulator class

templates for `SimpleList`. Declaring `SimpleListIterator` and `SimpleListManipulator` as embedded classes inside `SimpleList` would make a great deal of sense; then you could refer to them as `SimpleList<T>::Iterator` and `SimpleList<T>::Manipulator`. The only reason I avoided this is because most C++ compilers require the member functions of classes embedded in class templates be declared in-line. This would impact the readability of the code so badly that I decided to pull out the iterator and manipulator templates and declare their constructors **private**. Then, by declaring the `SimpleList` class template a **friend**, they can be autonomous and exclude access by anyone but `SimpleList` at the same time.

Listing 8.1.   `SimpleList` class template.

```
// ===========================================================
// list.h
//      Header file for SimpleList class template.
//      This class template implements unordered, singly-
//      linked lists that can have the following operations
//      performed on them:
//
//      Insert: Adds an item to the list.
//      Num: Returns the number of items in the list.
//      Query: looks through the list and, if it finds a
//             matching item, passes back a copy of it.
//             Query returns nonzero if the item is found.
//      Empty: Returns nonzero if the list is empty.
//      Head: Returns a pointer to the head element in
//            the list (if any).
//      ExtractHead: Extracts and returns the head element
//                   in the list.
//      Extract: Queries the given element and, if found,
//               passes back a pointer to it.
//
//      Iterator: Returns an iterator on the linked list.
//         The iterator can be used to examine items in
//         the list nondestructively.  The list cannot
//         be destroyed while an iterator is operating
//         on it.
//
// Copyright (C) 1995 by Nicholas Wilt.  All rights reserved.
// ===========================================================

#ifndef __SIMPLELIST__
```

```
#define __SIMPLELIST__

template<class T>
class SimpleListNode {
private:
    T contents;
    SimpleListNode<T> *next;

    SimpleListNode(const T& Contents, SimpleListNode *Next):
        contents(Contents), next(Next) { }

    friend class SimpleList<T>;
    friend class SimpleListIterator<T>;
    friend class SimpleListManipulator<T>;
};

template<class T>
class EXPORT
SimpleList {
public:

    enum ExceptionCause { ListIsEmpty,
                          IteratorAttached,
                          ManipulatorAttached };

    class Exception {
    public:
        int Why() const { return why; }
    private:
        Exception( int _why) { why = _why; }
        int why;
        friend SimpleList<T>;
    };

    SimpleList();
    SimpleList(const T& x);
    SimpleList(const SimpleList& x);
    SimpleList& operator=(const SimpleList& x);
    virtual ~SimpleList();

    virtual void Insert(const SimpleList<T>& x);
    virtual void Insert(const T& x);
    virtual T ExtractHead();
    virtual int Query(T *passbk) const;
```

(continued)

```
    virtual int Empty() const;
    virtual T *Head() const;
    virtual T *Extract(const T& x);

    virtual int Num() const { return n; }

    friend class SimpleListIterator<T>;
    virtual SimpleListIterator<T> Iterator() const;

    friend class SimpleListManipulator<T>;
    virtual SimpleListManipulator<T> Manipulator();

protected:
    int n;
    SimpleListNode<T> *head;

    int nIterators;
    int nManipulators;
};

template<class T>
class EXPORT
SimpleListIterator {
private:
    // Constructor is private.  These iterators can only be created
    // by the SimpleList class template.
    SimpleListIterator(SimpleList<T> *x);

    friend SimpleList<T>;
    friend SimpleListManipulator<T>;
public:

    enum ExceptionCause { InvalidDereference, NotAttached };

    // If the iterator throws an exception, it will be of this type.
    class Exception {
    public:
        int Why() const { return why; }
    private:
        Exception(int _why) { why = _why; }
        int why;
        friend SimpleListIterator<T>;
        friend SimpleListManipulator<T>;
    };
```

```
        // Copy constructor and assignment operator are publicly
        // accessible.
        SimpleListIterator(const SimpleListIterator<T>&);
        SimpleListIterator<T>& operator=(const SimpleListIterator<T>&);

        // Destructor.
        virtual ~SimpleListIterator();

        // Resets the iterator at the head of the list.
        virtual void Reset();

        // Detaches the iterator from the list.
        virtual void Detach();

        // Dereferencing operator works the same as the Contents
        // member function.
        virtual T& operator*();
        virtual const T& operator*() const;

        // Nonzero if the iterator points at a valid node.
        virtual operator int() const;

        // Increment operators move the iterator to point at the
        // next node.
        virtual void operator++(int);
protected:
        SimpleList<T> *list;
        SimpleListNode<T> *ptr;
};


template<class T>
class EXPORT
SimpleListManipulator : public SimpleListIterator<T> {
private:
        // Constructor is private.  These iterators can only be created
        // by the SimpleList class template.
        SimpleListManipulator(SimpleList<T> *x);

        friend SimpleList<T>;
public:
        // Copy constructor and assignment operator are publicly
        // accessible.
        SimpleListManipulator(const SimpleListManipulator<T>&);
        SimpleListManipulator<T>& operator=(const SimpleListManipulator<T>&);
```

(continued)

```
    // Destructor.
    virtual ~SimpleListManipulator();

    // Resets the manipulator at the head of the list.
    virtual void Reset();

    // Detaches the manipulator from the list.
    virtual void Detach();

    // Move to the next item on the list.
    virtual void operator++(int x);

    // Insert a node at the current position.
    virtual void Insert(const T&);

    // Delete the node at the current position.
    virtual void Delete();
protected:
    // Pointer to the node preceding the node pointed to by ptr.
    // This is needed in case the client wants to insert or
    // delete a node at the current position.
    SimpleListNode<T> *prev;
};

template<class T>
SimpleList<T>::SimpleList()
{
    head = 0;
    n = 0;
    nIterators = nManipulators = 0;
}

template<class T>
SimpleList<T>::SimpleList(const T& x)
{
    head = new SimpleListNode<T>(x, 0);
    n = 1;
}

template<class T>
SimpleList<T>::SimpleList(const SimpleList<T>& x)
{
    head = 0;
    n = 0;
```

```
        nIterators = nManipulators = 0;
        for (SimpleListNode<T> *sc = x.head; sc; sc = sc->next)
            Insert(sc->contents);
}


template<class T>
SimpleList<T>&
SimpleList<T>::operator=(const SimpleList<T>& x)
{
    SimpleListNode<T> *sc;
    for (sc = head; sc; ) {
        SimpleListNode<T> *temp = sc->next;
        delete sc;
        sc = temp;
    }
    head = 0;
    n = 0;
    nIterators = nManipulators = 0;
    for (sc = x.head; sc; sc = sc->next)
        Insert(sc->contents);

    return *this;
}


template<class T>
SimpleList<T>::~SimpleList()
{
    if (nIterators)
        throw Exception(IteratorAttached);
    if (nManipulators)
        throw Exception(ManipulatorAttached);
    SimpleListNode<T> *sc = head;
    while (sc) {
        SimpleListNode<T> *temp = sc->next;
        delete sc;
        sc = temp;
    }
}


template<class T>
void
SimpleList<T>::Insert(const SimpleList<T>& x)
{
    if (nIterators)
        throw Exception(IteratorAttached);
```

(continued)

```
    if (nManipulators)
        throw Exception(ManipulatorAttached);
    for (SimpleListNode<T> *sc = x.head; sc; sc = sc->next)
        Insert(sc->contents);
}

template<class T>
void
SimpleList<T>::Insert(const T& x)
{
    if (nIterators)
        throw Exception(IteratorAttached);
    if (nManipulators)
        throw Exception(ManipulatorAttached);
    head = new SimpleListNode<T>(x, head);
    n++;
}

template<class T>
T
SimpleList<T>::ExtractHead()
{
    if (nIterators)
        throw Exception(IteratorAttached);
    if (nManipulators)
        throw Exception(ManipulatorAttached);

    if (head) {
        T ret;
        SimpleListNode<T> *temp = head->next;
        ret = head->contents;
        delete head;
        head = temp;
        n--;
        return ret;
    }
    else
        throw Exception(ListIsEmpty);
}


template<class T>
int
SimpleList<T>::Query(T *passbk) const
```

```
{
    for (SimpleListNode<T> *sc = head; sc; sc = sc->next) {
        if (sc->contents == *passbk) {
            *passbk = sc->contents;
            return 1;
        }
    }
    return 0;
}

template<class T>
int
SimpleList<T>::Empty() const
{
    return head == 0;
}

template<class T>
T *
SimpleList<T>::Head() const
{
    if (head)
        return &head->contents;
    throw Exception(ListIsEmpty);
}

template<class T>
T *
SimpleList<T>::Extract(const T& x)
{
    SimpleListNode<T> *sc;
    for (sc = head; sc; sc = sc->next) {
        if (sc->contents == x)
            return &sc->contents;
    }
    return 0;
}

template<class T>
SimpleListIterator<T>
SimpleList<T>::Iterator() const
{
    if (nManipulators)
        throw Exception(ManipulatorAttached);
```

(continued)

```
        // Bitwise but not conceptual modification of a const object.
        ((SimpleList<T> *) this)->nIterators += 1;

        return SimpleListIterator<T>((SimpleList<T> *) this);
}

template<class T>
SimpleListManipulator<T>
SimpleList<T>::Manipulator()
{
        // Can't create a manipulator unless no iterators or
        // manipulators are attached.
        if (nIterators)
            throw Exception(IteratorAttached);
        if (nManipulators)
            throw Exception(ManipulatorAttached);

        // Bitwise but not conceptual modification of a const object.
        ((SimpleList<T> *) this)->nManipulators += 1;

        return SimpleListManipulator<T>((SimpleList<T> *) this);
}

template<class T>
SimpleListIterator<T>::SimpleListIterator(SimpleList<T> *x)
{
        list = x;
        ptr = x->head;
}

template<class T>
SimpleListIterator<T>::SimpleListIterator(const SimpleListIterator<T>& x)
{
        list = x.list;
        ptr = x.ptr;
        if (list)
            list->nIterators += 1;
}

template<class T>
SimpleListIterator<T>&
SimpleListIterator<T>::operator=(const SimpleListIterator<T>& x)
{
        list->nIterators -= 1;
        list = x.list;
```

```
        ptr = x.ptr;
        list->nIterators += 1;
        return *this;
}

template<class T>
SimpleListIterator<T>::~SimpleListIterator()
{
        if (list)
            list->nIterators -= 1;
}

template<class T>
void
SimpleListIterator<T>::Detach()
{
        if (! list)
            throw Exception(NotAttached);
        ptr = 0;
        list->nIterators -= 1;
        list = 0;
}

template<class T>
void
SimpleListIterator<T>::Reset()
{
        if (! list)
            throw Exception(NotAttached);
        ptr = list->head;
}

template<class T>
int
SimpleListIterator<T>::operator int() const
{
        return ptr != 0;
}

template<class T>
T&
SimpleListIterator<T>::operator*()
{
        if (! ptr)
```

(continued)

```
        throw Exception(InvalidDereference);
    return ptr->contents;
}


template<class T>
const T&
SimpleListIterator<T>::operator*() const
{
    if (! ptr)
        throw Exception(InvalidDereference);
    return ptr->contents;
}


template<class T>
void
SimpleListIterator<T>::operator++(int)
{
    if (! ptr)
        throw Exception(InvalidDereference);
    ptr = ptr->next;
}


template<class T>
SimpleListManipulator<T>::SimpleListManipulator(SimpleList<T> *x):
    SimpleListIterator<T>(x)
{
    prev = 0;
}


template<class T>
SimpleListManipulator<T>::~SimpleListManipulator()
{
    if (list)
        list->nManipulators -= 1;
    list = 0;
}


template<class T>
void
SimpleListManipulator<T>::Detach()
{
    list = 0;
    ptr = prev = 0;
    list->nManipulators -= 1;
}
```

```
template<class T>
void
SimpleListManipulator<T>::Reset()
{
    SimpleListIterator<T>::Reset();
    prev = 0;
}


template<class T>
void
SimpleListManipulator<T>::operator++(int)
{
    if (! ptr)
        throw Exception(InvalidDereference);
    prev = ptr;
    ptr = ptr->next;
}


template<class T>
void
SimpleListManipulator<T>::Insert(const T& x)
{
    if (list->Empty()) {
        list->Insert(x);
    }
    else {
        SimpleListNode<T> *newnode = new SimpleListNode<T>(x, ptr);
        prev->next = newnode;
        ptr = newnode;
    }
}


template<class T>
void
SimpleListManipulator<T>::Delete()
{
    if (! ptr)
        throw Exception(InvalidDereference);
    if (prev) {
        prev->next = ptr->next;
        delete ptr;
        ptr = prev->next;
    }
```

(continued)

```
    else {
        list->head = ptr->next;
        delete ptr;
        ptr = list->head;
    }
}

#endif
```

SimpleList is really a "kitchen sink" linked-list implementation. If you have an application where you just want to put items somewhere for safekeeping, chances are SimpleList will meet your needs. It keeps track of how many elements are in the list, so you can find that out in constant time whenever you like. The iterator and manipulator classes let you traverse and modify the elements in the list.

Finally, SimpleList implements safeguards to prevent programmers from writing code that may not work correctly. For example, the list may not be modified while an iterator or manipulator is attached to it. Also, a manipulator may not be attached if an iterator is already attached. (The manipulator is perfectly capable of deleting the node that the iterator is currently examining!) If any of these events occur, an exception is thrown. There are Exception classes embedded in each of the three class templates SimpleList, SimpleListIterator, and SimpleListManipulator. Each Exception class has only one **public** member: a member function called Why, which takes no arguments and returns an enum ExceptionCause to tell why the exception occurred.

Any of the following circumstances can elicit an exception.

Exception	Circumstance
SimpleList<T>:: IteratorAttached	Some operations are illegal if an iterator is still attached to the list. These include destruction, insertion, and removal of elements.
SimpleList<T>:: ManipulatorAttached	Some operations are illegal if a manipulator is attached to the list. These include destruction, insertion and removal of elements, and attaching an iterator or manipulator to the list.

`SimpleList<T>::` `  ListIsEmpty`	This exception is thrown if the list is empty when the `Head` or `RemoveHead` member functions are called to remove or examine the element at the head of the list.
`SimpleListIterator<T>::` `  InvalidDereference`	This exception is thrown if an iterator or manipulator is dereferenced after it has been incremented past the end of the list and no longer points at a valid element.
`SimpleListIterator<T>::` `  NotAttached`	This exception is thrown if an iterator or manipulator is operated on after it has been detached from a list.

Exception-handling Examples

The following example illustrates a fast and easy way to elicit an exception from the `SimpleList` class template.

```
SimpleList<int> list;          // Declare an empty list
int x = list.RemoveHead();     // Try to remove the
                               // item at the head
// The above line causes an exception of type
// SimpleList<int>::Exception to be thrown.
```

This example can be modified to catch the exception as follows.

```
SimpleList<int> list; // Declare an empty list
try {
    int x = list.RemoveHead();
}
catch (const SimpleList<int>::Exception&exc)
{
    if (exc.Why() == SimpleList<int>::ListIsEmpty)
        cerr << "Error: List was empty" << endl;
}
```

8.6.2 `DequeLList`: Doubly-linked Deque

The deque implementation is based on a doubly-linked list. That way, insertion and removal of items can be done in constant time

at either end of the list. Listing 8.2 gives DequeLLList, an implementation of deques. In the source code included with the book,
DequeLLList is given in <deque.h>.

Listing 8.2.   DequeLLList **class template.**

```
// ==========================================================
// deque.h
//      Header file for DequeLLList class template.
//      This class template implements a queue based on a
//      doubly-linked list.
//
// Copyright (C) 1995 by Nicholas Wilt.  All rights reserved.
// ==========================================================

#ifndef __DEQUE__

#define __DEQUE__

template<class T>
class DequeLLList {
public:
    class Node;

    // Constructors and destructor.
    DequeLLList();
    DequeLLList(const DequeLLList<T>&);
    DequeLLList<T>& operator=(const DequeLLList<T>&);
    virtual ~DequeLLList();

    // Fundamental operations: add to the head or tail,
    // remove from the head or tail.
    virtual void AddHead(const T& x);
    virtual void AddTail(const T& x);

    virtual T RemoveHead();
    virtual T RemoveTail();

    // Return nonzero if the queue is empty.
    virtual int Empty() const;

    // Examine head and tail of the queue.
    virtual T Head() const;
    virtual T Tail() const;
```

```
        enum Exception { DequeIsEmpty };

protected:
    class Node {
    public:
        T contents;
        Node *prev, *next;
        Node(const T& x, Node *Prev, Node *Next):
            contents(x), prev(Prev), next(Next) { }
    };

    Node *head, *tail;
};

template<class T>
DequeLList<T>::DequeLList()
{
    head = tail = 0;
}

template<class T>
DequeLList<T>::DequeLList(const DequeLList<T>& list)
{
    Node *prev = 0;

    head = tail = 0;
    for (Node *sc = list.head; sc; sc = sc->next) {
        tail = new Node(sc->contents, prev, 0);
        if (prev)
            prev->next = tail;
        prev = tail;
        if (! head)
            head = tail;
    }
}

template<class T>
DequeLList<T>::~DequeLList()
{
    for (Node *sc = head; sc; ) {
        Node *next = sc->next;
        delete sc;
        sc = next;
    }
}
```

(continued)

```
template<class T>
DequeLList<T>&
DequeLList<T>::operator=(const DequeLList& list)
{
    for (Node *sc = head; sc; ) {
        Node *next = sc->next;
        delete sc;
        sc = next;
    }
    Node *prev = 0;

    head = tail = 0;
    for (sc = list.head; sc; sc = sc->next) {
        tail = new Node(sc->contents, prev, 0);
        if (prev)
            prev->next = tail;
        prev = tail;
        if (! head)
            head = tail;
    }
    return *this;
}


template<class T>
void
DequeLList<T>::AddHead(const T& x)
{
    head = new Node(x, 0, head);
    if (head->next)
        head->next->prev = head;
    if (! tail)
        tail = head;
}


template<class T>
void
DequeLList<T>::AddTail(const T& x)
{
    tail = new Node(x, tail, 0);
    if (tail->prev)
        tail->prev->next = tail;
    if (! head)
        head = tail;
}
```

```
template<class T>
T
DequeLList<T>::RemoveHead()
{
    if (head) {
        T ret = head->contents;
        Node *next = head->next;
        delete head;
        head = next;
        if (! head)
            tail = 0;
        return ret;
    }
#ifdef EXCEPTIONS
    throw DequeIsEmpty;
#else
    return 0;
#endif
}

template<class T>
T
DequeLList<T>::RemoveTail()
{
    if (tail) {
        T ret = tail->contents;
        Node *prev = tail->prev;
        delete tail;
        tail = prev;
        if (! tail)
            head = 0;
        return ret;
    }
#ifdef EXCEPTIONS
    throw DequeIsEmpty;
#else
    return 0;
#endif
}

template<class T>
int
DequeLList<T>::Empty() const
{
```

(continued)

```
    return head == 0;
}

template<class T>
T
DequeLList<T>::Head() const
{
    if (head)
        return head->contents;
#ifdef EXCEPTIONS
    throw DequeIsEmpty;
#else
    return 0;
#endif
}

template<class T>
T
DequeLList<T>::Tail() const
{
    if (tail)
        return tail->contents;
#ifdef EXCEPTIONS
    throw DequeIsEmpty;
#else
    return 0;
#endif
}

#endif
```

DequeLList provides the following functions.

Function	Behavior
void AddHead(const T&);	Adds an element to the head of the deque.
void AddTail(const T&);	Adds an element to the tail of the deque.
T RemoveHead();	Removes an element from the head of the deque.

T Removetail();	Removes an element from the tail of the deque.
intEmpty() const;	Returns nonzero if the deque is empty.

If the exceptions are desired, the DequeLLList template will throw an exception (DequeLLList::Deque is Empty) if RemoveHead or RemoveTail is called when the deque is empty.

An embedded Node class implements the nodes of the doubly-linked list.

8.6.3 QueueLLList: Doubly-linked Queue

Since deques are more powerful than queues, and don't require any more memory if implemented using the same infrastructure (in this case, a doubly-linked list), we can reuse the deque implementation to reduce the amount of source code without compromising anything. Listing 8.3 gives QueueLLList, a class template that implements queues using the deque implementation already given. In the source code included with the book, QueueLLList is given in <queue.h>. QueueLLList provides the following functions.

Function	Behavior
void Add(const T&);	Adds an element to the queue.
T Remove();	Removes an element from the queue.
int Empty() const;	Returns nonzero if the queue is empty.

QueueLLList inherits its exception behavior from DequeLLList.

Listing 8.3. QueueLLList **class template.**

```
// ==========================================================
// queue.h
//      Header file for QueueLLList class template.
//      This class template implements a queue based on a
//      doubly-linked list.
//
// Copyright (C) 1995 by Nicholas Wilt.  All rights reserved.
// ==========================================================
```

(continued)

```cpp
#ifndef __QUEUE__

#define __QUEUE__

#include <deque.h>

template<class T>
class QueueLList {
public:
    // Constructors and destructor.
    QueueLList() { }

    // Fundamental operations: add to the head, remove
    // from the tail.
    virtual void Add(const T& x);
    virtual T Remove();

    // Return nonzero if the queue is empty.
    int Empty() const;
protected:
    DequeLList<T> deque;
};

template<class T>
void
QueueLList<T>::Add(const T& x)
{
    deque.AddHead(x);
}

template<class T>
T
QueueLList<T>::Remove()
{
    return deque.RemoveTail();
}

template<class T>
int
QueueLList<T>::Empty() const
{
    return deque.Empty();
}

#endif
```

8.6.4 `StackLList`: Singly-linked Stack

Listing 8.4 gives a class template called `StackLList`, which uses a singly-linked list to implement a simple stack class. In the source code included with the book, `StackLList` is given in `<stack.h>`. `StackLList` provides the following functions:

Function	Behavior
`void Push(const T&);`	Pushes an element onto the stack.
`T Pop();`	Pops an element from the stack top.
`int Empty() const;`	Returns nonzero if the stack is empty.
`T Top();`	Nondestructively examines the stack top.

If exceptions are desired, the `StackLList` template will throw an exception (`StackLList::StackIsEmpty`) if `Pop` is called when the stack is empty.

Listing 8.4. `StackLList` class template.

```
// ==========================================================
// stack.h
//      Header file for StackLList class template.
//      This class template implements a stack based on a
//      singly-linked list.
//
// Copyright (C) 1995 by Nicholas Wilt.  All rights reserved.
// ==========================================================

#ifndef __STACK__

#define __STACK__

// ----------------------------------------------------------
// StackLList
// Class template for a stack of T's.  The fundamental
// operations are Push, Pop, and Empty (which just
// tells you whether the stack is currently empty).
// ----------------------------------------------------------

template<class T>
class StackLList {
```

(continued)

```
public:
    // Constructors and destructor.
    StackLList() { top = 0;   }
    StackLList(const StackLList<T>&);
    StackLList<T>& operator=(const StackLList<T>&);
    virtual ~StackLList();

    // Fundamental operations.
    virtual void Push(const T& x);
    virtual T Pop();

    // Return nonzero if the stack is empty.
    virtual int Empty() const;

    // Nondestructively examine the stack top.
    virtual T Top();

    enum Exception { StackIsEmpty };

protected:
    // Embedded class implements the nodes in the linked
    // list that comprises the stack.
    class Node {
    public:
     T contents;
     Node *next;
     Node(const T& x, Node *Next):
     contents(x), next(Next) { }
    };
    Node *top;
};


// -------------------------------------
// Copy constructor.
// -------------------------------------
template<class T>
StackLList<T>::StackLList(const StackLList<T>& x)
{
    StackLList<T> temp;
    for (Node *sc = x.top; sc; sc = sc->next)
        temp.Push(sc->contents);
    top = 0;
    while (! temp.Empty())
```

```
        Push(temp.Pop());
}


// -----------------------------------
// Assignment operator.
// -----------------------------------
template<class T>
StackLList<T>&
StackLList<T>::operator=(const StackLList<T>& x)
{
    Node *sc = top;
    while (sc) {
        Node *next = sc->next;
        delete sc;
        sc = next;
    }
    StackLList<T> temp;
    for (sc = x.top; sc; sc = sc->next)
temp.Push(sc->contents);
    top = 0;
    while (! temp.Empty())
Push(temp.Pop());
    return *this;
}


// -----------------------------------
// Destructor.
// -----------------------------------
template<class T>
StackLList<T>::~StackLList()
{
    Node *sc = top;
    while (sc) {
        Node *next = sc->next;
        delete sc;
        sc = next;
    }
}


// -----------------------------------
// Push implementation.
//      Pushes the given item onto the
//      top of the stack.
// -----------------------------------
```

(continued)

```
template<class T>
void
StackLList<T>::Push(const T& x)
{
    top = new Node(x, top);
}


// ------------------------------------
// Pop implementation.
//       Removes and returns the item at
//       the top of the stack.
// ------------------------------------
template<class T>
T
StackLList<T>::Pop()
{
    if (top) {
        T ret = top->contents;
        Node *next = top->next;
        delete top;
        top = next;
        return ret;
    }
#ifdef EXCEPTIONS
    throw StackIsEmpty;
#else
    return 0;
#endif
}


// ------------------------------------
// Empty implementation.
//       Returns nonzero if the stack is
//       empty.
// ------------------------------------
template<class T>
int
StackLList<T>::Empty() const
{
    return top == 0;
}
```

```
// ------------------------------------
// Nondestructively examines the top of
// the stack.
// ------------------------------------
template<class T>
T
StackLList<T>::Top()
{
    if (top)
        return top->contents;
#ifdef EXCEPTIONS
    throw StackIsEmpty;
#else
    return 0;
#endif
}

#endif
```

8.7 Applications

There are myriads of applications for linear lists in computer programming. We will discuss a few here.

8.7.1 Singly-linked Lists: Sparse Matrices

A matrix is a two-dimensional, rectangular array of numbers. The matrix consists of *rows* and *columns*; an $M \times N$ matrix has M rows and N columns. The principal operation to perform on two matrices is matrix multiplication, where an $M \times N$ matrix is multiplied by an $N \times P$ matrix to yield an $M \times P$ matrix. Each cell in the output matrix consists of the sum of the products of corresponding elements in the row and column of the cell, as follows:

$$Out_{i,j} = \sum_{i=1}^{N} A_{i,k} B_{k,j}$$

A straightforward, $O(N^3)$ matrix multiplication algorithm is simple to implement. This implementation works well for small matrices. For larger matrices, more efficient algorithms have been described.

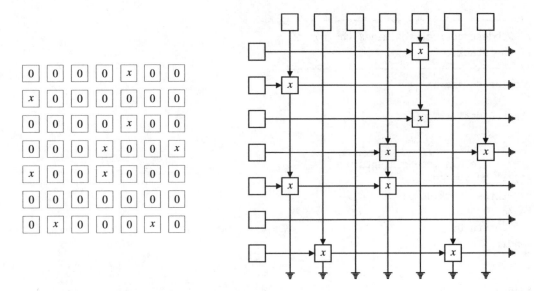

Figure 8.12.   Sparse matrix using linked lists.

And for matrices that are likely to contain many zero elements, it is more efficient not to store the elements at all. Instead, a sort of two-dimensional set of singly-linked lists can be used to bypass the zero elements in the array. This technique increases the complexity of implementation but also vastly decreases the memory storage requirements of these so-called "sparse" matrices.

Figure 8.12 depicts such an implementation of a sparse matrix. If we assume that each element in the naive matrix on the left is a **double**, it requires $49 * 8 = 392$ bytes of memory. Each nonzero element in the matrix on the right requires space for the double, plus space for the two Next pointers (to the elements on its right and bottom), plus space for two array indices (since the node must know where in the matrix it falls now). The 14 list heads also must be counted in the memory requirements for the sparse matrix on the right. Assuming an 8-byte **double**, 4-byte pointers, and 2-byte indices, the array on the right requires $9 * 16 + 14 * 4 = 200$ bytes of memory. As the matrices get larger (and sparser—the matrix shown has a much higher percentage of nonzero elements than truly sparse matrices), the space savings become much more dramatic.

As an added bonus, the matrix multiplication routine is faster because zero elements are not considered.

8.7.2 Stacks: Recursion Simulation

Functional recursion, as we have observed, should be avoided because it uses the machine stack in a nondeterministic way. For example, the most space-efficient Quicksort routine uses $O(\lg N)$ stack space; if Quicksort is called with large enough N, the machine stack will overflow, causing the program to crash. For algorithms like Quicksort that are nontrivial to implement iteratively, it is better to simulate recursion using a stack based on dynamic memory allocation.

8.7.3 Queues: I/O Buffers

One of the most prominent uses for queues is in I/O buffers. The original IBM PC, for example, had a 15-byte array in low memory that functioned as a queue for pending keystrokes. Whenever a keystroke occurred, it was added to head of the queue; whenever a keystroke was requested by an application program, it was removed from the tail of the queue. If the queue was full, the BIOS (basic I/O system) would cause the speaker to beep rather than overflow the queue. In this way, the order of the keystrokes was preserved and the queue was prevented from overflowing.

8.7.4 Doubly-linked Lists: Windowing Systems

Windowing systems such as Microsoft Windows and X Windows typically maintain a hierarchical list of the windows in the system. Each application has an application window, and all windows that belong to the application are "children" of the application window. These children are enumerated in a doubly-linked list, in no particular order. Under Windows, the linked list can be traversed by using the GetWindow system call with the GW_HWNDFIRST, GW_HWNDLAST, GW_HWNDNEXT, and GW_HWNDPREV constants.

A linked list is the ideal data structure for this application for a number of reasons. First, the window data structures (nodes in the linked list) usually can be allocated with a fixed-length allocator, making the implementation faster and less prone to heap fragmentation. Second, the order of the windows usually does not matter; usually they just need to be traversed and visited exactly once.

When the order does matter (as when determining the tab order of child windows in a dialog), the list can easily be modified to suit the programmer's needs.

8.7.5 Fingers: The `Clock` Page-Replacement Algorithm

A good example of an algorithm that uses fingers is the `Clock` page replacement algorithm for virtual memory management, described by Corbato [CORB68]. Before describing `Clock` in detail, a brief overview of page replacement algorithms is in order.

When a page fault occurs, the memory referenced is on disk and must be loaded into physical memory to satisfy the memory request. The operating system has to run a "page-replacement algorithm" to decide which page in physical memory should be evicted to make room for the incoming page. Page-replacement algorithms were an open problem in operating systems research for a long time, although they are fairly well understood by now.

The goal of the page-replacement algorithm is to avoid replacing a page that a process is currently using. If it replaces a page that a process needs, the process will access the just-evicted page soon and cause another page fault. As a rule, replacing a page that hasn't been used in a while is a good bet. The "least-recently-used," or LRU, algorithm for page replacement evicts the page that has been used least recently. LRU isn't feasible to implement, though, because no one builds computer hardware that keeps track of exactly when pages were accessed.

To approximate LRU, `Clock` puts the physical pages in memory into a circular linked list with a finger. Pages that have just been replaced are behind the finger; pages that probably can be replaced safely are ahead of the finger. When it comes time to replace a page, `Clock` executes the following algorithm.

```
1   Clock(Finger)
2       do
3           Finger←Finger.Next
4           if Finger.UseBit = TRUE then
5               Finger.UseBit←False
6               continue
7           if Finger.DirtyBit = TRUE then
8               SchedulePageForCleaning
```

```
9            continue
10           Suitable page has been found
11           break
12       ReplacePage
13       return
```

The UseBit and DirtyBit fields in the page pointed to by Finger are provided by the memory management hardware of any modern CPU. The use-bit is set when the page is accessed, and the dirty-bit of a page is set when the page is written to. These operations occur automatically without any intervention from the operating system.

If the use-bit is set, then the page has been accessed since Finger last traversed it. The page is probably not a good candidate for replacement because it has been accessed recently. To check on this page later, the use-bit is reset to 0. If the use-bit is still 0 the next time Finger sees this page, the process probably does not need that page in memory anymore.

If the dirty-bit is set, the page probably is not a good candidate for replacement either. However, because Finger traverses the circular list in one direction, it has been a long time since Clock last considered this page for replacement, and the page may not be in use anymore. Just in case, the page is scheduled for *cleaning*, a process that involves writing the page out to disk and resetting the page's dirty-bit to 0. If the page still isn't dirty the next time Clock considers it, the use-bit will determine whether it is a good candidate for replacement.

If Clock finds a page whose use- and dirty-bits are both 0, the page is suitable for replacement.

Figure 8.13 depicts Clock executing once to find a replaceable page. Each rectangle in the diagram is a page frame in the computer's physical memory. Clean pages that can be replaced are white. Lightly shaded pages have the USE-BIT set and should not be replaced. Dark pages have the USE-BIT and DIRTY-BIT set and should not be replaced, but need to be scheduled for cleaning when Finger encounters them.

The steps taken in Figure 8.13 are as follows.

1. Initially, Finger points at the last page replaced (in bold).
2. This page has the USE-BIT set; the bit is reset and we go on to the next page.

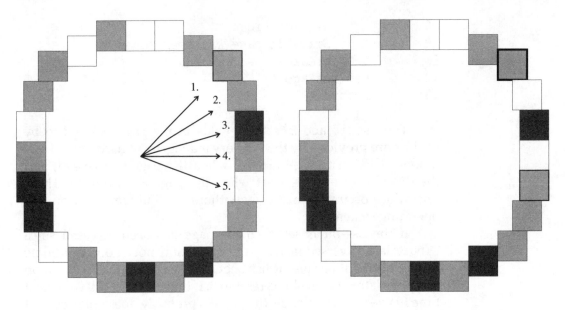

Steps during `Clock`   State after `Clock` has run

Figure 8.13.   Clock page replacement algorithm.

3. This page has the DIRTY-BIT set; we schedule the page for cleaning and go on to the next page.
4. This page has the USE-BIT set; the bit is reset and we go on to the next page.
5. This page is clean. Since it hasn't been accessed since `Finger` last considered it, it is a good candidate for replacement.

The right-hand diagram in Figure 8.13 shows the state of the page frames after `Clock` has run. The frames that had the use-bit set have been reset to white; the dirty page will be white as soon as it is cleaned. The last frame replaced is outlined in bold and, because an access was what caused the page fault in the first place, has the use-bit set.

`Clock` is guaranteed to terminate, since it resets the use-bits as it goes around the linked list. If it has to, it will go all the way around the list to where it started to find a page with a clear use-bit. If all the dirty-bits are set, `Clock` will have to wait until one has been cleaned before it can satisfy the page fault.

The only way that `Clock` will replace a page that has been accessed recently is if all the pages in memory are in use. In this case, Finger will traverse all the way around the available physical frames of memory to find a page suitable for replacement. If this happens, there probably is no way to keep all the processes in the system happy: Collectively they need more physical memory than the system has.

The Finger pointer separates the pages that have been accessed recently from pages that haven't been considered in a long time. By using a Finger pointer, the Clock algorithm implements a simple and specialized priority queue data structure to determine which page to replace.

Skip Lists

Pugh describes the *skip list*, an improved version of linked list with better asymptotic behavior [PUGH90, PUGH92]. Like singly-linked lists, each node only contains pointers to subsequent nodes, so the list can be traversed only from the head toward the tail. (Contrast this with the binary trees and other data structures discussed in subsequent chapters.) The nodes are maintained in sorted order, yet insertion, queries, and deletion can be performed in expected $O(\lg N)$ time as opposed to the $O(N)$ runtimes required to maintain sorted singly-linked lists.

Skip lists are *probabilistic*. In other words, they implement random behavior to prevent predetermined inputs from eliciting poor performance. Each node in a skip list contains a random number of Next pointers. Rather than eliminating the possibility of poor performance, the probabilistic nature of skip lists merely makes poor performance extremely unlikely. Randomizing the partitioning element in Quicksort, a technique discussed in Chapter 4, is also a probabilistic way to make poor performance unlikely.

Figure 9.1 depicts a skip list. The nodes in the skip list are enumerated in ascending order; each node's key is less than those of its successors. Every node in the skip list contains at least one Next pointer; these are designated Level 0, Level 1, and so on. Every node has a Level 0 pointer pointing at the next node in the skip list. Higher-level Next pointers, designated by Node.Next[Level], point at increasingly faraway nodes. These higher-level pointers are

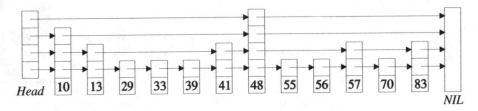

Figure 9.1. Skip list.

what make it possible to search skip lists faster than naive linked lists.

Each singly-linked list comprised by the skip list is terminated by a special node NIL that contains an "infinite" key guaranteed to be greater than any element to be inserted into the skip list. Because NIL is infinite, it preserves the order imposed by the skip list (that every node has a key less than its successors). While NIL will simplify our presentation of the algorithms to manipulate skip lists, we shall not use them in the implementation for reasons that will become clear in Section 9.6.

Skip lists are probabilistic because the number of Next pointers in a node is assigned randomly. Accordingly, they have a few parameters assigned that affect the behavior of this randomness. MaxLevel is the maximum number of Next pointers per node. A probability p describes the number of pointers per node, as follows.

```
1   RandomLevel(p, MaxLevel)
2        Level←1
3        while Random(0, 1) < p and Level < MaxLevel
4             Level←Level+1
5        return Level
```

The call to Random returns a real value between 0 and 1. p is a real value as well; the probability that a new node will contain N Next pointers is p^n. Thus, for $p = 0.5$, half of all nodes have one pointer; one-quarter have two pointers; one-eighth have three; and so on. The average number of Next pointers per node is $1/(1 - p)$ (2 for $p = 0.5$, $\frac{4}{3}$ for $p = 0.25$, etc.). RandomLevel isn't guaranteed to terminate without help, so we refuse to give any node more than MaxLevel Next pointers.

MaxLevel should be chosen according to how many elements are expected to be placed in the skip list. Pugh suggests setting

MaxLevel $= \log_{1/p} N$, where N is the maximum number of nodes to be inserted (for example, setting MaxLevel=24 for skip lists with $p = 0.5$ should accommodate up to 2^{24} or about 16.8 million elements).

Section 9.1 discusses the query operation, the key procedure used to maintain skip lists. Sections 9.2 and 9.3 discuss insertion and deletion of items in skip lists. Section 9.4 discusses skip list performance and how the parameters affect it in more detail. Section 9.5 discusses variations on skip list implementations and how they can affect the time and space requirements of skip list maintenance. Finally, Section 9.6 describes the skip list implementation in this book.

9.1 Query

To query a node Q, a pointer Scan into the skip list begins at the top level and scans across that level of the linked list until $Q<$ Scan.Next[Level].Contents. Thus, Scan points at a node whose key is strictly less than Q and the span from Scan to Scan.Next encompasses the node being queried. At that point, Scan drops down a level and continues scanning; since the Scan now occurs at a lower level, it has a higher granularity than before. When Scan reaches the lowest level, it no longer skips any nodes, so when the loop terminates, either Scan.Next points at Q or there is no instance of Q in the skip list. Pseudocode for the operation is as follows.

```
1   Query(List, Q)
2       Level←List.MaxLevel
3       Scan←NIL
4       while Level ≥ 0 do
5           if Scan = NIL then Scan←List.Head[Level]
6           while Scan ≠ NIL and
                    Q < Scan.Next[Level].Contents do
7               Scan←Scan.Next[Level]
8           Level←Level-1
9       if Scan.Contents = Q then
10          return Scan.Contents
11      else return NOT-FOUND
```

Figure 9.2 depicts a query into a skip list. The element being queried is 83. The shaded block shows how Scan traverses the skip

Query: 83

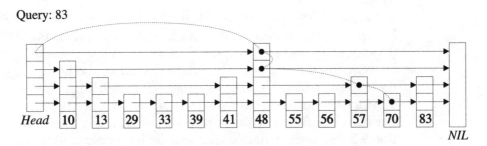

Head   10   13   29   33   39   41   48   55   56   57   70   83

                                                                                    NIL

Figure 9.2.   Skip list query.

list to find it. When the query ends, Scan points at 70; its Next pointer points at the node being queried.

Note that the query can begin at any level of the skip list, and it will work properly. At the lowest level, it is equivalent to traversing a singly-linked list; as the initial level increases, the speedup due to skipping elements increases.

9.2 Insertion

Insertion is done by constructing a vector Update of Next pointers. Update contains MaxLevel elements that are initialized to NIL. Update works much like the pointer Scan did during the query, except that Update remembers the values of the final values of Scan at each level during the query. Instead of just dropping Scan down by a level, we set Update[level] to Scan and then drop Scan down by a level. After the query operation has completed, Update contains a vector of pointers to the nodes that precede the location where the new node should be inserted. (NULL pointers in Update indicate that the new node should be inserted at the head.) Pseudocode for the Update procedure is as follows.

```
1   Insert(List, AddMe)
2      Level←List.MaxLevel
3      Scan←NIL
4      while Level ≥ 0 do
5        if Scan = NIL then Scan←List.Head[Level]
6        while Scan ≠ NIL and
            AddMe < Scan.Next[Level].Contents do
7          Scan←Scan.Next[Level]
8        Update[Level]←Scan
```

```
9        Level←Level-1
10       NewLevel←RandomLevel(List)
11       NewNode←new Node(AddMe, NewLevel)
12       for Level←NewLevel downto 0 do
13         if Update[Level] ≠ NIL do
14           NewNode.Next[Level]←Update[Level].Next
15           Update[Level].Next←NewNode
```

Figure 9.3 depicts insertion into a skip list.

The number of Next pointers in the new node is then randomly determined. This procedure has a number of parameters: MaxLevel, the maximum number of Next pointers per node, and a probability p. Given these parameters, the number of Next pointers is determined as follows.

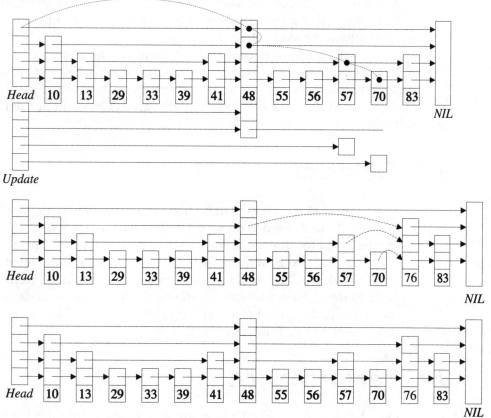

Figure 9.3. Skip list insertion.

```
1   RandomLevel(List)
2      Level←1
3      while Random(0, 1) < List.p and
            Level < List.MaxLevel
4         Level←Level+1
5      return Level
```

The call to Random returns a real value between 0 and 1. p is a real value as well; the probability that a new node will contain N Next pointers is p^N. Thus, for $p = 0.5$, half of all nodes have one pointer; one-quarter have two pointers; one-eighth have three; and so on.

Using this scheme, there is a small chance of an extremely high-level node being generated that adds overhead without greatly helping query operations. For example, a level-14 node does not help much if the next-highest level in the skip list is 4. As an alternative, Pugh suggests capping the level at one higher than the highest level currently in the skip list.

Once the new node has been created, the elements in the Update vector are used to wire it into the skip list. The new node's Next pointers are set to the Next pointers of the Update pointers; the Next pointers of the Update nodes are set to point at the new node.

9.3 Deletion

Just as the Update vector can be used to wire a new node into the skip list, it can be used to remove a node from the skip list. Update is computed as for insertion. The lowest L vectors ($0..L - 1$ inclusive) of Update then point at the node to delete, where L is the level of the node to delete. Copying the corresponding Next pointers from the node to the elements in Update effectively removes the node from the skip list. The node can then be deleted. Figure 9.4 depicts the deletion of a node from a skip list.

9.4 Performance

Our discussion of skip list performance follows Pugh [PUGH90]. Programmers more interested in practical runtimes may wish to

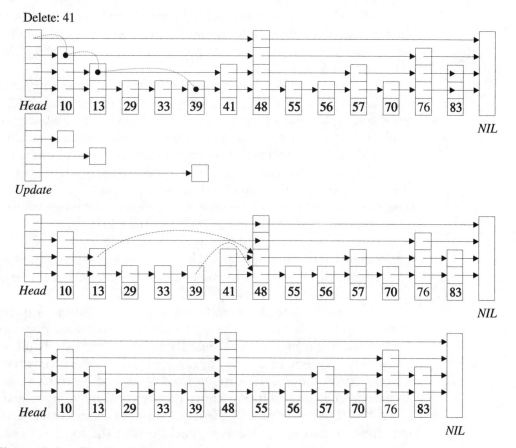

Delete: 41

Head 10 13 29 33 39 41 48 55 56 57 70 76 83

NIL

Update

Head 10 13 29 33 39 41 48 55 56 57 70 76 83

NIL

Head 10 13 29 33 39 48 55 56 57 70 76 83

NIL

Figure 9.4. Skip list deletion.

turn to Chapter 13 to examine the performance characteristics of the skip list implementation included with this book.

The performance of skip lists is incumbent on the performance of the query operation. Once a query has been performed, an insertion or deletion can be performed in $O(k)$ time. Since we have limited k to a small integer, $O(k)$ is effectively $O(1)$, or constant time. This runtime is quickly dwarfed by the time required to query the desired location in the skip list.

To explore the runtimes of skip list queries, we will utilize two probability distributions, the binominal distribution $B(t, p)$, and the negative binomial distribution $NB(s, p)$.

$B(t, p)$ denotes the number of successes seen in a series of t independent random trials where the probability of a success in a trial is p. The average and variance of $B(t, p)$ are tp and $tp(1 - p)$.

$NB(s, p)$ denotes the number of failures seen before the sth success in a series of independent random trials where the probability of success in a trial is p. The average and variance of $NB(s, p)$ are $s(1 - p)/p$ and $s(1 - p)/p^2$.

The utility of $NB(s, p)$ becomes obvious when, for example, we wish to calculate the average number of Next pointers per node. If we think of iterations through the while loop in RandomLevel as "failures" and the termination condition to be a "success," adding one to $NB(1, 1 - p)$ yields the average number of Next pointers per node. (We add one because if zero failures are encountered before the first success, that means there is one Next pointer, and so on.) The average value of $NB(1, 1 - p)$ is $p/(1 - p)$, so the average number of Next pointers per node is $1 + [p/(1 - p)]$, or $1/(1 - p)$.

Another mathematical tool we will need to analyze skip list performance is the function $L(n) = \log_{1/p} n$. For a skip list containing N elements, this is the approximate factor by which the number of nodes decreases as the level increases.

Now, to analyze the number of steps taken during a query into a skip list, we start at the query element and work our way back toward the highest-level Head pointer in the list. Think of the backward climb as a series of random independent trials with success corresponding to a move up a level and a failure corresponding to a move left. We know that we will move up exactly MaxLevel ($L(N) - 1$) times—the exact number of successes to be experienced during our traversal back toward the top-level Head where the query started. The number of leftward moves required to move up to level $L(N)$ can be thought of as the number of failures seen before reaching the $(L(N) - 1)$th success; the probability of a success on each trial is p. This is a negative binomial distribution: $NB(L(N) - 1, p)$. The total number of moves to climb to level $L(N)$ is thus: $(L(N) - 1) + NB(L(N) - 1, p)$.

We have assumed that we would reach level $L(N)$ in our backward climb before hitting the head of the skip list. This corresponds to assuming that the list extends infinitely to the left. Since the list does not actually do this, the number of moves we computed serves as an upper bound on the number of moves required to climb to level $L(N)$.

Once having moved to level $L(N)$, the number of leftward movements is bounded from above by the number of nodes at that level. The number of such nodes is given by the binomial distribution $B(N, (1/p)N)$.

The final step is to compute a probabilistic bound on M, the maximum level in a list of N elements. The probability that the level of a given node is greater than k is p^k. Therefore, the probability that $M > k$ is $1 - (1 - p^k)^N$. To reconstruct what's going on here, $(1 - p^k)^N$ is the probability that *no* node will have a level greater than k. Subtracting this probability from 1 yields the probability that *some* node will have a level greater than k. This probability can be bounded by the number of nodes in the list with levels greater than k: $1 - (1 - p^k)^N < Np^k$.

Using the identities $N = p^{\log_p N}$ and $\log_a N = \log_b N / \log_b a$, Np^k can be rewritten as $p^{k - \log_{1/p} N}$ or $p^{k - L(N)}$. Recalling that $p^i = \Pr\{NB(1, 1 - p) + 1 > i\}$, we can write $p^{k - L(N)} = \Pr\{NB(1, 1 - p) + 1 > k - L(N)\}$.

We can obtain a probabilistic bound on the maximum level in a list of N elements by $L(N) + NB(1, 1 - p) + 1$.

The cost of the entire search, then, is the cost to climb up to level $L(N)$, plus the number of leftward movements to reach the head:

$$Cost = (L(N) - 1) + NB(L(N) - 1, p) + B(N, \tfrac{1}{p}N) + NB(1, 1 - p) + 1$$

$$= L(N) + NB(L(N) - 1, p) + B(N, \tfrac{1}{p}N) + NB(1, 1 - p)$$

The average and variance of this cost can be obtained by plugging into the expressions given in the definitions of the binomial and negative binomial distributions.

$$Average\ cost = \frac{L(N)}{p} + \frac{1}{1 - p} + 1$$

So for a skip list with $p = 0.5$ containing 256 elements, the average number of steps required to query a node is $[(\log_2 256)/0.5] + [1/(1 - 0.5)] + 1 = 19$.

Since the last two terms are constant for a given skip list, the cost of a skip list query is expected to increase logarithmically with N. In other words, the cost to query, insert, or delete an element in a skip list is $O(\log_{1/p} N)$. The base of the logarithm varies, but this only affects performance by a constant factor.

Just for fun, we also can compute the variance of the cost from the definitions of binomial and negative binomial distributions.

$$Variance\ of\ cost = \frac{(L(N) - 1)(1 - p)}{p^2} + \frac{1 - \tfrac{1}{p}N}{p} + \frac{p}{(1 - p)^2}$$

The variance gives a measure of how consistent the performance of the skip list will be. Intuitively, decreasing p should increase the variance as it becomes less likely that high-level pointers will assist a given inquiry. This intuition is confirmed by the formula.

9.5 Variations

Depending on the requirements of the application, it may be appropriate to modify the basic skip list data structure just described.

9.5.1 Reducing Comparisons

If comparisons are extremely expensive (as when comparing strings or complicated records), comparing the same elements more than once can be avoided by keeping track of the last node that was compared with the query node. Pseudocode for the operation follows.

```
1   QueryMinComparisons(List, Q)
2       Level←List.MaxLevel
3       Scan←NIL
4       AlreadyChecked←NIL
5       while Level ≥ 0 do
6           if Scan = AlreadyChecked then
7               Level←Level-1
8               continue
9           if Scan = NIL then Scan←List.Head[Level]
10          while Scan ≠ NIL and
                  Q < Scan.Next[Level].Contents do
11              Scan←Scan.Next[Level]
12          Level←Level-1
```

9.5.2 Other Probability Distributions

To reduce the space requirements of a skip list, Pugh suggests introducing an additional parameter k, the number of iterations for RandomLevel to execute before increasing the level of the node. The probability of a node having i Next pointers is then p^{i+k-1}. The average number of pointers per node using this distribution is $1 + [p^{k+1}/(1 - p)]$.

Performance does not unduly suffer from this optimization; the average number of comparisons required to perform a query becomes $[L(N) - k - 1 + (1/p^k)]/p$. Like the performance in the standard case, this expression increases as the log of the number of elements in the skip list.

9.5.3 Selection

An efficient algorithm for selecting the kth highest element in the skip list can be implemented by associating a distance traversed with each Next pointer in the nodes of the skip list. (This distance is 1 if the node pointed to is the immediately subsequent one.)

```
1   Select(List, k)
2        Level←List.MaxLevel
3        Scan←NIL
4        Pos←0
5        while Level ≥ 0 do
6             if Scan = NIL then Scan←List.Head[Level]
7             while Scan ≠ NIL and
                    Pos+Scan.fDistance[Level] ≤ k do
8                  Pos←Pos+Scan.fDistance[Level]
9                  Scan←Scan.Next[Level]
10            Level←Level-1
11       return Scan.Contents
```

9.5.4 Merge

An algorithm to merge two skip lists into one (while destroying both lists) is straightforward. For skip lists *list1* and *list2*, construct an Update vector for *list1* that corresponds to a query for the first element in *list2*. This Update vector can then be used to append *list2* to *list1*. Then construct an Update vector for *list2* that corresponds to a query for the head element in the remainder of *list1* and use it to append *list1* to *list2*. By repeating this process, the skip lists can be destructively merged in expected $O(\log N)$ time where N is the total number of elements in both skip lists. Pugh [PUGH90] describes this algorithm and how it compares favorably with algorithms to merge balanced trees in more detail.

9.6 Implementation

The implementation of skip lists presented here is straightforward. It consists of a class template `SkipList`. Two related class templates, `SkipListNode` and `SkipListIterator`, help complete the skip list implementation. `SkipListNode` implements a node in the skip list; `SkipListIterator` implements an iterator on the skip list. Both of these class templates have **private** constructors and declare `SkipList` a **friend**, so only `SkipList` can create instances of them or access their contents. Both class templates might have been implemented better as embedded classes. However, no C++ compiler I am aware of can parse member functions of classes embedded in templates unless they are implemented in-line. In the interest of readability, I separated out `SkipListNode` and `SkipListIterator` so their member functions could be declared and implemented separately in the header file.

9.6.1 Representation

The biggest difference between the high-level description of skip lists given earlier and the implementation is that the latter avoids using a sentinel node at the tail of the list. The tail sentinel NIL simplifies things at the end by eliminating any need to worry about boundary conditions if explicit NULL pointers terminate the lists at different levels. Because the NIL node has a value of infinity, it's impossible for any query to seek beyond it. The sentinel is good for highlighting the features of the algorithms without overwhelming the reader with details.

We avoided the use of sentinels in all of the data structures in this book, however. Sentinels are not appropriate for a truly general-purpose implementation for two reasons. First, the sentinel nodes in the data structure require extra space. Because one of the members of each node is an instance of a user-provided class, this places a greater burden on clients of the skip list implementation. Second, the user-provided class must have not only its copy constructor, assignment operator, and < operator defined; it also must have a default constructor guaranteed to run quickly and generate a class instance that doesn't take up much space.

As if that weren't enough, the class also must have an infinity value. For some data types, such as unsigned integers, an infinity value is not possible without restricting the possible values clients can use. Even if we assume this is a reasonable restriction, it remains an open question how to communicate to the skip list implementation exactly what that infinity value is.

That said, it should be pointed out that sentinels are useful in a broad variety of contexts. Most classes have default constructors, and most metrics for comparisons have "infinities" that can be used without perceptibly degrading the utility of the implementation. (If unsigned integers are being used as keys, for example, excluding the largest one and using it as a sentinel value usually isn't a problem.) The descriptions of skip lists given here should be sufficient to let readers modify the source code and incorporate a sentinel node at the end if they wish.

Listing 9.1 gives the definitions for the `SkipList` class template, the related template `SkipListNode`, and the implementations of the constructors and assignment operator for `SkipList`. In the source code included with the book, the skip list implementation is given in `<skiplist.h>`.

Listing 9.1. `SkipList` class template definitions.

```
// ==========================================================
// skiplist.h
//       Header file for SkipList class template.
//       This class template implements skip lists, a
//       probabilistic augmentation of singly linked lists.
//
// Copyright (C) 1995 by Nicholas Wilt.  All rights reserved.
// ==========================================================

template<class T>
class SkipList {
public:
    SkipList(int p = RAND_MAX/2, int MaxLevel = 15);
    SkipList(const SkipList<T>&);
    SkipList<T>& operator=(const SkipList<T>&);
    virtual ~SkipList();

    virtual void Insert(const T&);
    virtual void Delete(const T&);
    virtual T *Query(const T&);
    virtual void Print() const;
    virtual void PrintAll() const;
    virtual void CheckInvariant() const;
```

(continued)

```
public:
    SkipListNode<T> *Head(int i) { return head[i]; }
    SkipListNode<T> *QueryNode(const T& x);
protected:
    int p, level, MaxLevel;
    SkipListNode<T> **head, **update;

    int RandomLevel() const;
    void CopyList(const SkipList<T>&);
};

template<class T>
class SkipListNode {
private:
    // Constructors, destructor and assignment operator
    SkipListNode();
    SkipListNode(const T& _contents, int _level);
    virtual ~SkipListNode();

    // Copy constructor and assignment operator: declared
    // BUT NOT IMPLEMENTED (at least, by default). There
    // should never be a need for these functions.  The
    // reason I didn't want to include them by default is
    // because they require the level member to be in every
    // node of the skip list, which is very wasteful of space.
    // If for some reason you need them, remove the
    // #if 0/#endif preprocessor directives around their
    // implementations below. You will need to compile with
    // the EXCEPTIONS define set.
    SkipListNode(const SkipListNode&);
    SkipListNode<T>& operator=(const SkipListNode&);

    // Manipulation of Next pointers
    SkipListNode *Next(int i);
    void SetNext(int i, SkipListNode<T> *nxt);

    // Access grant to contents
    T *Contents();

    // Members
    T contents;
    SkipListNode **next;
```

```
#ifdef EXCEPTIONS
    // If exceptions are enabled, store the level so we
    // can validate access of the array of next pointers.
    int level;
#endif

    friend class SkipList<T>;
    friend class SkipListIterator<T>;
public:
    enum ExceptionCause { InvalidNext };

    class Exception {
    private:
int cause;
    Exception(enum ExceptionCause _cause):
        cause(_cause) { }
    friend SkipListNode<T>;
    public:
        int Why() const { return cause; }
    };
};

// -------------------------------------
// Copy constructor.
// -------------------------------------
template<class T>
SkipList<T>::SkipList(const SkipList<T>& x)
{
    CopyList(x);
}

// -------------------------------------
// Assignment operator.
// -------------------------------------
template<class T>
SkipList<T>&
SkipList<T>::operator=(const SkipList<T>& x)
{
    for (SkipListNode<T> *sc = head[0]; sc; ) {
        SkipListNode<T> *next = sc->Next(0);
        delete sc;
        sc = next;
    }
    CopyList(x);
```

(continued)

```
        return *this;
}


// ------------------------------------
// Destructor.
// ------------------------------------
template<class T>
SkipList<T>::~SkipList()
{
    for (SkipListNode<T> *sc = head[0]; sc; ) {
        SkipListNode<T> *next = sc->Next(0);
        delete sc;
        sc = next;
    }
}


// ===========================================================
// SkipListNode implementation
// ===========================================================


// ------------------------------------
// Default constructor
// ------------------------------------
template<class T>
SkipListNode<T>::SkipListNode()
{
    next = 0;
}


// ------------------------------------
// Constructor
// ------------------------------------
template<class T>
SkipListNode<T>::SkipListNode(const T& _contents, int _level)
{
    contents = _contents;
#ifdef EXCEPTIONS
    level = _level;
#endif
    next = new SkipListNode *[_level];
    for (int i = 0; i < _level; i++)
        next[i] = 0;
}

#if 0
```

```
// Un-comment this out only if you need to--you should never need the copy
// constructor or assignment operator for SkipListNode. If you ever do, you
// will have to store the level of each node so these functions know how many
// Next pointers to allocate in the new node.


// ------------------------------------
// Copy constructor
// ------------------------------------
template<class T>
SkipListNode<T>::SkipListNode(const SkipListNode& x)
{
    contents = x.contents;
#ifdef EXCEPTIONS
    level = x.level;
#endif
    next = new SkipListNode *[x.level];
    for (int i = 0; i < x.level; i++)
        next[i] = x.next[i];
}


// ------------------------------------
// Assignment operator
// ------------------------------------
template<class T>
SkipListNode<T>&
SkipListNode<T>::operator=(const SkipListNode& x)
{
    if (next) delete[] next;
    contents = x.contents;
    next = new SkipListNode *[level = x.level];
    for (int i = 0; i < x.level; i++)
        next[i] = x.next[i];
    return *this;
}
#endif


// ------------------------------------
// Destructor
// ------------------------------------
template<class T>
SkipListNode<T>::~SkipListNode()
{
    if (next)
        delete[] next;
}
```

In the SkipList class template, p is an integer that is some fraction of RAND_MAX such that the skip list's parameter p is p/RAND_MAX. (RAND_MAX, the maximum value that can be returned by rand(), is declared in the standard ANSI C header <stdlib.h>.) That way, the skip list implementation of RandomLevel can call the rand() library function and compare directly to p. p has a default value of RAND_MAX/2 (equivalent to $p = 0.5$). This default can be overridden, of course.

Besides p, SkipList contains level (the maximum level of any node in the list) and MaxLevel (maximum level of the list) parameters. MaxLevel has a default value of 15. Pugh suggests setting MaxLevel to $\log_{1/p} N$, where N is the maximum number of nodes expected to reside in the skip list at any time. For the default value of p, the default MaxLevel is good for up to $2^{15} = 32768$ elements.

9.6.2 Query

The query operation is implemented as described in Section 9.1. The biggest difference between the implementation given and the implementation described in Section 9.1 is that, when beginning Scan's trek across the skip list, if it hits an element equal to the query element Q, it returns immediately. This is because Scan is initially set to NULL (0 in C++); this indicates that a Head pointer has not yet been found that points to an element less than the query element. As Scan drops down levels, if it is still NULL it starts at the Head pointer of that level to try and find an element less than Q. If Scan drops to the lowest level and still can't find a Head pointer less than Q, that could mean one of two things: Q is not in the skip list, or Q is the first element in the skip list. Unfortunately, because each skip list is terminated with a NULL, Scan also could wind up NULL because Q is larger than any element in the skip list. There's no way to tell the difference after the loop has finished, so we head off the first possibility at the pass by returning Q if it's at the head of any level of the skip list. The extra comparisons required are minimal, since they are performed only at the head.

Listing 9.2 gives SkipList<T>::Query.

Listing 9.2. Query member function.

```
// ------------------------------------------------------------
// SkipList<T>::Query
//      Queries the skip list for the given element and, if
```

```
//      found, returns a pointer to it. Otherwise returns 0.
// ------------------------------------------------------------
template<class T>
T *
SkipList<T>::Query(const T& x)
{
    SkipListNode<T> *Node = QueryNode(x);

    return (Node) ? Node->Contents() : 0;
}


// ------------------------------------------------------------
// SkipList<T>::QueryNode
//      Queries the skip list for the given element and, if
//      found, returns a pointer to the node. Otherwise
//      returns 0.
// ------------------------------------------------------------
template<class T>
SkipListNode<T> *
SkipList<T>::QueryNode(const T& x)
{
    SkipListNode<T> *sc = 0;
    for (int i = MaxLevel - 1; i >= 0; i -= 1) {
        if ((! sc) && head[i]) {
            if (*head[i]->Contents() == x) return head[i];
            if (*head[i]->Contents() < x) sc = head[i];
        }
        while (sc && sc->Next(i) && *sc->Next(i)->Contents() < x)
            sc = sc->Next(i);
        }
        if (sc) {
            sc = sc->Next(0);
            if (sc && *sc->Contents() == x)
            return sc;
        }
        return 0;
}
```

9.6.3 Insertion

SkipList<T>::Insert begins by computing the level of the new
node by calling RandomLevel. Then it constructs the Update vector
for the new node as described in Section 9.2, with one catch: If the
Head pointer for a given level is NULL, it is set to point at the new
node. The corresponding element in Update then is set to NULL to

indicate that the node is already wired into the skip list at that level. After Update has been constructed, it is used to wire the new node into the skip list. Finally, the level of the skip list is set to the new node's level if it is greater.

Listing 9.3 gives SkipList<T>::Insert.

Listing 9.3. Insert member function.

```
// ----------------------------------------------------------
// SkipList<T>::Insert
//      Inserts the given element into the skip list.
// ----------------------------------------------------------
template<class T>
void
SkipList<T>::Insert(const T& x)
{
    int lvl = RandomLevel();
    SkipListNode<T> *sc = 0;
    SkipListNode<T> *addme = new SkipListNode<T>(x, lvl);
    for (int i = lvl - 1; i >= 0; i -= 1) {
      if (head[i]) {
          sc = head[i];
          while (sc && sc->Next(i) && *sc->Next(i)->Contents() < x)
              sc = sc->Next(i);
          if (x < *sc->Contents()) {
              // Prepend to list
              addme->SetNext(i, sc);
              head[i] = addme;
              update[i] = 0;
              continue;
          }
          update[i] = sc;
      }
      else {
          head[i] = addme;
          update[i] = 0;
      }
    }
    if (lvl > level) {
        for (i = level; i < lvl; i++)
          update[i] = 0;
        level = lvl;
    }
    for (i = 0; i < lvl; i++) {
```

```
      if (update[i]) {
        addme->SetNext(i, update[i]->Next(i));
        update[i]->SetNext(i, addme);
      }
    }
}
```

9.6.4 Deletion

As with `SkipList<T>::Insert`, the deletion implementation is complicated somewhat by maintenance of the `Head` vector. The `Update` vector is constructed as before, with NULL elements where the head of a certain level's sublist is less than the element to be deleted Q. Then, when using `Update` to rewire the skip list to exclude Q, NULL elements in `Update` mean one of two things: Either the corresponding `Head` pointer points at Q, in which case it should be updated to Q's corresponding `Next` pointer, or Q is not present in that level of the skip list and the skip list need not be updated at that level.

Once the `Update` vector has been used to exclude Q from the skip list, the node can be deleted.

Listing 9.4 gives `SkipList<T>::Delete`.

Listing 9.4. `Delete` member function.

```
// ------------------------------------------------------------
// SkipList<T>::Delete
//      Deletes the given node from the skip list.
// ------------------------------------------------------------
template<class T>
void
SkipList<T>::Delete(const T& x)
{
    SkipListNode<T> *sc = 0;
    for (int i = level - 1; i >= 0; i -= 1) {
      if (head[i]) {
          sc = head[i];
          while (sc && sc->Next(i) && *sc->Next(i)->Contents() < x)
            sc = sc->Next(i);
          if (x < *sc->Contents()) {
            // Update vector won't help us here.
            update[i] = 0;
            continue;
```

(continued)

```
            }
            update[i] = sc;
        }
        else {
            update[i] = 0;
        }
    }
    if (! (sc->contents == x)) {
        sc = sc->Next(0);
        if (! sc)
            return;
        if (! (sc->contents == x))
            return;
    }
    for (i = 0; i < level; i++) {
        if (head[i] == sc)
            head[i] = sc->Next(i);
        else if (update[i] && update[i]->Next(i) == sc)
            update[i]->SetNext(i, sc->Next(i));
    }
    delete sc;
    while (level > 1 && head[level-1] == 0)
        level -= 1;


}
```

9.6.5 Iterators

The SkipListIterator class template implements a straightforward iterator on the skip list. Instances of the iterator can be created by calling SkipList<T>::Iterator.

SkipListIterator overloads the dereferencing operator (operator*) to return the contents of the node currently pointed to by the iterator. SkipListIterator overloads operator int to return whether the iterator currently points at a valid node. It also overloads the prefix and postfix increment operators ++ to go on to the next node. Thus, a skip list skiplist can easily be traversed as follows.

```
for (SkipListIterator<T> iter(skiplist);
     iter;
     iter++) {
     // *iter now returns the contents of iter
}
```

In addition to these overloaded operators, the skip list iterator class provides member functions Query (which points the skip list at a given element, or invalidates it if the query element is not present in the list) and Restart (which points the iterator back at the head of the skip list).

SkipListIterator trusts its clients not to misuse it. Deleting the node pointed to by an iterator is possible; calling operator* would then cause an invalid pointer to be dereferenced. A safeguard similar to the ones used in the SimpleList implementation in Chapter 8 could prevent destructive operations on the skip list while iterators are attached.

SkipListIterator also permits clients to modify the node contents through operator*; this could be used to change the skip list so the nodes are no longer in sorted order. At the cost of generality, operator* could be changed to return a **const** reference to the node contents. The current implementation assumes that clients of SkipList might want to modify the satellite data in the nodes and trusts them not to modify the keys.

Listing 9.5 gives the class template definition and implementation of SkipListIterator.

Listing 9.5. SkipListIterator class template.

```
template<class T>
class SkipListIterator {
public:
    SkipListIterator(SkipList<T>& _list);
    virtual ~SkipListIterator() { }

    // Operator int returns "true" if the iterator points
    // to a valid node.
    virtual operator int() const;

    // Dereferencing operator returns the contents of the
    // node currently pointed to by the iterator.
    virtual T& operator*() const;

    // Increment operators go on to the next item in the list.
    virtual void operator++();
    virtual void operator++(int);

    // Restart: points the iterator back at the list head.
    virtual void Restart();
```

(continued)

```
    // Query: points the iterator at the given element.
    virtual void Query(const T&);

#ifdef EXCEPTIONS
    enum ExceptionCause { InvalidDereference };

    class Exception {
    private:
        Exception(int _cause): cause(_cause) { }
        int cause;
        friend SkipListIterator<T>;
    public:
        int Why() const;
    };
#endif

protected:
    SkipList<T> *list;
    SkipListNode<T> *ptr;
};

// ============================================================
// SkipListIterator implementation
// ============================================================


// -------------------------------------
// Constructor
// -------------------------------------

template<class T>
SkipListIterator<T>::SkipListIterator(SkipList<T>& _list)
{
    list = &_list;
    ptr = list->Head(0);
}

template<class T>
SkipListIterator<T>::operator int() const
{
    return ptr != 0;
}

template<class T>
void
SkipListIterator<T>::operator++(int)
```

```
{
    if (ptr)
        ptr = ptr->Next(0);
}

template<class T>
void
SkipListIterator<T>::operator++()
{
    (*this)++;
}

template<class T>
T&
SkipListIterator<T>::operator*() const
{
#ifdef EXCEPTIONS
    if (! ptr)
        throw Exception(InvalidDereference);
#endif
    return ptr->contents;
}

template<class T>
void
SkipListIterator<T>::Restart()
{
    ptr = list->Head(0);
}

template<class T>
void
SkipListIterator<T>::Query(const T& x)
{
    ptr = list->QueryNode(x);
}
```

9.6.6 Miscellaneous Functions: `CheckInvariant`, `Print`, `PrintAll`

Skip lists have a number of invariants that can be verified. The most important is that every sublist in the skip list enumerates the elements in ascending order. Also, every sublist of level *i* is a strict

subset of the level $i - 1$. The CheckInvariant member function
verifies that these invariants hold for the skip list and complains to
cerr if they do not. CheckInvariant was used to help implement
the skip list and may prove useful to readers who intend to modify
the implementation.

Print and PrintAll are also member functions of largely diagnostic value. Print prints the elements of the skip list to cout by
traversing the level 0 Next pointers. PrintAll prints each level of
the skip list in decreasing order.

Listing 9.6 gives the implementation of CheckInvariant,
Print, and PrintAll.

Listing 9.6.   CheckInvariant, Print, and PrintAll **member functions.**

```
// ----------------------------------------------------------
// SkipList<T>::CheckInvariant
//       Checks to make sure the skip list is valid.
//       Complains to cerr if not.
// ----------------------------------------------------------
template<class T>
void
SkipList<T>::CheckInvariant() const
{
    for (int i = 0; i < level; i++) {
        SkipListNode<T> *sc = head[i];
        while (sc) {
            if (sc->Next(i) && *sc->Next(i)->Contents() < *sc->Contents() )
                cerr << "Invariant failed on skip list\n";
            sc = sc->Next(i);
        }
    }
}


// ----------------------------------------------------------
// SkipList<T>::Print
//       Prints the contents of the skip list in order to cout.
// ----------------------------------------------------------
template<class T>
void
SkipList<T>::Print() const
{
    SkipListNode<T> *sc = head[0];
    while (sc) {
        cout << sc->contents << ' ';
```

```
        sc = sc->next[0];
    }
    cout << '\n';
}


// ----------------------------------------------------------
// SkipList<T>::PrintAll
//      Prints the contents of each level of the skip list
//      in order to cout.
// ----------------------------------------------------------
template<class T>
void
SkipList<T>::PrintAll() const
{
    for (int i = level-1; i >=0 ; i--) {
        SkipListNode<T> *sc = head[i];
        cout << "Level " << i << ": ";
        while (sc) {
            cout << sc->contents << ' ';
            sc = sc->next[i];
        }
        cout << '\n';
    }
}
```

Binary Trees

Binary trees are a dynamic data structure that efficiently support the following operations:

- Insertion
- Deletion
- Query
- Minimum and maximum
- Traversal

If the data in the binary tree is uniform and random, these operations all take $O(\lg N)$ time to perform. As we shall see, this runtime can degrade to $O(N)$. A more elaborate data structure is needed to guarantee fast performance. Red-black trees, a form of balanced binary tree, guarantee $\Theta(\lg N)$ performance for every operation. Splay trees, another form of binary tree, perform at least as well as binary trees and far better in most applications. However, these data structures require extra time to maintain. If the data being manipulated is uniform and random, you might as well use a naive binary tree and avoid the costs of maintaining a more sophisticated data structure.

10.1 Characteristics and Terminology

The binary tree has a number of characteristics that are always true.

- The tree consists of nodes. Each node contains an element in the data structure.

- Every node can have up to two children (this is where the term "binary" comes from), a left child and a right child. The node with children is referred to as the parent of those child nodes.

- The left child of every node, if present, has a key less than the node.

- The right child of every node, if present, has a key greater than the node.

The node at the top of the binary tree, which has no parent, is called the *root*. The tree can be completely described by a pointer to the root node, since any other node in the binary tree can be found by traversing the tree from the root.

Nodes with children are called *interior nodes*. Nodes with no children are called *leaf nodes*. The *height* of the binary tree is the distance from the root to the farthest leaf node. Virtually every operation that can be performed on binary trees is $O(h)$, where h is the binary tree's height.

Figure 10.1 shows an example binary tree.

Any node in the binary tree can be thought of as the root of another, smaller binary tree. These smaller subtrees are the basis for recursive formulations of the algorithms to manipulate binary trees. Everything in the left subtree of a node has a key less than that of the node. Everything in the right subtree of a node has a key greater than that of the node. In fact, sometimes we don't even need to think of the individual nodes in the subtrees, only of the subtrees themselves. Figure 10.2 shows a partial binary tree with subtrees delineated by triangles. We'll use this notation more extensively in subsequent chapters, when we talk about ways to balance binary trees.

The height of a binary tree that contains N nodes can range from $\lceil \lg N \rceil$ to N. A binary tree whose height approaches $\lg N$ is called well balanced, and most operations can be performed on it

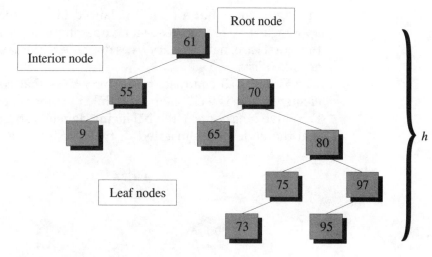

Figure 10.1. Binary tree.

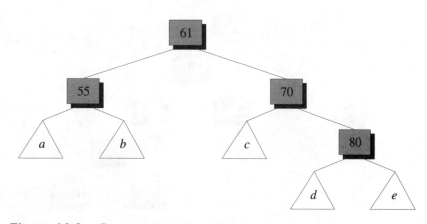

Figure 10.2. Binary tree with subtrees.

in $O(\lg N)$ time. But a poorly balanced binary tree, whose height approaches N, forces those same operations to take $O(N)$ time. In the worst case, naive binary trees degrade to the same performance as linked lists.

Figure 10.3 contrasts two binary trees that contain the same elements. One is well balanced, while the other is poorly balanced. For naive binary trees, the balancing depends strictly on the order that the nodes were inserted. If they are inserted more or less in

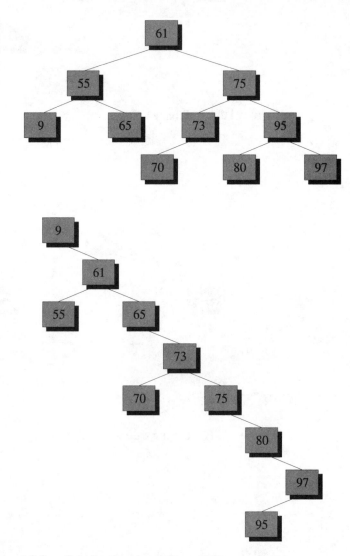

Figure 10.3.   Balanced and unbalanced binary trees.

random order, the binary tree will likely be well balanced. However, if the nodes are inserted in sorted order, the binary tree will be poorly balanced and exhibit poor performance.

While binary trees are not necessarily useful on their own, they lay an important framework for related data structures that have better performance. You see, there's no way to improve on the basic structure of the binary tree. For example, it may seem logical to give nodes more than two children. The leftmost child would then be less than the middle child, which was less than the rightmost child. This would decrease the height of the tree and presumably increase the tree's performance. However, having k children per node yields a minimum tree height of $\lceil \log_k N \rceil$, which is only a constant factor better than the $\lceil \lg N \rceil$ minimum height of a binary tree. Then you have to worry about how to traverse the tree efficiently, which will almost certainly cost more than having more than two children per node bought you in the first place. So the binary, two-child structure of the tree is difficult to improve upon. What is needed is to balance the tree.

In fairness, having more than two children per node can pay off for disk-based data structures. Bayer and McCreight describe the *B-tree*, a balanced tree data structure that strives to minimize disk accesses [BAYE72]. You can consult one of the algorithms texts mentioned in Section 1.2.6 for more information on B-trees.

We will examine ways to balance binary trees in subsequent chapters, but first we'll cover all the fundamental operations that can be performed on binary trees in $O(h)$ time. As long as the basic structure of the binary tree is the same, these operations will work whether the tree is balanced or not.

10.2 Searching

Pseudocode for searching a binary tree looks like this.

```
1   Query(Tree, q)
2       Node←Tree.Root
3       while Node ≠ NULL do
4           if Node.Key = q then
5               return Node
6           if q < Node.Key then
```

```
7                Node←Node.Left
8            else
9                Node←Node.Right
10       return NOT-FOUND
```

Figure 10.4 shows a binary tree being searched.

The maximum number of comparisons that will be performed is $h - 1$, where h is the tree's height. Thus, Query runs in $O(h)$ time.

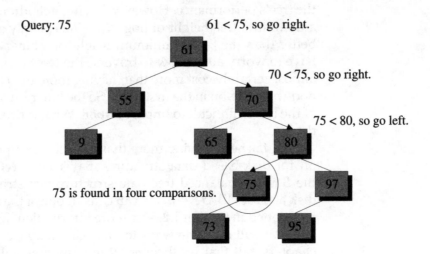

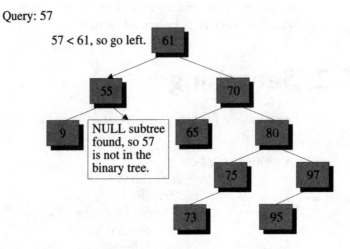

Figure 10.4.   Binary tree query.

10.3 Minimum and Maximum

The minimum node in a binary tree is the leftmost node from the root. It can be found by executing the following pseudocode.

```
1  Minimum(Tree)
2      x←Tree.Root
3      while x ≠ NULL and x.Left ≠ NULL
4          x←x.Left
5      return x;
```

Similarly, the maximum node is the rightmost node from the root.

```
1  Maximum(Tree)
2      x←Tree.Root[Tree]
3      while x ≠ NULL x.Right ≠ NULL
4          x←x.Right
5      return x;
```

As you can see from the pseudocode, Maximum and Minimum are very similar routines. In the literature, they are referred to as *symmetric*: Given one, you can easily derive the other by swapping references to Left and Right. In general, we will not give pseudocode for symmetric routines. Rather, we'll give pseudocode for one and mention the symmetric case. Both cases are implemented in the source code, of course.

Minimum and Maximum perform at most $h - 1$ operations on a binary tree of height h, so they run in $O(h)$ time.

10.4 Iterators for Binary Trees

Iterators are objects that allow users of classes to examine instances of the class nondestructively. Like iterators for linked lists, iterators for binary trees encapsulate the concept of traversing the data structure. An iterator for a binary tree contains a pointer to a node in that binary tree. The iterator can then operate on the subtree rooted at that node or point itself at another node. Operations on the subtree include Minimum and Maximum; operations to point to other nodes include Predecessor and Successor, which point the iterator at the node whose key immediately precedes or succeeds the current node's key.

If each node contains a pointer to its parent, then it is easy to define iterators on binary trees that support Predecessor and Successor operations. Given a node in a binary tree, its successor is found as follows.

```
1   Successor(x)
2       if x.Right ≠ NULL then
3           return Minimum(x.Right)
4       y←x.Parent
5       while y ≠ NULL and x = y.Right do
6           x←y
7           y←y.Parent
8       return y
```

If the node has a right child, then its successor is the leftmost node in the right subtree. Otherwise, the parent nodes are examined successively until one is found that is the left child of its parent. Since Successor traverses the tree in one direction (downward toward the minimum of the right subtree or upward toward the root), it is clearly $O(h)$, where h is the height of the tree.

Finding the predecessor node is symmetric to finding the successor node.

Note that the entire binary tree can be traversed iteratively by finding the minimum node, then calling Successor repeatedly to enumerate the nodes in sorted order until Successor returns NULL. Although we have proven an upper bound of $O(h)$ on Successor's performance when called in isolation, we can establish a more favorable bound when it is called iteratively as described. The algorithm traverses every edge in the tree exactly twice: For every subtree rooted at a node, the left edge is traversed once as nodes preceding the subtree root are considered, then again as Successor executes lines 4 to 8 of the pseudocode to find the subtree root. If the subtree root has a right child, the right edge is traversed once as successor nodes are considered, then again as Successor executes lines 4 to 8 of the pseudocode to find the successor of the subtree's maximum node. If the subtree root has a parent, Successor traverses that edge as it seeks the successor of the subtree's maximum; we already counted that edge traversal when we said that the parent's left edge would be considered exactly twice.

The number of edges in the binary tree is proportional to the number of nodes, so the traversal algorithm is $\Theta(N)$ for a tree containing N elements.

10.5 Insertion

To add a node to a binary tree, begin by searching the tree. At each interior node, compare the candidate key (the key to be added) with the node's key. If the candidate key is less than the node's key, the candidate must be added to the left subtree; otherwise it must be added to the right. When a NULL subtree is found, the new node can be inserted in its place. Pseudocode for the operation is as follows.

```
1    Insert(Tree, Add)
2          if Tree.Root = NULL then
3                return new Node(Add)
4          x←Tree.Root
5          y←NULL
6          while x ≠ NULL
7                y←x
8                if Add.Key < x.Key then x←x.Left
9                else x←x.Right
10         if Add.Key < y.Key then
11                y.Left←new Node(Add)
12         else y.Right←new Node(Add)
13         return Tree.Root
```

The contents of the new node are given as Add. If the tree is empty, the root is replaced with a pointer to the new node; otherwise the tree is traversed with x and y until x finds the new location of the node (y keeps track of x's parent). The new node is then inserted according to whether it is less than or greater than the NULL subtree's parent.

Figure 10.5 shows insertion in action. Given this naive algorithm, it is easy to see how an unbalanced tree can result; consider what happens when you insert elements into a binary tree in increasing order. Each new element is inserted on the right, and the tree contains no left-hand children. The tree height is linear rather than $O(\lg N)$, severely degrading the data structure's performance.

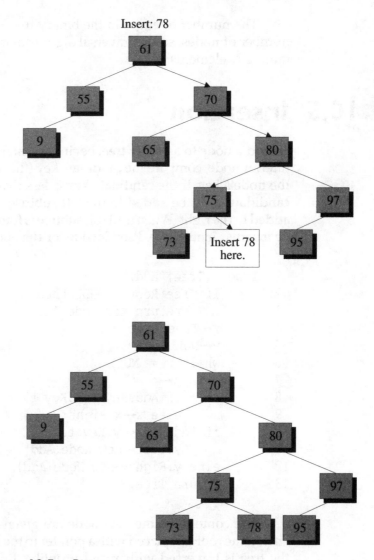

Figure 10.5. Binary tree insertion.

10.6 Deletion

Deleting a node from a binary tree consists of searching for that node, then splicing it out of the tree. Three cases have to be dealt with when splicing the node out:

1. The node has no children. In this case, the node can be deleted without incident.
2. The node has one child. The node's child can be spliced to the node's parent.
3. The node has two children. The node's successor (which has at most one child) is spliced out and the node's contents are replaced by those of its successor.

The following pseudocode illustrates how Delete is done. It takes the tree to delete from and the node to delete, and returns the new root of the tree.

```
1   Delete(Tree, z)
2        if z = NULL then return Tree.Root
3        if z.Left = NULL or z.Right = NULL then
4             y←z
5        else
6             y←Successor(z)
7        if y.Left ≠ NULL then x←y.Left
8        else x←y.Right
9        if x ≠ NULL then x.Parent ← y.Parent
10       Slice out y
11       if y.Parent ≠ NULL then
12            if y = y.Parent.Left then
13                 y.Parent.Left ← x
14            else
15                 y.Parent.Right ← x
16       else
17            Tree.Root ← x
18       if y ≠ z
19            z.Contents ← y.Contents
20       return Tree.Root
```

Figure 10.6 shows the three cases of deletion from a binary tree.

10.7 Traversal

Traversing a binary tree consists of visiting every node in the tree exactly once. Binary trees can be traversed in a variety of ways. The three basic algorithms are recursive, as follows.

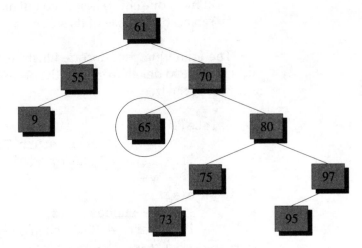

Case 1. 65 (no child nodes) can be deleted without incident.

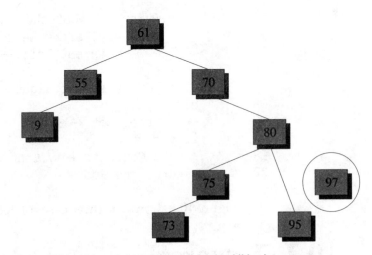

Case 2. 97 (one child node) can be deleted by splicing its child to its parent.

Figure 10.6.   Binary tree deletion.

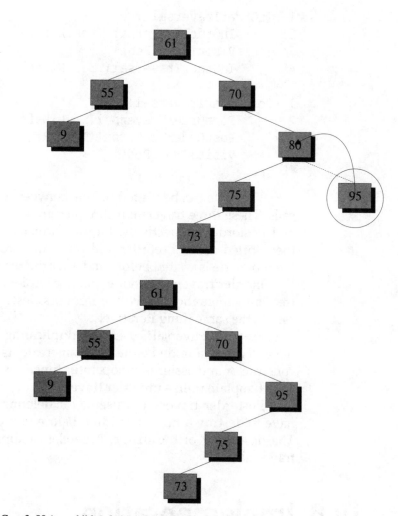

Case 3. 80 (two child nodes) can be deleted by splicing out its successor and replacing its contents with those of its successor.

Figure 10.6. Binary tree deletion (*continued*).

```
1   PreOrderTraversal(Tree)
2       Visit(Tree.Root)
3       PreOrderTraversal(Tree.Left)
4       PreOrderTraversal(Tree.Right)

1   InOrderTraversal(Tree)
2       InOrderTraversal(Tree.Left)
3       Visit(Tree.Root)
4       InOrderTraversal(Tree.Right)

1   PostOrderTraversal(Tree)
2       PostOrderTraversal(Tree.Left)
3       PostOrderTraversal(Tree.Right)
4       Visit(Tree.Root)
```

The node can be visited before, between, or after the recursive calls. These three traversal techniques are called preorder, inorder, and postorder, respectively. Inorder traversal visits the nodes in their sorted order. Preorder and postorder are so named because the root node is visited before and after the recursive calls.

Inorder traversal is not explicitly implemented in our binary tree implementation, since the iterators described in Section 10.4 can do the same thing iteratively.

Preorder traversal is useful for duplicating an existing tree: You have to create a node before you can create its children. The copy constructor and assignment operator functions for the BinaryTree class template utilize preorder traversal.

Postorder traversal is useful for deleting a binary tree: You have to destroy a node's children before you can destroy a node. The destructor of the BinaryTree class template uses postorder traversal.

10.8 Implementation

The BinaryTree class template in <btree.h> implements binary trees as described in this chapter. Two related class templates assist BinaryTree: BinaryNode implements a node in the binary tree, and the embedded Iterator class implements an iterator to traverse a binary tree.

BinaryTree implements naive binary trees that are subject to worst-case behavior (for example, when nodes are inserted in sorted order). Thus, the BinaryTree class template probably will not be well suited to general-purpose dynamic searching applications. However, naive binary trees lay an important framework to work with. Self-balancing binary trees are based on naive binary trees. For example, BinaryTree<T>::Minimum and BinaryTree<T>::Maximum need never change for naive binary trees, red-black trees, or splay trees. This is because everything we've said about binary trees applies whether they are self-balancing or not.

It must be evident by now that nodes wield most of the power in binary trees. Every node roots a subtree, and the root node roots the whole binary tree. Our implementation reflects that the nodes in a binary tree are where most of the interesting operations should be implemented.

Binary tree nodes are self-referential, meaning they contain pointers to other binary tree nodes. Conceptually, the class template for a binary node would be as follows.

```
template<class T>
class BinaryNode {
    T contents;
    BinaryNode<T> *left, *right, *parent;
};
```

But we've already pointed out that binary trees form a conceptual framework for other, more sophisticated data structures. Red-black trees, for example, avoid the worst case $O(N)$ behavior of binary trees by balancing themselves after each insertion and deletion. Yet there is a great deal of functionality we would like to borrow from BinaryNode—searching red-black trees is identical to searching naive binary trees, for example. So is finding the minimum and maximum, and finding the predecessor and successor for a node. Therefore, we can just inherit RedBlackNode from BinaryNode.

```
template<class T>
class RedBlackNode : public BinaryNode<T> {
    enum RedBlack { Red, Black };
    enum RedBlack clr;
};
```

RedBlackNode inherits all of the functionality in BinaryNode, including the contents, left, right, and parent members and all member functions. Because BinaryNode<T>::Insert and BinaryNode<T>::Delete are virtual, RedBlackNode can overload their behaviors (explicitly calling BinaryNode<T> implementations when appropriate) and leave untouched the features of BinaryNode (such as Minimum) that do not change.

There is a subtle problem with this scheme, however. The self-referential pointers in BinaryNode are declared as pointers to BinaryNode, but they actually point to RedBlackNodes. What happens when we want the color of the left child of a RedBlackNode? The left member points to a BinaryNode, as far as the compiler is concerned, and while it is willing to implicitly cast a RedBlackNode to BinaryNode, it will not do the converse. (A real-world analogy would be that a "child" is a "person," but a "person" is not necessarily a "child.") You can do the conversion explicitly with a typecast, but this drastically decreases readability. ((RedBlackNode<T> *) left)->clr is much less readable than left->clr.

We can use templates to solve this problem. Besides a template parameter T that tells the type of the node's contents, another parameter Node gives the type of the nodes contained in the self-referential BinaryNode data structure. This class template is doubly generic: Not only can it contain any type, but it can refer to itself as any node type. To use this class template, you inherit from it and specify the node type.

```
template<class T, class Node>
class BinaryNodeHelper {
    T contents;
    Node *left, *right, *parent;
};
```

Most of the functionality for binary trees is implemented by BinaryNodeHelper. Everywhere that a pointer to a child or parent node is called for, the Node parameter is used instead. Besides making the code more flexible, using Node instead of BinaryNode<T> drastically increases the code's readability. Also, references to this are explicitly cast to Node *, since **this** is a BinaryNode<T> * and we know that it actually points to a Node (which may be a derived class of Node.)

The actual `BinaryNode` class template inherits from `Binary-NodeHelper`, as follows.

```
template<class T>
class BinaryNode<T> : public BinaryNodeHelper<T,
BinaryNode<T> > {
};
```

The `BinaryTree` class template has the same problem: It implements a lot of functionality that other, balanced tree implementations would like to borrow, but it contains a pointer to the root node whose type has to be parameterized as well. So `BinaryTreeHelper` is a class template that takes `T` and `Node` parameters, and `BinaryTree` inherits from `BinaryTreeHelper`.

Figure 10.7 shows the class hierarchy for the `BinaryTree`, `RedBlackTree`, and `OSTree` (order statistics tree, described in Chapter 15) families of class templates.

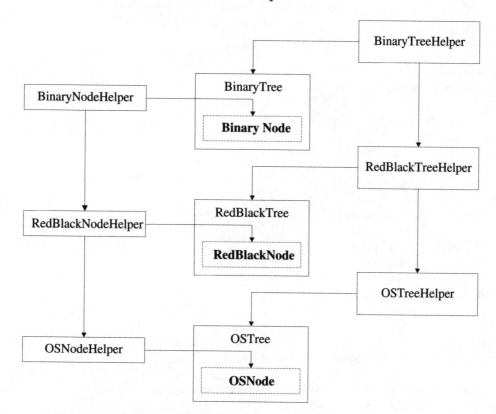

Figure 10.7. Binary tree class hierarchy.

10.8.1 Definition and Memory Management

Listing 10.1 gives the class template definitions for BinaryNode-Helper, BinaryNode, BinaryTreeHelper, and BinaryTree. In the source code included with the book, the binary tree implementation is given in <bintree.h>. The BinaryTreeHelper and BinaryTree class templates bear the same relationship as the BinaryNodeHelper and BinaryNode class templates. Just as BinaryNode is a BinaryNodeHelper whose self-referential pointers happen to point to BinaryNode<T> *s, BinaryTree is a BinaryTreeHelper whose root pointer happens to point to a BinaryNode<T> *.

Listing 10.1. BinaryTree class template definitions.

```
// ------------------------------------------------------------
// Helper class template, BinaryNode, contains most of the
// functionality in binary trees.
// ------------------------------------------------------------
template<class T, class Node>
class BinaryNodeHelper {
public:
    // Constructors and destructor
    BinaryNodeHelper() { }
    BinaryNodeHelper(const T& _contents,
             Node *_parent = 0,
             Node *_left = 0,
             Node *_right = 0);
    virtual ~BinaryNodeHelper() { }

    // Subtree manipulations
    virtual Node *Duplicate(Node *_parent) const;
    virtual void DeleteSubtree();
    virtual Node *LeftRotate(Node *root);
    virtual Node *RightRotate(Node *root);

    // Return 0 if something is wrong with the binary tree.
    virtual int CheckInvariant(const Node *);

    // Return nonzero if the node is a left or right child.
    virtual int IsLeftChild() const;
    virtual int IsRightChild() const;
```

```
    // Insertion and deletion
    virtual Node *Insert(const T& x);
    virtual Node *Delete(Node *z);

    // Query
    virtual Node *Query(const T& x);
    virtual Node *QueryNearest(const T& x);

    // Traversal
    virtual Node *Minimum();
    virtual Node *Maximum();
    virtual Node *Predecessor();
    virtual Node *Successor();

    // Miscellaneous
    virtual T *Contents();
    virtual void Print() const;

public:
    T contents;
    Node *left, *right, *parent;

};


template<class T>
class BinaryNode : public BinaryNodeHelper<T, BinaryNode<T> > {
public:
    // Constructors and destructor
    BinaryNode() { }
    BinaryNode(const T& contents,
               BinaryNode<T> *parent = 0,
               BinaryNode<T> *left = 0,
               BinaryNode<T> *right = 0):
        BinaryNodeHelper<T, BinaryNode<T> >(contents, parent, left, right) { }
    virtual ~BinaryNode() { }
};


template<class T, class Node>
class BinaryTreeHelper {

public:
    // Constructors and destructor
    BinaryTreeHelper();
    BinaryTreeHelper(const BinaryTreeHelper<T, Node>&);
```

(continued)

```
BinaryTreeHelper<T, Node>& operator=(const BinaryTreeHelper<T, Node>&);
virtual ~BinaryTreeHelper();

// Primitives
virtual void Insert(const T&);        // Insert a node
virtual void Delete(const T&);        // Delete a node
virtual T *Query(const T& q);
virtual int IsEmpty() const { return root == 0; }

// Traverses the binary tree in-order and sends it to cout.
// This is largely for debugging purposes.
virtual void Print() const;

// Traverses the binary tree and checks its invariants.
virtual int CheckInvariant();

// Grants of access.  These are really for the Iterator
// class.
virtual Node *IteratorRoot() const;
virtual Node *IteratorQuery(const T& x) const;

// Different ways to iterate on the binary tree.
enum StartOrder { AtBeginning, AtRoot, AtEnd };

// Embedded iterator class lets people access
// the binary tree nondestructively.
class Iterator {

public:
    // Constructor for the iterator.  Besides the tree
    // to iterate on, this function optionally takes
    // the place to start: the minimum or maximum node
    // of the tree, or the root.  The default is to
    // start at the minimum node.
    Iterator(const BinaryTreeHelper<T, Node>& _tree,
            enum StartOrder start = AtBeginning)
    {
        tree = (BinaryTreeHelper<T, Node> *) (&_tree);
        StartAt(start);
    }

    // Start iterator over at the minimum, maximum or
    // root node of the binary tree.
    void StartAt(enum StartOrder start)
```

```
{
    ptr = tree->IteratorRoot();
    if (start == AtBeginning)
        ptr = ptr->Minimum();
    else if (start == AtEnd)
        ptr = ptr->Maximum();
}


// Empty destructor, but can be overloaded by classes
// that inherit from this one.
virtual ~Iterator() { }


// Previous points the iterator at the previous node in the
// sorted order, or 0 if the current node is the minimum.
virtual void Previous()
{
    if (ptr)
        ptr = ptr->Predecessor();
}


// Next points the iterator at the "next" node in the sorted
// order, or 0 if the current node is the maximum.
virtual void Next()
{
    if (ptr)
        ptr = ptr->Successor();
}


// Parent points the iterator at the parent node of the
// current node, or 0 if the current node is the root.
virtual void Parent()
{
    if (ptr)
        ptr = ptr->parent;
}


// Query points the iterator at the specified node in the
// tree.  The previous contents of the iterator are
// destroyed after this call, even if the query is
// unsuccessful (in which case the iterator points at NULL).
virtual void Query(const T& x)
{
    ptr = tree->IteratorQuery(x);
}
```

(continued)

```
    // Operator int returns "true" if the iterator points
    // to a valid node.
    virtual operator int() const
    {
        return ptr != 0;
    }


    // Dereferencing operator returns the contents of the
    // node currently pointed to by the iterator.
    virtual T operator*() const
    {
        if (! ptr)
            return 0;
        return ptr->contents;
    }


    // Contents returns a pointer to the contents of the
    // node currently pointed to (as opposed to returning
    // a copy of the node, as the dereferencing operator
    // above does).
    virtual const T *Contents() const
    {
        if (ptr)
            return &ptr->contents;
        return 0;
    }
    virtual T *Contents()
    {
        if (ptr)
            return &ptr->contents;
        return 0;
    }


    // Increment and decrement operators are the same as
    // Next and Previous.
    virtual void operator++() { Next(); }
    virtual void operator++(int) { Next(); }
    virtual void operator--() { Previous(); }
    virtual void operator--(int) { Previous(); }

protected:
    Node *ptr;
    BinaryTreeHelper<T, Node> *tree;
};
```

```
protected:
    Node *root;
};


template<class T>
class BinaryTree : public BinaryTreeHelper<T, BinaryNode<T> > {
public:
    BinaryTree() { }
};


// ---------------------------------------------------------
// BinaryNodeHelper implementation.
// ---------------------------------------------------------
template<class T, class Node>
BinaryNodeHelper<T, Node>::BinaryNodeHelper(const T& _contents,
                            Node *_parent,
                            Node *_left,
                            Node *_right)
{
    contents = _contents;
    parent = _parent;
    left = _left;
    right = _right;
}


template<class T, class Node>
Node *
BinaryNodeHelper<T, Node>::Duplicate(Node *_parent) const
{
    Node *ret = new Node( *((Node *) this));
    if (left)
        ret->left = left->Duplicate(ret);
    if (right)
        ret->right = right->Duplicate(ret);
    ret->parent = _parent;
    return ret;
}
```

Implementing a single binary tree-derived data structure requires four class templates: two to implement its functionality in a way that can be derived, and two to explicitly implement its functionality.

Most of the functions to be discussed next are members of BinaryNodeHelper.

10.8.2 Minimum and Maximum

Listing 10.2 gives the implementation of the Minimum and Maximum member functions of the BinaryNodeHelper class template.

Listing 10.2.   Minimum and Maximum member functions.

```
template<class T, class Node>
Node *
BinaryNodeHelper<T, Node>::Minimum()
{
    Node *sc = (Node *) this;
    while (sc && sc->left)
        sc = sc->left;
    return sc;
}


template<class T, class Node>
Node *
BinaryNodeHelper<T, Node>::Maximum()
{
    Node *sc = (Node *) this;
    while (sc && sc->right)
        sc = sc->right;
    return sc;
}
```

10.8.3 Traversal

Listing 10.3 gives the implementation of the Predecessor and Successor member functions of the BinaryNodeHelper class template.

Listing 10.3.   Predecessor and Successor member functions.

```
template<class T, class Node>
Node *
BinaryNodeHelper<T, Node>::Predecessor()
{
    if (left)
        return left->Maximum();
    Node *x = (Node *) this;
    Node *y = parent;
    while (y && x == y->left) {
        x = y;
        y = y->parent;
```

```
    }
    return y;
}


template<class T, class Node>
Node *
BinaryNodeHelper<T, Node>::Successor()
{
    if (right)
        return right->Minimum();
    Node *x = (Node *) this;
    Node *y = parent;
    while (y && x == y->right) {
        x = y;
        y = y->parent;
    }
    return y;
}
```

Listing 10.1 gave the definition of the embedded Iterator class in the BinaryNodeHelper class template. An Iterator can be created pointing at the minimum, maximum, or root nodes of the binary tree. The user of the class can then "dereference" the iterator to examine the contents of its current node, or update the iterator to point at the current node's predecessor, successor, or parent. This Iterator class is reused by the RedBlackTree, SplayTree, and OSTree class templates; for more information on how to use it, refer to Chapter 13 and the searching sample programs described in Appendix B.

10.8.4 Query

The Query member function given in Listing 10.4 implements a query into the binary tree as described in Section 10.1. It returns a pointer to the contents of the node queried if found, or 0 if the query element is not found in the tree.

Listing 10.4. Query and QueryNearest member functions.

```
template<class T, class Node>
Node *
BinaryNodeHelper<T, Node>::Query(const T& x)
{
    Node *sc = (Node *) this;
```

```
    while (sc) {
        if (x == sc->contents)
            return sc;
        if (x < sc->contents)
            sc = sc->left;
        else
            sc = sc->right;
    }
    return 0;
}


template<class T, class Node>
Node *
BinaryNodeHelper<T, Node>::QueryNearest(const T& x)
{
    Node *sc = (Node *) this;
    Node *prev = 0;
    while (sc) {
        prev = sc;
        if (x < sc->contents)
            sc = sc->left;
        else
            sc = sc->right;
    }
    return prev;
}
```

QueryNearest, also given in Listing 10.4, works just like Query except that it returns the parent of the first NULL subtree found, whether it is equal to the query node or not.

10.8.5 Insertion

The Insert member function given in Listing 10.5 implements insertion into the binary tree as described in Section 10.4. It uses the QueryNearest member function (see above) to find the node that should serve as the parent of the new node.

Listing 10.5.   Insert member function.

```
template<class T, class Node>
Node *
BinaryNodeHelper<T, Node>::Insert(const T& x)
{
    Node *nearest = QueryNearest(x);
```

```
    if (x < nearest->contents)
        nearest->left = new Node(x, nearest);
    else
        nearest->right = new Node(x, nearest);
    return (Node *) this;
}
```

10.8.6 Deletion

The Delete member function given in Listing 10.6 implements deletion from the binary tree as described in Section 10.5.

Listing 10.6. Delete member function.

```
template<class T, class Node>
Node *
BinaryNodeHelper<T, Node>::Delete(Node *z)
{
    Node *root = (Node *) this;
    Node *x, *y;
    if (! z)
        return root;
    if (! z->left || ! z->right)
        y = z;
    else
        y = z->Successor();
    if (y->left)
        x = y->left;
    else
        x = y->right;
    if (x)
        x->parent = y->parent;
    if (y->parent) {
        if (y == y->parent->left)
            y->parent->left = x;
        else
            y->parent->right = x;
    }
    else
        root = x;
    if (y != z)
        z->contents = y->contents;
    delete y;
    return root;
}
```

11

Red-Black Trees

Red-black trees, as described by Cormen et al. [CORM90], are derived from binary trees, but they are immune to the worst-case behavior evinced by naive binary trees. Red-black trees *guarantee* $O(\lg N)$ operation for insertion, deletion, minimum, maximum, and other operations. They do this by performing balancing operations after each insertion or deletion.

Red-black trees have all the characteristics of binary trees.

- The tree consists of nodes. Each node contains an element in the data structure.

- Every node can have up to two children, a "left" child and a "right" child.

- The left-hand child of every node has a key less than the node.

- The right-hand child of every node has a key greater than the node.

In addition, red-black trees have the following characteristics.

1. Every node is colored "red" or "black."
2. Every NULL child is black.
3. If a node is red, then both its children are black.
4. Every simple path from a node to a descendant leaf contains the same number of black nodes. The number of black nodes

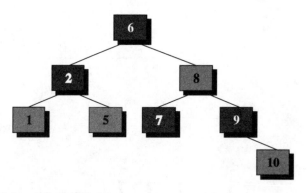

Figure 11.1.   Red-black tree.

to any leaf node is called the "black height" of the red-black tree.

Properties 3 and 4 guarantee that red-black trees are efficient. Since every path to a leaf contains the same number of black nodes, and any red node has black children, the longest possible path is composed of $\lceil 2\lg N \rceil + 1$ nodes that alternate red and black. Since the smallest possible height for a binary tree with N nodes is $\lceil \lg N \rceil$, red-black trees offer performance that is twice optimal in the worst case.

Figure 11.1 shows an example red-black tree. You may want to take a moment to verify that the red-black properties hold for it.

If we can maintain the red-black properties without compromising the asymptotic runtime, we get near-optimal performance no matter what order the nodes are inserted in. The only binary tree operations that need to be modified to enforce the red-black properties are insertion and deletion. All the other operations, including Minimum, Maximum, Predecessor, Successor, and Query, are identical to those for binary trees.

Before describing how to implement red-black trees, we will take a moment to examine rotations, which are used to balance the tree after insertion or deletion.

11.1   Rotations

Rotations are pointer manipulation primitives that are used to balance binary trees. A rotation does not affect the binary tree charac-

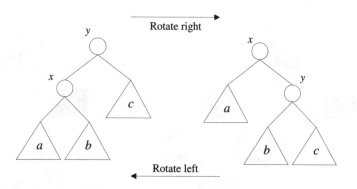

Figure 11.2. Rotation.

teristics, only the arrangement of the nodes in the tree. Rotations are constant-time operations.

Figure 11.2 shows symmetric left and right rotations. The nodes involved are not being rotated so much as the edge between the two nodes.

11.2 Insertion

To insert a node into a red-black tree, the initial steps proceed as if it is an unadorned binary tree: The tree is traversed and, when an empty node is encountered, it is replaced with the new node. For red-black trees, the node is colored red. Coloring the new node red minimizes the impact on the red-black tree properties, since it does not increase the black height of the subtree. Also in accordance with the red-black tree properties, the new red node's children are both black, since NULL children are considered black. If the newly inserted node's parent is red, however, Property 3 is violated. In this case, we must propagate color changes up toward the root of the tree until the red-black properties hold. This is done by designating the newly inserted node x and considering the following cases.

- Case 1: x and its parent are both red. If x's uncle is red, we can recolor it and x's parent black and move x toward the root of the tree to recheck Property 3. Figure 11.3 shows a red-black tree insertion where Case 1 applies. An ellipse delineates the two red nodes that violate Property 3.

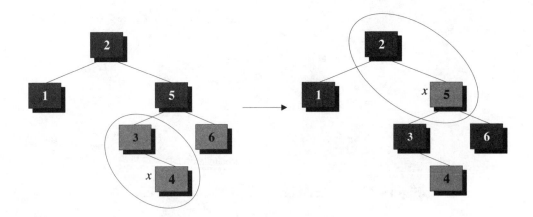

Figure 11.3.   Red-black tree insertion (Case 1).

- Case 2: x and its parent are both red, and x's parent is a
  left child. In this case, x's parent and grandparent can be
  recolored black and red, respectively. A right rotation is then
  performed to balance the tree, yielding a valid red-black
  tree. Figure 11.4 shows a red-black tree insertion where Case
  2 applies.

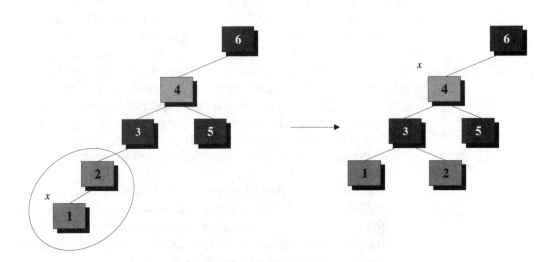

Figure 11.4.   Red-black tree insertion (Case 2).

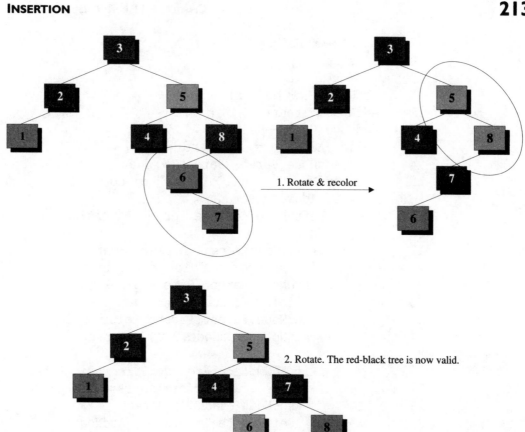

Figure 11.5. Red-black tree insertion (Case 3).

- Case 3: x and its parent are both red, and x's parent is a right child. This can be transformed to Case 2 by performing a left rotation with x's parent. Figure 11.5 shows a red-black tree insertion where Case 3 applies.

- Cases 4–6: These are symmetric to Cases 1 to 3. You can derive Cases 4 to 6 by taking the cases above and swapping "left" with "right" and vice versa.

```
1   Insert(Tree, Add)
2     x←Tree.Root
3     y←0
4     while x ≠ 0 do
5         y←x
6         if Add < x.Contents then
```

```
7          x←x.Left
8       else
9          x←x.Right
10    AddNode←new Node(x)
11    AddNode.Parent←y
12    AddNode.Color←Red
13    while (AddNode ≠ Root and
14         AddNode.Parent.Parent ≠ 0 and
15         AddNode.Parent.Color = Red) do
16         if AddNode.Parent =
17           LeftChild(AddNode.Parent.Parent) then
18           Case 1
19           y←AddNode.Parent.Parent.Right
20           if y ≠ 0 and y.Color = Red then
21             AddNode.Parent.Color←Black
22             y.Color←Black
23             AddNode.Parent.Parent.Color←Red
24             AddNode←AddNode.Parent.Parent
25           else
26             if AddNode = AddNode.Parent.Right then
27               Case 2: transform so case 3 applies
28               AddNode←AddNode.Parent
29               LeftRotate(Tree.Root, AddNode)
30           Case 3
31           AddNode.Parent←Black
32           if AddNode.Parent.Parent ≠ 0 then
33             AddNode.Parent.Parent.Color←Red
34             RightRotate(Tree.Root,
35                             AddNode.Parent.Parent)
36       else
37         Cases 4-6 are symmetric to Cases 1-3
38    Tree.Root.Color←Black
```

The **while** loop terminates if Cases 2 or 3 are executed, since executing either of these cases is guaranteed to yield a valid red-black tree. In the worst case, Case 1 will be executed repeatedly, recoloring nodes up the tree until the root is reached. This operation is linear in the height of the tree, or $\Theta(\lg N)$ for a red-black tree that contains N elements.

11.3 Deletion

Deletion from a red-black tree starts out just like deletion from a binary tree: The node is found, and, if it has fewer than two children, it is spliced out with its parent. Otherwise the node's successor is spliced out and the contents of the current node are replaced by those of its successor. The pseudocode for this deletion routine is as follows.

```
1   Delete(Tree, z)
2     if z.Left = NULL or z.Right = NULL then
3        y←z
4     else
5        y←Successor(z)
6     if y.Left ≠ NULL then
7        x←y.Left
8     else
9        x←y.Right
10    if x ≠ NULL then
11       x.Parent←y.Parent
12    Splice x out
13    if y.Parent ≠ NULL then
14       if y=y.Parent.Left then
15          y.Parent.Left←x
16       else
17          y.Parent.Right←x
18    else
19       Tree.Root←x
20    if y ≠ z then
21       z.Contents←y.Contents
22    if y.Color = Black then
23       DeleteFixup(Tree, x, y.Parent)
24       delete y
```

DeleteFixup is called if the spliced-out node was black; deleting a black node affects the red-black properties because it decreases the black height of all nodes in the subtree by one. We need to increment the black height again by finding a suitable red node and recoloring it black. (Any red node in the subtree will do, since there are no constraints on the colors of black nodes' children.) If no red

node can be found, it may be necessary to rotate and recolor the tree
to make it conform to the red-black properties again.

```
 1  DeleteFixup(Tree, x, p)
 2    while x ≠ Tree.Root and x.Color = Black do
 3      if x = p.Left then
 4        w←p.Right
 5        if w ≠ NULL then
 6          return
 7        if w.Color = Red then
 8          Case 1
 9          w.Color←Black
10          p.Color←Red
11          LeftRotate(Tree, p)
12          w←p.Right
13          if p = NULL or w = NULL then
14            return
15        else
16          if w.Left.Color = Black and
             w.Right.Color = Black then
17            Case 2
18            w.Color←Red
19            x←p
20            p←p.Parent
21            continue
22          else
23            if w.Right.Color=Black then
24              Case 3
25              w.Left.Color←Black
26              w.Color←Red
27              RightRotate(Tree, w)
28              w←p.Right
29              if p = NULL or w = NULL then
30                return
31            Case 4
32            w.Color←p.Color
33            if p ≠ NULL then
34                p.Color←Black
35            w.Right.Color←Black
36            if p ≠ NULL then
37                LeftRotate(Tree, p)
```

```
38                    x←Root
39      else
40        (Lines 4-38 again with Left and Right swapped)
41      x.Color←Black
```

DeleteFixup works x toward the root of the tree, resolving situations where the black height of w's subtree is greater than that of x's subtree. w is x's "sibling," the other child of x's parent. w roots the sibling subtree whose black height we would like to decrement.

The four cases considered by DeleteFixup are as follows.

Case 1 occurs if w is red. We then know its children are black. (This is a red-black tree property.) In this case, w can be recolored black and left-rotated with its parent. x's sibling (the new w) is then red, so Case 1 has been transformed into one of the other cases. Figure 11.6 depicts a situation where Case 1 applies.

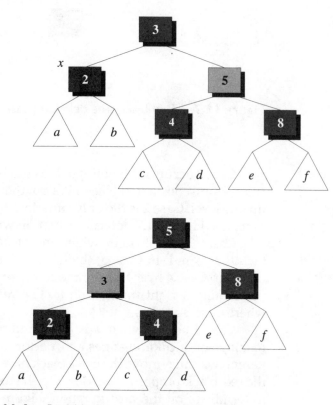

Figure 11.6. Red-black tree deletion (Case 1).

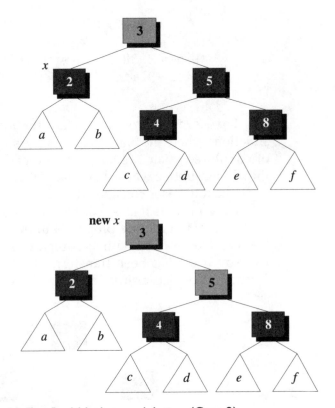

Figure 11.7.   Red-black tree deletion (Case 2).

Case 2 occurs if w's children are both black. (Remember, NULL subtrees are considered black.) We can then color w red and move x up one level. Case 2 is the only situation that causes the **while** loop to repeat. Figure 11.7 depicts a situation where Case 2 applies.

Cases 3 and 4 occur when one of w's children is black and the other is red. In Case 3, the left child is red. We can transform Case 3 to Case 4 by switching the colors of w and its left child, then performing a right rotation on w. Figure 11.8 depicts a situation where Case 3 applies.

Case 4 occurs when w is black and w's right child is red. By making some color changes and performing a left rotation on x's parent, we can remove the extra black on x without violating any of the red-black properties. Setting x to the root causes the **while** loop to terminate on the next iteration. Figure 11.9 depicts a situation where Case 4 applies.

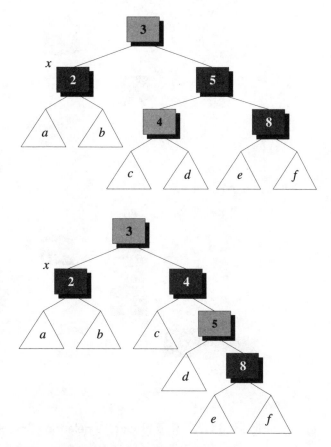

Figure 11.8. Red-black tree deletion (Case 3).

Like its cousin for naive binary trees, Delete is $O(h)$, and, since the height of a red-black tree with N nodes is $O(\lg N)$, it runs in $\Theta(\lg N)$ time. If Delete calls DeleteFixup, we must also take that runtime into account; if DeleteFixup were to take more than $O(\lg N)$ time, it would impact the overall runtime of the operation. Fortunately, DeleteFixup moves only toward the root of the red-black tree, performing constant-time operations at each level, so it runs in time proportional to the tree height. The overall runtime to delete a node from a red-black tree is therefore $\Theta(\lg N)$.

11.4 Implementation

Red-black trees, whose implementation is given in <rbtree.h>, use the same class template structure as naive binary trees. Four class

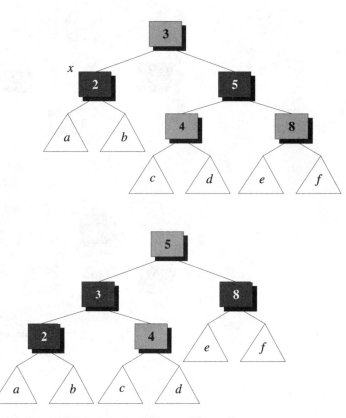

Figure 11.9. Red-black tree deletion (Case 4).

templates cooperate to offer a flexible implementation that can be reused through inheritance. (The order statistics tree class template described in Chapter 15 inherits from the family of RedBlackTree class templates.) Listing 11.1 gives the class template definitions for RedBlackNodeHelper, RedBlackNode, RedBlackTreeHelper, and RedBlackTree. In the source code included with the book, the red-black tree implementation is given in <rbtree.h>.

Listing 11.1. RedBlackTree class template definitions.

```
template<class T, class Node>
class RedBlackNodeHelper : public BinaryNodeHelper<T, Node> {
public:
    // enum contains the node color.
    enum RedBlack { Black, Red } clr;

    // Constructors.  Node always starts out red.
    RedBlackNodeHelper() { clr = Red; }
```

```
    RedBlackNodeHelper(const T& X,
                Node *P = 0,
                Node *L = 0,
                Node *R = 0):
        BinaryNodeHelper<T, Node>(X, P, L, R) { }
    RedBlackNodeHelper(const T& X, enum RedBlack Clr, Node *P = 0,
            Node *L = 0, Node *R = 0):
        BinaryNodeHelper<T, Node>(X, P, L, R), clr(Clr) { }
    virtual ~RedBlackNodeHelper() { }

    // Tree manipulations used during insertion and deletion
    virtual Node *DeleteFixup(Node *x, Node *p);

    // Operations defined on binary trees.  All run in O(lgN) time.
    virtual Node *Insert(const T& AddMe);
    virtual Node *Delete(Node *z);

    // Returns 0 if the red-black invariant holds.
    virtual int CheckInvariant(const Node *);
};

template<class T>
class RedBlackNode : public RedBlackNodeHelper<T, RedBlackNode<T> > {
public:
    // Constructors.  Node always starts out red.
    RedBlackNode() { }
    RedBlackNode(const T& X,
                RedBlackNode<T> *P = 0,
                RedBlackNode<T> *L = 0,
                RedBlackNode<T> *R = 0):
        RedBlackNodeHelper<T, RedBlackNode<T> >(X, P, L, R) { }
    RedBlackNode(const T& X, enum RedBlack Clr, RedBlackNode<T> *P = 0,
            RedBlackNode<T> *L = 0, RedBlackNode<T> *R = 0):
        RedBlackNodeHelper<T, RedBlackNode<T> >(X, clr, P, L, R) { }
    virtual ~RedBlackNode() { }
};

template<class T>
class RedBlackTree : public RedBlackTreeHelper<T, RedBlackNode<T> > {
public:
    RedBlackTree() { }
};

// -----------------------------------------------------------
// RedBlackTreeHelper class template.
// -----------------------------------------------------------
```

(continued)

```
template<class T, class Node>
class RedBlackTreeHelper : public BinaryTreeHelper<T, Node> {
    // The following is accessible only to classes that inherit
    // from RedBlackTreeHelper, since they deal directly with RedBlackNodes.
    protected:
        virtual Node *QueryNode(T q) const
            { return (root) ? (Node *) root->Query(q) : 0; }
};
```

Figure 11.10 depicts how the red-black tree class templates interact with each other and with the class templates for binary trees. RedBlackNodeHelper inherits from BinaryNodeHelper and implements most of the functionality required for red-black trees. Because much of this functionality is inherited from binary nodes, just a few member functions of BinaryNodeHelper need to be overloaded. RedBlackNode inherits from RedBlackNodeHelper<T, RedBlackNode<T> >, just as BinaryNode<T> inherits from Binary NodeHelper<T, BinaryNode<T> >. Section 10.7 describes why the hierarchy of binary tree implementations is implemented this way.

The color of each node in a red-black tree is contained in RedBlackNodeHelper and is declared as follows:

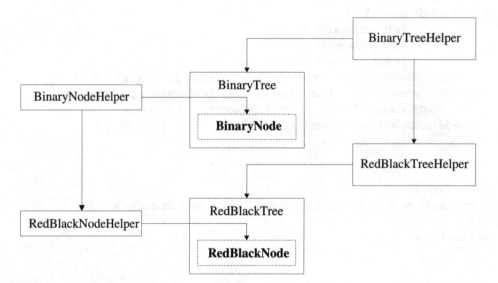

Figure 11.10.   Red-black tree class hierarchy.

```
enum RedBlack { Red, Black } clr;
```

The `clr` member contains the color of the node.

11.4.1 Rotations

Rotations are simple pointer manipulations not specific to red-black trees (splay trees, discussed in Chapter 12, also use rotations), so they are implemented in the `BinaryNodeHelper` class template. `BinaryNodeHelper<T>::LeftRotate` and `BinaryNodeHelper<T>::RightRotate` each operate on the node that the member function is called on.

11.4.2 Insertion

Listing 11.2 gives `RedBlackNodeHelper<T,Node>::Insert`, which overloads `BinaryNode<T, Node>::Insert`. It implements insertion as described in Section 11.2.

Listing 11.2. `Insert` member function.

```
template<class T, class Node>
Node *
RedBlackNodeHelper<T, Node>::Insert(const T& AddMe)
{
    Node *root = (Node *) this;
    Node *x = (Node *) this;
    Node *y = 0;
    while (x) {
        y = x;
        x = (AddMe < x->contents) ? x->left : x->right;
    }
    Node *addme = new Node(AddMe, y);
    if (! y)
        root = addme;
    else {
      if (AddMe < y->contents)
          y->left = addme;
      else
          y->right = addme;
    }
    addme->clr = Red;
    while (addme != root &&
```

(continued)

```
        addme->parent->parent &&
        addme->parent->clr == Red) {
Node *y;

if (addme->parent == addme->parent->parent->left) {
    y = addme->parent->parent->right;
    if (y && y->clr == Red) {
        // Case 1: x's uncle is red
        addme->parent->clr = Black;
        y->clr = Black;
        addme->parent->parent->clr = Red;
        addme = addme->parent->parent;
    }
    else {
        if (addme == addme->parent->right) {
            // Case 2: x is a right child
            // Rotate to transform to case 3
            addme = addme->parent;
            root = addme->LeftRotate(root);
        }
        // Case 3: x is a left child
        addme->parent->clr = Black;
        if (addme->parent->parent) {
            addme->parent->parent->clr = Red;
            root = addme->parent->parent->RightRotate(root);
        }
        // The while loop will terminate
        // on the next iteration.
    }
}
else {
    y = addme->parent->parent->left;
    if (y && y->clr == Red) {
        addme->parent->clr = Black;
        y->clr = Black;
        addme->parent->parent->clr = Red;
        addme = addme->parent->parent;
    }
    else {
        if (addme == addme->parent->left) {
          addme = addme->parent;
          root = addme->RightRotate(root);
        }
        addme->parent->clr = Black;
        if (addme->parent->parent) {
```

```
                    addme->parent->parent->clr = Red;
                    root = addme->parent->parent->LeftRotate(root);
                }
            }
        }
    }
    root->clr = Black;
    return root;
}
```

11.4.3 Deletion

Listing 11.3 gives RedBlackNodeHelper<T, Node>::Delete, which overloads BinaryNode<T, Node>::Delete. It implements deletion as described in Section 11.3. RedBlackNodeHelper<T, Node>::-DeleteFixup is used by Delete to fix up the red-black tree properties after the deletion.

Listing 11.3. Delete member function.

```
template<class T, class Node>
Node *
RedBlackNodeHelper<T, Node>::DeleteFixup(Node *x, Node *p)
{
    Node *root = (Node *) this;

    while (x != root && (! x || x->clr == Black)) {
        Node *w;
        if (x == p->left) {
            if (! p)
                return root;
            w = p->right;
            if (! w)
                return root;
            if (w->clr == Red) {
                w->clr = Black;
                p->clr = Red;
                root = p->LeftRotate(root);
                w = p->right;
                if (! p || ! w)
                    return root;
            }
            if ( ((! w->left) || w->left->clr == Black) &&
                  ((! w->right) || w->right->clr == Black)) {
```

(continued)

```
                w->clr = Red;
                x = p;
                p = p->parent;
                continue;
            }
            else if ((! w->right) || w->right->clr == Black) {
                w->left->clr = Black;
                w->clr = Red;
                root = w->RightRotate(root);
                w = p->right;
                if (! p || ! w)
                    return root;
            }
            w->clr = p->clr;
            if (p)
                p->clr = Black;
            w->right->clr = Black;
            if (p)
                root = p->LeftRotate(root);
            x = root;
        }
        else {
            if (! p)
                return root;
            w = p->left;
            if (! p || ! w)
                return root;
            if (w->clr == Red) {
                w->clr = Black;
                p->clr = Red;
                root = p->RightRotate(root);
                w = p->left;
                if (! p || ! w)
                    return root;
            }
            if ( ((! w->right) || w->right->clr == Black) &&
                 ((! w->left) || w->left->clr == Black)) {
                w->clr = Red;
                x = p;
                p = p->parent;
                continue;
            }
            else if ((! w->left) || w->left->clr == Black) {
                w->right->clr = Black;
```

```
                    w->clr = Red;
                    root = w->LeftRotate(root);
                    w = p->left;
                    if (! p || ! w)
                        return root;
                }
                w->clr = p->clr;
                if (p)
                    p->clr = Black;
                w->left->clr = Black;
                if (p)
                    root = p->RightRotate(root);
                x = root;
            }
        }
    if (x)
        x->clr = Black;
    return root;
}

template<class T, class Node>
Node *
RedBlackNodeHelper<T, Node>::Delete(Node *z)
{
    Node *root = (Node *) this;
    Node *x, *y;

    if (! z)
        return root;
    y = (! z->left || ! z->right) ? z : (Node *) z->Successor();
    x = (y->left) ? y->left : y->right;

    if (x)
        x->parent = y->parent;

    if (y->parent) {
        if (y == y->parent->left)
            y->parent->left = x;
        else
            y->parent->right = x;
    }
    else
        root = x;
    if (y != z)
        z->contents = y->contents;
```

(continued)

```
    if (y->clr == Black) {
        if (root)
            root = root->DeleteFixup(x, y->parent);
    }
    delete y;
    return root;
}
```

11.4.4 Invariants

Listing 11.4 gives RedBlackNodeHelper<T, Node>::CheckInvariant, which overloads BinaryTreeHelper's implementation of CheckInvariant. The same invariants as those used for binary trees still apply, but RedBlackNodeHelper also checks the red-black properties to make sure they hold. This process is extremely time-consuming, so it should be used only for debugging purposes; it is well worth doing whenever the red-black tree implementation has been changed.

Listing 11.4. CheckInvariant member function.

```
template<class T, class Node>
int
RedBlackNodeHelper<T, Node>::CheckInvariant(const Node *_parent)
{
    static int BlackHeight;

    if (_parent == 0)
        BlackHeight = -1;

    // Check binary tree properties.
    if (parent != _parent)
        return 0;
    if (left) {
        if (contents < left->contents)
            return 0;
    }
    if (right) {
        if (right->contents < contents)
            return 0;
    }

    // Now check red-black tree properties.
```

```
// If a node is red, then both its children are black
// (NULL nodes are black).
if (clr == Red) {
    if ((left && left->clr != Black) ||
        (right && right->clr != Black))
        return 0;
}

// The black-heights of all leaf nodes are equal.
int bh = 0;

if ((! left) && (! right)) {
    // Compute black-height of node
    for (Node *sc = (Node *) this; sc; sc = sc->parent)
        if (sc->clr == Black)
            bh += 1;

    if (BlackHeight == -1) {
        BlackHeight = bh;
    }
    else {
        if (bh != BlackHeight)
            return 0;
    }
}
if (left && (! left->CheckInvariant((Node *) this)))
    return 0;
if (right && (! right->CheckInvariant((Node *) this)))
    return 0;
return 1;
}
```

Splay Trees

Splay trees are a self-adjusting binary tree data structure described by Sleator and Tarjan [SLEA85]. They optimize access times by propagating accessed nodes to the root of the tree.

Splay trees work well because of locality of reference: By their very nature, computer programs access the same data more than once in a short time. Locality of reference is a theme that appears often in computer science. For example, the code executed most often by the processor is usually in small loops, so even a small processor cache can have a dramatic effect on performance. Disk caches and translation lookaside buffers are other structures that take advantage of locality of reference to deliver higher performance.

Splay trees, unlike red-black trees, make no guarantee on worst-case performance. If they are accessed in a suboptimal way, the access times may drop to the worst-case $O(N)$ runtime. The time to access a node approaches $\Theta(1)$, however, when a small subset of the nodes are accessed in a short period of time.

12.1 Splay and Query

Every time a node is queried for any reason, it is splayed to the root of the tree by performing the following splaying step repeatedly until x is the root of the tree. Figure 12.1 depicts how these three cases are resolved.

Case 1. p is root.

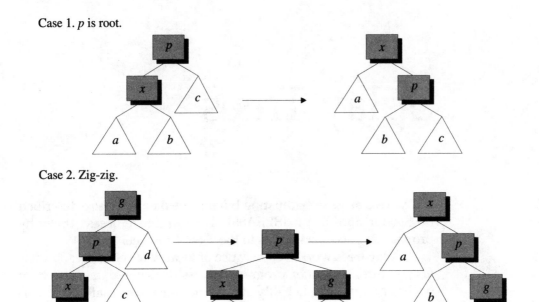

Case 2. Zig-zig.

Case 3. Zig-zag.

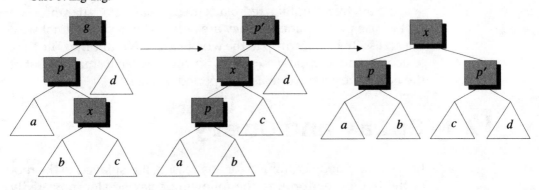

Figure 12.1.   Splaying steps.

- Case 1. If x's parent p is the root, rotate x with p. Since x then becomes the root, this is the last step in the splaying process.

- Case 2. Zig-zig: If p is not the root and x and p are both left or both right children, rotate p with its parent g (the grandparent of x), then rotate x with its parent p.

- Case 3. Zig-zag: If p is not the root and x is a left child and p is a right child (or vice versa), rotate x with p, then rotate x with its new parent p'.

Splaying is $O(d)$, where d is the distance from the root of the node being splayed. Thus, like most other binary tree operations described previously, splaying is $O(h)$ where h is the height of the tree.

Pseudocode for the splaying operation is as follows.

```
1    Splay(Tree, x)
2      while x.Parent ≠ NULL do
3        p←x.Parent
4        g←p.Parent
3        if p = Tree.Root then
4          Rotate(p, x)
5        else if p and g are both left or right children
6          Zig-zig
7          Rotate(g, p)
8          Rotate(p, x)
9        else
10         Zig-zag
11         Rotate(p, x)
12         Rotate(x.Parent, x)
13       x←p
14       if x.Parent ≠ NULL then
15         x←x.Parent
```

During our discussion of red-black trees, we described *rotations*, primitive operations that can be used to balance a tree. In the context of splay trees, left children are always right-rotated with their parents and right children are always left-rotated with their parents. This operation is termed `Rotate` in the pseudocode.

The `Query` operation on a splay tree is followed by a `Splay` operation, propagating the queried node to the root of the tree.

As we shall see, making the queried node the root can be used to implement insertion and deletion easily. In addition, it makes the just-queried node quickly available if it is queried again in the near future.

The splaying operation balances the tree as a side effect: It approximately halves each node's distance to the root as it propagates upward. Figure 12.2 shows how a splaying operation affects a poorly balanced tree when the bottom node is accessed. In both cases, the tree height is approximately halved as a result of the splaying.

12.2 Split and Insert

Insertion is performed on a splay tree with a primitive operation called Split. If the new node is greater than the current root, we can make the current root node the left subtree of the node being inserted; the right subtree of the root then becomes the right subtree of the new root. If the new node is less than the current root, the split occurs symmetrically.

We can't just perform Split to insert a node, however; we probably won't be able to retain the binary tree property. There may be nodes in the left subtree that are greater than the node being inserted, or vice versa. We can ensure that the binary tree property will hold by splaying its closest neighbor up to the root of the tree. This operation works by traversing the tree and branching at each node as if the node to be inserted were being queried. When a NULL branch is encountered, its parent is splayed up to the root.

Once the nearest node has been propagated to the root, we know that the binary tree property will hold for the node being inserted. The new node can then be inserted at the root using Split. Figure 12.3 depicts splay tree insertion using Split.

Note that this Insert operation adheres to the splay tree's commitment to deliver the last-accessed node (in this case, the node just inserted) in constant time.

12.3 Join and Delete

An operation called Join can be used to implement deletion in splay trees. Join merges two subtrees, the left subtree and the right sub-

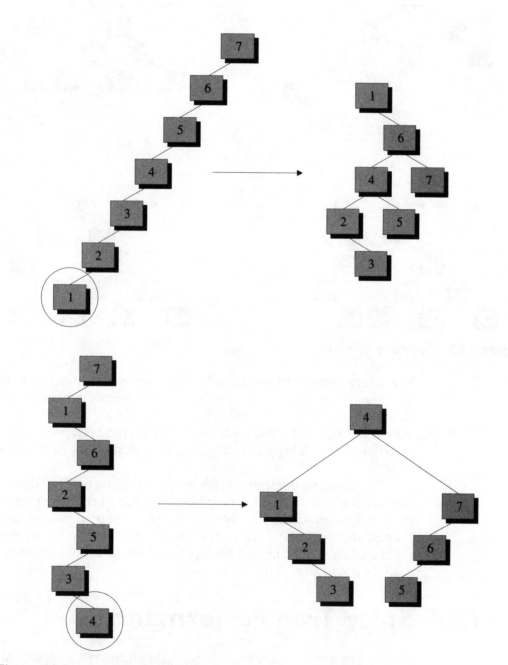

Figure 12.2. Splaying unbalanced trees.

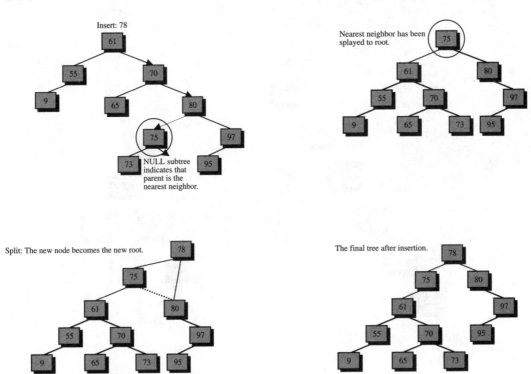

Figure 12.3.   Splay tree insertion.

tree. Every element in the left subtree is guaranteed to be less than any element in the right subtree. Join first queries the maximum element in the left subtree and splays it up to the root. The resulting subtree has no right child, since the maximum has been propagated up to the root. The right subtree can then become the new root's right child.

The Delete operation works by querying the node to delete; this has the side effect of propagating the node up to the root of the tree. The left and right subtrees of the root are then merged into a single tree with the Join operation. The former root of the tree can then be deleted. Figure 12.4 depicts a deletion being performed with the Join operation.

12.4 Splay Tree Performance

The performance of splay trees is more complicated to analyze than that of red-black trees. With red-black trees, once it is shown that the tree height can never exceed twice optimal, a strong upper bound

1. Delete: 75

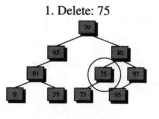

2. Splay 75 to root.

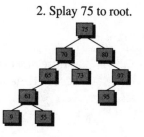

3. Remove the node from the root.

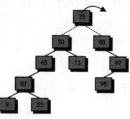

4. Join the two subtrees at the root.

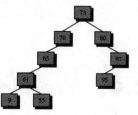

Figure 12.4.   Splay tree deletion.

can be proven on the various operations. (They all take time proportional to the height.) To analyze the performance of splay trees, which can attain the worst-case height N for a tree containing N nodes, Sleator and Tarjan rely on a technique called *amortized analysis*. Amortized analysis describes the behavior of a data structure over many operations, rather than giving time complexity bounds on a single operation. A detailed description of amortized analysis is not within the scope of this book (see Cormen et al. [CORM90] for an excellent discussion), but we can cover the high points of Sleator and Tarjan's analysis of splay trees. The proofs for these theorems are given in their paper [SLEA85].

12.4.1 Balance Theorem

The total amortized time to perform m accesses on an N-*node* splay tree is $O((m+N)\lg N+m)$. Since the time to perform m accesses on an optimally balanced binary tree is $O(m \lg N)$, the Balance Theorem implies that a splay tree is as efficient as any form of uniformly balanced tree.

12.4.2 Static Optimality Theorem

If every item is accessed at least once, then the total amortized access time is:

$$O\left(m + \sum_{i=1}^{N} q(i) \lg\left(\frac{m}{q(i)}\right)\right)$$

where $q(i)$ is the number of times item i was accessed. Since the total access time for any fixed tree is

$$\Omega\left(m + \sum_{i=1}^{N} q(i) \log\left(\frac{m}{q(i)}\right)\right)$$

[ABRA83, as cited by Sleator and Tarjan], the Static Optimality Theorem implies that a splay tree is as asymptotically efficient as any fixed search tree, including the optimum tree for the given access sequence.

12.4.3 Working Set Theorem

This theorem studies how the access time for an item behaves as the time since the last access was performed. Let $t(j)$ be the number of different items accessed before access j since the last access of item i_j (or since the beginning of the sequence, if j is the first of item i_j). The total amortized access time is then

$$O\left(N \log N + m + \sum_{j=1}^{m} + \lg(t(j) + 1)\right)$$

The Working Set Theorem implies what we already know by intuition: If an element has been accessed recently, it can be accessed very quickly. As other items are accessed, they push the item away from the root of the tree. The theorem lets us get specific about the performance implications of subsequent accesses: The access time to retrieve an item increases as the logarithm of the number of accesses to other elements since the given item was last accessed.

Like naive binary trees, splay trees respond poorly to systematic behavior by their clients. Inserting elements into a splay tree in sorted order results in a degenerate tree (where the height of the splay tree approaches the number of elements in it). Similarly, sequentially accessing elements in the splay tree can result in a degenerate tree. If these situations are likely to arise, a red-black tree would probably be a better solution. But in practical searching applications, a splay tree is almost certainly a better choice.

12.5 Applications

Splay trees can be used in any searching application that exhibits locality of reference. Most searching applications do; here are a few examples.

12.5.1 Virtual Memory Management

The virtual memory manager of an operating system typically uses a splay tree to resolve virtual addresses. Technically, the operating system has to convert the virtual address into a physical address whenever a memory reference occurs. In practice, doing so would be prohibitively slow. Instead, the processor has a cache of address translations called the translation lookaside buffer (or TLB) that the operating system maintains. When a memory reference occurs, the processor automatically performs the translation if the address is in the TLB. If the TLB cannot resolve a virtual address, control is transferred to the operating system, which results in several possible outcomes: The virtual address may reside on disk, so the memory has to be swapped in before the translation to a physical address can be done; the address may be invalid, so the operating system has to throw an exception of some kind; or, most likely, the address is in physical memory but just wasn't in the TLB.

In the latter case, the operating system uses a splay tree to find the address mapping and update the TLB. A splay tree is the perfect data structure for this task: Because memory accesses exhibit locality of reference, the page the operating system is looking for is likely to be near the root. If it is not, it gets splayed up to the root in anticipation of the next time.

12.5.2 Heap Management

Another application for splay trees is the heap manager. The heap manager is a set of library function calls that perform dynamic memory allocation. (In ANSI C, the two most important heap management functions are malloc and free; in C++, these are usually supplanted by the new and delete operators.)

When someone calls malloc for the first time, it requests a large block of memory from the operating system. (This operation is system dependent: UNIX systems may call brk, while Windows systems would call GlobalAlloc.) This block of memory can then be diced into pieces for clients of malloc. malloc operates this way for performance reasons: brk and GlobalAlloc are quite slow to call, so they should not be called unless it is absolutely necessary. In the case of 16-bit Windows, GlobalAlloc can be called only 8,000 times or so, anyway, so dicing up memory allocated with GlobalAlloc is a necessity.

When free is called, giving back the block of memory that malloc requested from the operating system usually is not an option: Parts of that memory block are probably still being used by other clients of the heap manager. So malloc stores a description of the freed block of memory (base pointer and length of the block) in a *free list*. On subsequent calls to malloc, it checks through the free list to see if it already has a suitable block of memory. According to one popular heuristic, the first block of memory large enough to satisfy the request is used. If no single block of memory is large enough, malloc may consolidate adjacent blocks of memory in the free list. malloc will request more memory from the operating system only if it is absolutely necessary.

A splay tree makes an excellent data structure to store the heap manager's free list. It allows malloc to search for a suitable memory block quickly and, if the implementor so chose, it would allow fast consolidation of adjacent blocks in the free list as well.

12.5.3 Everything Else

Most searching applications exhibit locality of reference. If you think your application does, splay trees are probably your best bet. The way the sample code is laid out, it should be trivial for you to try all of the different tree implementations and experiment to see which one best suits your application.

12.6 Future Work

Many alternatives to the splay tree data structure described here can be derived. If the splay tree implementation given here is not suitable, one of the following variations might work out.

12.6.1 Semi-Adjusting Splay Trees

One way to save some work when adjusting a splay tree is to perform only one rotation in the zig-zag case but take two steps up the tree anyway. This will rebalance the tree almost as well as full-blown splaying but requires less time because only one rotation is done in the zig-zag case. Pseudocode for this algorithm follows.

```
1   SemiSplay(Tree, x)
2   while x.Parent ≠ NULL do
3     p←x.Parent
4     g←p.Parent
3     if p = Tree.Root then
4       Rotate(p, x)
5     else if p and g are both left or right children
6       Zig-zig
7       Rotate(g, p)
8       Rotate(p, x)
9     else
10      Zig-zag
11      Rotate(p, x)
12    x←p
13    if x.Parent ≠ NULL then
14      x←x.Parent
```

12.6.2 Top-Down Splaying

If having a parent pointer reside in the node consumes too much memory, splay trees can be modified to perform the splaying from the top down. This obviates the need for a parent pointer in each node. Top-down splaying performs the query and subsequent splaying operation concurrently. For a query element q, the subtree being queried is split into three parts: the left subtree, which contains items known to be less than q; the right subtree, which contains items greater than q; and the middle subtree, which consists of the subtree rooted at the current node on the access path. The middle subtree contains the query element, if it is in the tree at all.

Initially, the left and right subtrees are empty and the root node roots the middle subtree. As we search down the tree, a leftward move relegates the subtree rooted by the element just considered to the right subtree; the subtree is added to the right subtree by making it the left child of the right subtree's root. If two moves are made in the same direction, a rotation is performed before splicing the rejected tree into the right subtree. Figure 12.5 depicts how the three trees interact during top-down splaying. The symmetric case

Zig: y is the accessed node.

Zig-zig:

Zig-zag:

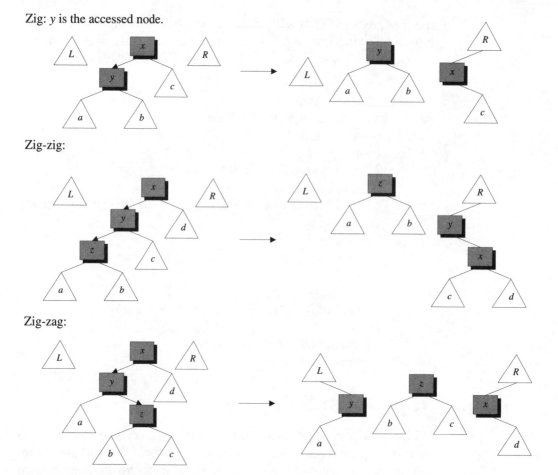

Figure 12.5.   Top-down splaying.

applies as well; everywhere "left" and "right" were just mentioned, swap them and the code must implement those cases as well.

After finally finding the query node (or its nearest neighbor), the trees are reassembled. Figure 12.6 depicts this operation.

12.6.3 Splaying Occasionally

Another way to save some work when maintaining splay trees is by splaying only on special occasions, when it will do the most good. One such method would be to splay only when the access depth is "abnormally long." A variety of metrics are possible to decide whether an access depth is long; one is to compare the access depth to the optimal height for the tree and splay if the access

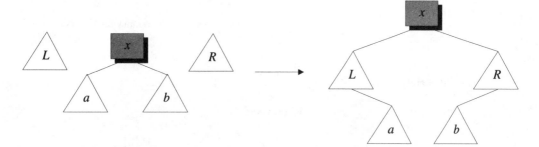

Figure 12.6. Resolution of top-down splaying.

depth is k times greater. (k would be some constant determined by the application.) Such a method would require that the splay tree implementation keep track of the number of nodes in the tree, however.

12.6.4 Suspension of Splaying

For a static searching application, the splaying step may become redundant after a certain number of accesses. If this happens, it may make sense to splay on the first k accesses, then stop splaying altogether on the assumption that the tree structure is good enough to efficiently satisfy future queries. As with the last method described, deciding on a suitable value for k is application-specific.

12.7 Implementation

Splay trees are implemented much as are red-black trees. Four related class templates inherit from the four `BinaryTree` class templates and overload relevant functions to modify their behavior. Figure 12.7 depicts the relationships between these four class templates and their bases. `SplayNodeHelper` inherits from `BinaryNodeHelper` and implements most of the functionality of splay trees. `SplayNode` inherits from `SplayNodeHelper`. `SplayTreeHelper` inherits from `BinaryTreeHelper`, and `SplayTree` inherits from `BinaryTree`. All these class templates would not be necessary if we just wanted to implement splay trees using the existing `BinaryTree` functionality; we stick to the paradigm laid down in the `BinaryTree` and `RedBlackTree` implementations in anticipation of someday reusing this code, which implements splay trees as well.

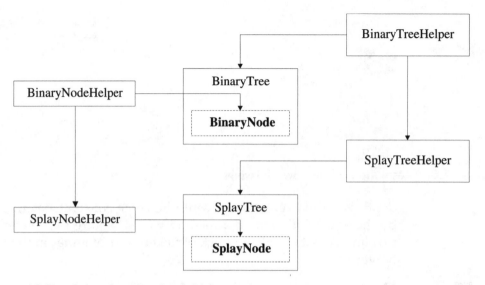

Figure 12.7.   Splay tree class hierarchy.

The SplayTree class template inherits BinaryTree's Iterator class. Since splay trees have the same basic structure as naive binary trees, Iterator can be used to examine elements in the splay tree without any trouble.

Listing 12.1 gives the definitions for the four class templates that implement splay trees. In the source code included with the book, the splay tree implementation is given in <splay.h>.

Listing 12.1.   SplayTree class template definitions.

```
template<class T, class Node>
class SplayNodeHelper : public BinaryNodeHelper<T, Node> {
public:
    // Constructors and destructor
    SplayNodeHelper() { }
    SplayNodeHelper(const T& X,  Node *P = 0,
                    Node *L = 0, Node *R = 0):
        BinaryNodeHelper<T, Node>(X, P, L, R) { }
    virtual ~SplayNodeHelper() { }

    // Insertion and deletion
    virtual Node *Insert(const T& x);
    virtual Node *Delete(Node *z);

    // Query
    virtual Node *QueryNearest(const T& x);
```

```
        // Rotate depending on whether node is right or left child.
        // Rotate left if node is a right child, or right if the
        // node is a left child.
        virtual Node *RotateNode(Node *root);

        // Splaying operation propagates the node pointed to by
        // "this" to the root.  The current root is passed in, and
        // the new root is returned.
        virtual Node *Splay(Node *root);

        // Call this on the root; the left and right subtrees
        // are passed back in the parameters.
        virtual void Split(const T& x, Node **left, Node **right);

        // Join two trees into a single tree.
        // Left root is assumed to be less than right root.
        virtual Node *Join(Node *left, Node *right);
};

template<class T>
class SplayNode : public SplayNodeHelper<T, SplayNode<T> > {
public:
        // Constructors.  Node always starts out red.
        SplayNode() { }
        SplayNode(const T& X,
                  SplayNode<T> *P = 0,
                  SplayNode<T> *L = 0,
                  SplayNode<T> *R = 0):
            SplayNodeHelper<T, SplayNode<T> >(X, P, L, R) { }
        virtual ~SplayNode() { }
};

template<class T, class Node>
class SplayTreeHelper : public BinaryTreeHelper<T, Node> {
public:
        SplayTreeHelper() { }
        virtual void Insert(const T&);
        virtual void Delete(const T&);
        virtual T *Query(const T&);
        virtual Node *IteratorQuery(const T&) const;
};

template<class T>
class SplayTree : public SplayTreeHelper<T, SplayNode<T> > {
```

(continued)

```
public:
    SplayTree() { }
};
```

12.7.1   RotateNode, Splay, QueryNearest, and Query

RotateNode is a simple function that right-rotates a node with its parent if it is a left child, or left-rotates with its parent if it is a right child. This is the rotation primitive utilized by the splaying operation.

Splay is the splaying operation as described in Section 12.1. It propagates the node up to the root, rotating as it goes to rebalance the tree.

QueryNearest is a helper function that queries the nearest element to a given query element. It is useful not only for querying a particular element, but for preparing the tree to be inserted into, since it causes the queried node to be splayed to the root.

Query locates the nearest element to a given query element and splays it up to the root. If the elements are the same, Query returns a pointer to the element that was just splayed up to the root; otherwise it returns 0.

Listing 12.2 gives the listings for RotateNode, Splay, QueryNearest, and Query.

Listing 12.2.   RotateNode, Splay, QueryNearest and Query member functions.

```
template<class T, class Node>
Node *
SplayNodeHelper<T, Node>::RotateNode(Node *root)
{
    if (IsLeftChild())
        return parent->RightRotate(root);
    else
        return parent->LeftRotate(root);
}

template<class T, class Node>
Node *
SplayNodeHelper<T, Node>::Splay(Node *root)
{
    // "this" is the node to propagate to the root.
    Node *prop = (Node *) this;
```

```
    if (! prop->parent)
        return prop;

    while (prop->parent && prop->parent->parent) {
        // Parent of x isn't the root, zig-zig or zig-zag.
        if ((prop->IsLeftChild() && prop->parent->IsLeftChild()) ||
            (prop->IsRightChild() && prop->parent->IsRightChild())) {
            // zig-zig
            root = prop->parent->RotateNode(root);
            root = prop->RotateNode(root);
        }
        else {
            // zig-zag
            root = prop->RotateNode(root);
            root = prop->RotateNode(root);
        }
    }
    return (prop->parent) ? prop->RotateNode(root) : prop;
}

template<class T, class Node>
Node *
SplayNodeHelper<T, Node>::QueryNearest(const T& x)
{
    // Splay the closest node to the query up to the root.
    Node *sc = (Node *) this;
    Node *prev = 0;
    while (sc != 0) {
        prev = sc;
        if (sc->contents == x) {
            sc->Splay((Node *) this);
            return sc;
        }
        if (x < sc->contents)
            sc = sc->left;
        else
            sc = sc->right;
    }
    if (prev)
        return prev->Splay((Node *) this);
    return 0;
}

template<class T, class Node>
```

(continued)

```
T *
SplayTreeHelper<T, Node>::Query(const T& x)
{
    Node *q = root->QueryNearest(x);
    if (q) {
        root = q;
        if (q->contents == x)
            return &q->contents;
    }
    return 0;
}
```

12.7.2 Split and Insert

Split implements the Split operation as described in Section 12.2. It is used by the Insert function, which inserts a new element into the splay tree.

Insert first calls QueryNearest to splay the nearest element up to the root. The root element must be the new element's predecessor or successor before the tree can be operated on using Split; otherwise the binary tree properties may not hold. QueryNearest is guaranteed to propagate the new element's predecessor or successor up to the root of the tree. After splaying this adjacent element up to the root, Insert splits the tree and sews it back together with the newly inserted element as the root.

Listing 12.3 gives the listings for Split and Insert.

Listing 12.3.   Split and Insert **member functions.**

```
template<class T, class Node>
void
SplayNodeHelper<T, Node>::Split(const T& x, Node **pleft, Node **pright)
{
    if (contents < x) {
        *pleft = (Node *) this;
        *pright = (Node *) right;
        right = 0;
    }
    else {
        *pright = (Node *) this;
        *pleft = (Node *) left;
        left = 0;
    }
```

```
    if (*pleft)  (*pleft)->parent = 0;
    if (*pright) (*pright)->parent = 0;
}

template<class T, class Node>
Node *
SplayTreeHelper<T, Node>::Insert(const T& x)
{
    Node *sleft, *sright, *ret;

    // Splay x or its closest neighbor up to root.
    Node *root = QueryNearest (x);
    root->Split (x, &sleft, &sright);
    if (sleft && sright) {
        if (x < sleft->contents)
            Swap (sleft, sright);
    }
    else {
        if ((sleft && x < sleft->contents ||
        (sright && sright->contents < x))
        Swap (sleft, sright);
    }
    ret = new Node (x, 0, sleft, sright);
    if (sleft) sleft->parent = ret;
    return ret;
}
```

12.7.3 Join and Delete

Join implements the Join operation as described in Section 12.3. It splices the root node out of the tree and queries the maximum node of the left subtree. As a side effect of the query, the maximum node is propagated up to the root, where it is guaranteed to have no right child (since it is the maximum). The root of the right subtree then can be made the right child of the left subtree's root.

Delete implements splay tree deletion by querying the element to delete (thus propagating it up to the root), then splicing it out using Join.

Listing 12.4 gives the listings for Join and Delete.

Listing 12.4. Join and Delete member functions.

```
template<class T, class Node>
Node *
```

(continued)

```
SplayNodeHelper<T, Node>::Join(Node *left, Node *right)
{
    // Make left and right their own subtrees
    if (left)
        left->parent = 0;
    if (right)
        right->parent = 0;

    // If one subtree is empty, return the other
    if (left == 0)
        return right;
    if (right == 0)
        return left;
    // Propagate maximum node to root of left.
    // The right subtree of the resulting root node is empty.
    left = left->Maximum()->Splay(left);

    // Right is guaranteed to be greater than any node in left,
    // so just make it the right-hand child.
    left->right = right;
    right->parent = left;
    return left;
}


template<class T, class Node>
Node *
SplayTreeHelper<T, Node>::Delete(Node *x)
{
    if (x == (node *) this) {
        Node *ret = Join (x->left, x->right);
        delete x;
        return ret;
    }
    else
        return 0;
}
```

Searching Wrapup

This chapter describes how to utilize the data structures for searching and reviews the performance implications of using the different data structures.

13.1 Using the Data Structures for Searching

The various data structures for searching implemented in this book solve basically the same set of problems but in different ways. Taken as a whole, data structures for searching that can be inserted into, deleted from, queried, and so on are called *dictionaries*. The various class templates for searching implemented in this book are all dictionary classes, and their interfaces are fairly uniform so users don't have to modify code to figure out which is the best data structure for the job.

Every dictionary class in this book is implemented as a class template, so they can be used as follows:

```
BinaryTree<int> btree;
```

This line of C++ instantiates two things. First, it declares a new instance of the `BinaryTree` class template: `BinaryTree<int>`, a class that implements a binary tree of `int`s. `BinaryTree<UserDefined-`

Type> declares a different instance of the BinaryTree class template, a class distinct from BinaryTree<int> that implements a binary tree of UserDefinedTypes. These instances of the class template are true classes; you can inherit from them, declare them **friends**, and otherwise interact with them exactly as with other classes.

Second, of course, the line of code declares an instance of the class BinaryTree<int>. btree is a binary tree that ints can be inserted into, deleted from, queried from, and otherwise manipulated.

Virtually any well-implemented class can be manipulated by these dictionary classes, but it must have the following: a copy constructor and assignment operator (if the default memberwise implementations provided by the compiler do not suffice), a destructor, and overloaded < and == operators. The < operator should take two parameters x and y and return int: nonzero if x precedes y in the sorted order, otherwise 0. This operator is used to order the items so they can be retrieved quickly later. The == operator takes two parameters x and y and returns int: nonzero if x is equal to y, otherwise 0. This operator is used to verify that a queried item is "equal" to the one passed in as a template for the query.

13.1.1 Insertion

Every dictionary class has an Insert member function that is used to insert items into the dictionary.

```
void Insert(const T& x);
```

13.1.2 Deletion

Every dictionary class has a Delete member function that is used to delete a given item from the dictionary.

```
void Delete(const T& x);
```

Note: The item is located using the T class's < operator; before deletion, the item is compared with the == operator. It may make sense to think of x as a "template" for the item to delete: It need only contain the key information required to locate and delete the item. None of the satellite information normally associated with an instance of the class T has to be included in the instance passed to `Delete`.

13.1.3 Queries

Every dictionary class has a `Query` member function that is used to query a given item from the dictionary.

```
T *Query(const T& x);
```

   As with deletion, the desired item is located using the < operator and verified with the == operator, and the instance passed into `Query` is only a "template" to locate the desired element. If the element is located, `Query` returns a pointer to it; otherwise `Query` returns 0 (the C++ equivalent to NULL, the guaranteed-invalid pointer).

   The pointer `Query` returns is to the element in the data structure. This pointer is not **const**, so the object can be modified by the client if desired. Take pains not to modify the key data through **this** pointer; doing so will invalidate the data structure. The key is used to locate not only this element, but other elements in the data structure; changing it is generally a global process that must be done by deleting the element and reinserting it with the new key. The current implementation chooses generality over robustness: it is error-prone if clients change the key of the element returned, but it may be useful to be able to change the satellite data.

13.1.4 Traversal (Trees)

The different data structures support traversal in different ways. The tree-based dictionary classes (`BinaryTree`, `RedBlackTree`, and `SplayTree`) all support `Predecessor` and `Successor` operations as well as `Query` and in-order traversal (visiting each node in the sorted order). The `SkipList` iterator class supports `Successor`, `Query`, and in-order traversal; unfortunately, this data structure does not lend itself to finding the predecessor of a node efficiently. We'll describe the iterator class for `BinaryTree` and its derivatives first.

   All of the tree-based data structures use the same embedded `Iterator` class from `BinaryTree`: `BinaryTree<T>::Iterator`. The constructor takes the instance of `BinaryTree` (or class derived from it) to iterate on and, optionally, the node to begin at (an instance of the embedded enum StartOrder: AtBeginning, AtRoot, or AtEnd). Different member functions then serve to point the iterator at different nodes, restart the iterator at a new location in the tree, or retrieve the contents of the node pointed at by the iterator:

Function	Behavior
void StartAt(enum-StartOrder start);	Restarts the iterator at the minimum, root, or maximum node in the tree.
void Previous();	Points the iterator at the previous node, or 0 if the current node is the minimum.
void Next();	Points the iterator at the next node, or 0 if the current node is the maximum.
void Parent();	Points the iterator at the parent node of the current node, or 0 if the current node is the root.
void Query(const T& x);	Points the iterator at the specified node in the tree, or 0 if the given node is not found.
operator int() const;	Returns nonzero if the iterator points at a valid node.
T operator*() const;	The dereferencing operator returns the contents of the node currently pointed to by the iterator. It invokes the copy constructor for the class T.
const T *Contents()-const;	Returns a **const** pointer to the contents of the node currently pointed to (which avoids the overhead of returning a copy of the node contents).
T *Contents();	Returns a non-**const** pointer to the contents of the node currently pointed to (which avoids the overhead of returning a copy of the node contents). It also gives the opportunity to modify the satellite data in the node. Modi-

fying the key will invalidate the data structure.

```
void operator++();
void operator++(int)
void operator--();
void operator--(int);
```
The increment and decrement operators behave like Next and Previous, respectively. No distinction is made between prefix and postfix operation.

For the sake of simplicity, the safeguards in the iterator classes for `SimpleList` are not present in `BinaryTree<T>::Iterator`. Items pointed to by an iterator can be deleted out from under the iterator if you aren't careful.

The most common idiom made available by this class interface is to traverse the tree in order.

```
for (BinaryTree<T>::Iterator iter(btree); iter; iter++)
{
    // Use operator* or Contents member functions
    // to examine node contents
}
```

Traversing in reverse order is just as trivial.

```
for (BinaryTree<T>::Iterator iter(btree,
BinaryTree<T>::AtEnd);
        iter;
        iter--)
{
    // Use operator* or Contents member functions
    // to examine node contents
}
```

For derivatives of binary trees, you can simply declare `Iterator` as if it were embedded in those classes. For example:

```
for (SplayTree<T>::Iterator iter(splaytree);
        iter;
        iter++)
{
    // Use operator* or Contents member functions
    // to examine node contents
}
```

13.1.5 Traversal (Skip Lists)

The skip list iterator class is implemented somewhat differently from the iterators for the tree-based data structures. It supports the same basic operations except for Predecessor. (Skip lists do not support this operation particularly efficiently.) However, unlike the binary tree iterators, SkipListIterator is implemented as a separate class. Traversing a skip list in order can be done as follows.

```
for (SkipListIterator<T> iter(list); iter; iter++) {
    // Use * operator to examine contents of node
}
```

The skip list iterator operations are as follows:

Function	Behavior
operator int() const;	Returns nonzero if the iterator points at a valid node.
T& operator*() const;	Returns the contents of the node currently pointed to by the iterator.
operator++(); operator++(int);	The increment operators go on to the next item in the list. No distinction is made between prefix and postfix operators.
void Restart();	Points the iterator back at the list head.
void Query(const T&);	Points the iterator at the given node.

SkipListIterator declares an embedded class, Exception, that is used to implement exceptions if desired. SkipListIterator will currently generate only one exception (InvalidDereference). This exception is thrown if a client attempts to dereference an iterator that does not point at a valid node.

13.2 Searching Wrapup

Here we discuss the performance tradeoffs associated with the different data structures for searching. Each data structure is appropriate for a particular range of applications. To review:

- Linear lists are good for keeping unsorted lists of items.

- Skip lists are a generalization of singly-linked lists that support insertion, deletion, and query in expected $O(\lg N)$ time.

- Binary trees are a good data structure for keeping ordered sets of items. They support insertion, deletion, and query in expected $O(\lg N)$ time, assuming the incoming data is random.

- Red-black trees are a form of binary tree that offer *guaranteed* $O(\lg N)$ performance, at a cost of some runtime (to balance the tree) and space (to color the nodes).

- Splay trees are a form of adaptive binary tree that rearrange themselves to optimize the access time of frequently accessed nodes. The access time for recently accessed nodes starts out at $O(1)$ and degrades as the logarithm of the number of other accesses that have been performed since the last one.

Binary trees, splay trees, and skip lists all respond poorly to systematic behavior by their clients.

- All of them behave poorly if items are inserted in sorted order.

- Binary trees and splay trees behave poorly if items are inserted in reverse-sorted order.

- Splay trees behave poorly if the items are accessed in sorted or reverse-sorted order. (The tree is reordered to behave like a linked list.) Ironically, splay trees are the best-suited trees for practical searching applications, since most such applications evince locality of reference rather than referring to items in order. In short, if ordered data is likely to be encountered, red-black trees are probably the best choice because they offer guaranteed optimal asymptotic performance (at the cost of a constant factor).

PART

Selection

The median of a data set is the middle element in the sorted order. For example, the median of $\{12, 1, 5, 10, 7\}$ is 7. The median is a useful statistic because it is robust. The median household income of an area is usually a much more useful number than the average household income. While a few wealthy families can grossly distort the average household income, they barely affect the median.

A naive algorithm for computing the median of a data set is to sort the data, then pick out the middle element. That's much more work than is required. Comparison-based sorting is $\Omega(N \lg N)$, but comparison-based median algorithms are $\Omega(N)$, and optimal algorithms for computing the median have been derived.

The median is a special case of a more general idea, the *order statistic*. The ith order statistic of a data set is the ith element in the sorted order. (Therefore, the median is the $(N/2)$th order statistic.) In computer algorithms jargon, computing an order statistic is called *selection*.

Blum et al. [BLUM73] give an interesting history of the selection problem, referring to an article written by Lewis Carroll in 1883 protesting that the runner-up in single-elimination tennis tournaments was not necessarily the second-best player. (Any player who lost to the winner may have been the second best.) Fairly determining the second-best player in the tournament corresponds to selection of the second-highest element. An optimal algorithm to select this element has been derived; it requires exactly $N + \lceil \lg N \rceil - 2$ comparisons. (To return to the tournament jargon, the algorithm

259

involves having a second knockout tournament among the players who lost to the winner.) This algorithm is clearly linear, but it is valid only for the special case of $i = 2$. Deriving linear-time algorithms for selection of arbitrary elements is much more difficult and was the subject of the paper by Blum et al. We will discuss their results in Chapter 14.

Our discussion of selection approximately follows that of Cormen et al. [CORM90]. Chapter 14 discusses the special cases of minimum and maximum and introduces two algorithms for selection: one very practical, expected-linear time selection algorithm and a somewhat slower worst-case linear time selection algorithm. Chapter 15 discusses the order statistics tree, a data structure based on binary trees that is well suited to computing order statistics on dynamic data sets. Finally, Chapter 16 discusses the performance tradeoffs in our selection implementations and a number of alternative implementations of selection, including optimizing for small cases and using histograms for selection.

14

Linear-Time Selection

This chapter discusses selection of an element from an array. All of the algorithms given herein can select an element from an array in linear time. Section 14.1 examines the special case of selecting the minimum and maximum element from an array. Section 14.2.1 discusses an expected-linear selection algorithm related to Hoare's Quicksort [HOAR62]. Like Quicksort, this selection algorithm has a runtime of $O(N^2)$ in the worst case; however, like Quicksort, it is very practical to use because it has an extremely small constant factor and its worst-case runtime can be made very difficult to elicit. For those who insist on linear time in the worst case, Section 14.2.2 discusses a more complicated algorithm that is guaranteed to run in linear time.

14.1 Minimum and Maximum

The minimum and maximum are two special cases of order statistics for which trivial $O(N)$ algorithms can be written. Listing 14.1 gives a function template to return a pointer to the minimum element of an array. The algorithm to compute the maximum is identical, with the sense of the comparison reversed. In the source code included with the book, the `Minimum`, `Maximum`, and `MinMax` function templates are all given in `<order.h>`.

Listing 14.1.   Minimum function template.

```
// -------------------------------------------------------------
// Minimum function template
//      Computes minimum element in an array.
//
// Parameters:
//      T *base         Base of the array.
//      const int n     Number of elements in the array.
//
// Return value: T *
//      Pointer to the minimum element in the array.
//
// Requires:
//      operator< must be defined on the class T.
//
// Runtime:
//      O(N) for an N-element array.
// -------------------------------------------------------------

template<class T>
T *
Minimum(T *base, const int n)
{
    T *ret = base;
    for (int i = 1; i < n; i++)
        if (base[i] < *ret)
            ret = base + i;
    return ret;
}
```

As Cormen et al. [CORM90] point out, if you want to compute *both* the minimum and the maximum, you can do better than to run Minimum and Maximum on the array. The function template MinMax, given in Listing 14.2, takes two elements at a time, compares them, and compares only the smaller with the minimum and the larger with the maximum. This still uses $O(N)$ comparisons, but only about $(3/2)N$ comparisons instead of the $2N - 2$ comparisons performed when Minimum and Maximum are run separately. MinMax uses the optimal number of comparisons for unordered input.

Listing 14.2.   MinMax function template.

```
// -------------------------------------------------------------
// MinMax function template
```

```
//      Simultaneously computes the minimum and maximum
//      elements in an array.
//
// Parameters:
//      T *base          Base of the array.
//      const int n      Number of elements in the array.
//      T **min          Passback for the minimum.  On exit,
//                       the T * pointed to by this parameter
//                       will point at the minimum element in
//                       the array.
//      T **max          Passback for the maximum.  On exit,
//                       the T * pointed to by this parameter
//                       will point at the maximum element in
//                       the array.
//
// Return value: None
//
// Runtime:
//      O(N) for an N-element array.
// ------------------------------------------------------------

template<class T>
void
MinMax(T *base, const int n, T **min, T **max)
{
    int i;
    *min = *max = base;
    for (i = 1; i < n - 1; i += 2) {
        if (base[i] < base[i+1]) {
            if (base[i] < **min)
        *min = base + i;
            if (**max < base[i+1])
                *max = base + i + 1;
        }
        else {
            if (base[i+1] < **min)
                *min = base + i + 1;
            if (**max < base[i])
                *max = base + i;
        }
    }
    // We may have skipped over the last element in the array
    // without checking it against the min and max.
    if (i == n - 1) {
```

(continued)

```
          if (base[i] < **min)
              *min = base + i;
          if (**max < base[i])
              *max = base + i;
      }
}
```

14.2 Selection in Linear Time

This chapter explores the general problem of selecting a given element from a data set. As with the Minimum and Maximum functions,
the input is an array of some type T; however, the element being
selected is specified by an index i in the range $[0, N - 1]$. All of
the algorithms described here run in expected–or worst case–linear
time, which is much more efficient than sorting the input array.

14.2.1 Hoare's Algorithm: Expected–Linear Selection

The same paper by C. A. R. Hoare that introduced Quicksort
[HOAR62] also introduced an efficient, expected–linear time algorithm for selection. Listing 14.3 shows a recursive C++ function
template that implements Select. In the source code included with
the book, the various selection routines are given in <order.h>.

```
1   Select(A, N, i)
2       if N=1 then return A[0]
3       Midpoint←Partition(A, N)
4       if i<Midpoint then
5            return Select(A, Midpoint, i)
6       else
7            return Select(A+Midpoint, N-Midpoint,
                          i-Midpoint)
```

    Like Quicksort, Select partitions the array about an element
T into two subarrays with elements ≤T and ≥T. In fact, the routine
Partition called in the pseudocode just given is identical to the
partitioning routine utilized by Quicksort. After partitioning the
array, we can figure out which side of the partition the element we
are looking for is on. If we are selecting the fifth-highest element in

Listing 14.3. SelectRecursive function template.

```
// ------------------------------------------------------------
// SelectRecursive function template
//
//      Performs selection on an array.  "Selection" is computing
//      the i'th element in the sorted order; for example, the
//      median of a set of values can be computed by selecting
//      the N/2'th element in an N-element array.
//
//      This recursive implementation is simpler but less
//      efficient than the Select function below.  Since this
//      routine is tail-recursive, it can be rewritten using
//      an iterative loop.
//
// References:
//      Cormen, Leiserson and Rivest, p. 187.
//
// Parameters:
//
//      T *base         Base of the array.
//      int N           Number of elements in the array.
//      int inx         Index of the element to select.  This
//                      must be in the range [0, n-1].
//
// Return value: T *
//      The return value points at the inx'th element in the
//      sorted order of the array.
//
// Runtime:
//      Expected O(N) for an N-element array, worst-case O(N^2).
//
// ------------------------------------------------------------
template<class T>
T *
SelectRecursive(T *base, int N, int inx)
{
    // We've found the element if there's only one...
    if (N == 1)
        return base;
    int part = Partition(base, N);
    if (inx < part)
        return SelectRecursive(base, part, inx);
    else
        return SelectRecursive(base + part, N - part, inx - part);
}
```

the array and the left-hand subarray contains seven elements, then we know that the element we are looking for is the fifth-highest element in the left-hand subarray. The other case occurs if we are looking for the fifth-highest element and the left-hand subarray contains only four elements. In that case, we know that the element we are looking for is the second-highest element in the right-hand subarray. In this way, the selection algorithm can narrow down the location of the element being selected.

Figure 14.1 shows the selection algorithm at work. After repeatedly discarding the portions of the array that do not contain the element being selected, Select has narrowed the array down to a one-element subarray that contains the element being selected.

Select vs. Quicksort

Because of their shared heritage, there are many similarities between Select and Quicksort. Like Quicksort, Select degrades to an $O(N^2)$ runtime if an unfavorable partition is chosen every time. Like Quicksort, we can decrease the likelihood of this happening by randomizing the partitioning element. Also like Quicksort, Select is tail-recursive and can be improved by implementing it as a loop. A randomized, iterative implementation of Select is shown in Listing 14.4.

Unlike Quicksort, however, Select considers only one of the subarrays after partitioning. This allows us to completely replace all recursion in the algorithm, unlike Quicksort, where we had to leave one of the recursive calls intact. Considering only one subarray also impacts the expected runtime of Select: While Quicksort has an expected runtime of $O(N \lg N)$, the expected runtime of Select is $O(N)$.

We can make the worst-case performance of Hoare's selection algorithm very unlikely by randomizing the partitioning element. Alternatively, we could compare a few elements in the input array and choose a partitioning element from them. This is similar to the median-of-three partitioning scheme implemented for Quicksort.

Floyd and Rivest [FLOY75] describe an oft-cited technique for choosing a better partitioning element. I investigated it but didn't find it to offer much advantage over the randomized implementation given here. It is included in <order.h> as a function template called SelectFR.

Select: 6th highest element (26).

24	86	63	26	62	18	48	91	53	44	94	20	23	32	10

1. Partition about 24.

10	23	20	18	62	26	48	91	53	44	94	63	86	32	24

First partition contains only four elements, so 6th
element is (6-4)=2nd element of second partition.

2. Partition about 62.

10	23	20	18	24	26	48	32	53	44	94	63	86	91	62

First partition contains 6 elements, so the element
we are looking for is somewhere in it.

3. Partition about 32, keep narrowing the input array.

10	23	20	18	24	26	32	48	53	44	94	63	86	91	62

4. Partition about 24.

5. When we have narrowed to a one-element subarray, it's the one we are looking for.

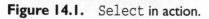

Figure 14.1. Select in action.

Listing 14.4. Select function template.

```
// -------------------------------------------------------------
// Select function template
//
//      Performs selection on an array.  "Selection" is computing
//      the i'th element in the sorted order; for example, the
//      median of a set of values can be computed by selecting
//      the N/2'th element in an N-element array.
//
// References:
//      Cormen, Leiserson and Rivest, p. 187.
//
// Parameters:
//
//      T *base         Base of the array.
//      int N           Number of elements in the array.
//      int inx         Index of the element to select.  This
//                      must be in the range [0, N-1].
//
// Return value: T *
//      The return value points at the inx'th element in the
//      sorted order of the array.
//
// Runtime:
//      Expected O(N) for an N-element array, worst-case O(N^2).
//
// -------------------------------------------------------------

template<class T>
T *
Select(T *base, int N, int inx)
{
    int left = 0;
    int right = N;

    // This while loop terminates when base[left..right]
    // defines a 1-element array.
    while (right > left + 1) {

        // Select a random element to partition about.
        int q = left + rand() % (right - left);

        Swap(base[left], base[q]);
        int part = left + Partition(base + left, right - left);
```

```
        // Now focus attention on the partition containing
        // the order statistic we're interested in.
        if (inx < part - left)
            // Throw away the right-hand partition; we know it
            // doesn't contain the i'th order statistic.
            right = part;
        else {
            // Throw away the left-hand partition; we know it
            // doesn't contain the i'th order statistic.
            // Now we're looking for the inx - part - left'th
            // order statistic of the right-hand partition.
            inx -= part - left;
            left = part;
        }
    }
    // base[left] is the element we want, return pointer to it.
    return base + left;
}
```

14.2.2 Worst-Case Linear Selection

Hoare's expected–linear time selection algorithm described in Section 14.2.1 will fulfill almost any need for a selection algorithm. Eliciting the worst-case $O(N^2)$ behavior from that algorithm can be made extremely unlikely by randomizing the partitioning element. It is iterative, so it uses $O(1)$ auxiliary space. It has a small constant factor, so it is efficient. In general, we have avoided exploring alternative methods when such an attractive method has been described already.

I couldn't resist implementing a selection algorithm by Blum et al. [BLUM73], however. This algorithm is generally slower than Hoare's expected–linear selection algorithm, but it does not have the unfavorable worst-case runtime. SelectLinear runs in linear time in the worst case, no matter what the input. Our presentation of the algorithm follows that of Cormen et al. [CORM90].

SelectLinear works similarly to Select, in that it partitions the array and recursively considers one of the subarrays. However, it does some extra work in order to guarantee that the partitioning element used is a good one.

1. Divide the N elements of the input array into $\lfloor N/s \rfloor$ groups of s elements each and one group of N mod s elements. s is

a small odd integer greater than 3. (5 is used in the C++ implementation.) If there are fewer than 2*s* elements in the input array, simply sort them and access the array to find the desired order statistic; this is a constant-time operation because *s* is a small constant.

2. Find the median of each group. This is a constant-time operation for each group, so the runtime for this step is $O(N)$. The suggested method of finding this median is by running Insertion Sort on each group and selecting the middle element. If the leftover group has an even number of elements, the larger element is selected.

3. Find the median of the $\lceil N/s \rceil$ medians computed in Step 2.

4. Partition the input array around the median-of-medians using a modified version of Partition that takes the element to partition about as input. (In the header file part.h, this implementation of Partition is called `Partition2`.)

5. Recursively consider the left subarray if the element being selected is less than or equal to the partition; otherwise recursively consider the right subarray.

Steps 4 and 5 are the heart of Hoare's selection algorithm. Steps 1 to 3 are dedicated to finding a good element to partition about.

See Listing 14.5 for a C++ implementation of `SelectLinear` with $s = 5$.

Listing 14.5.   `SelectLinear` function template.

```
// ------------------------------------------------------------
// SelectLinear function template
//
//      Performs selection on an array.  This routine has the
//      same interface as Select, but is guaranteed to run in
//      linear time.  Select has an expected-linear runtime,
//      but may degenerate to O(N^2) in the worst case.
//
// References:
//      Cormen, Leiserson and Rivest, p. 189-191.
//
// Parameters:
//
//      T *base         Base of the array.
//      int n           Number of elements in the array.
```

```
//      int inx          Index of the element to select.  This
//                       must be in the range [0, n-1].
//
// Return value: T *
//      The return value points at the inx'th element in the
//      sorted order of the array.
//
// Runtime:
//      O(N) for an N-element array.
//
// -------------------------------------------------------------

template<class T>
T *
SelectLinear(T *base, int n, int inx)
{
    int i, j;

    int n5 = (n + 4) / 5;

    if (n5 < 2) {
        InsertionSort(base, n);
        return base + inx;
    }

    T *temp = new T[n5];
    j = 0;
    for (i = 0; i <= (n - 5); i += 5)
        temp[j++] = Median5(base+i);
    if (i < n) {
        InsertionSort(base + i, n - i);
        temp[j] = base[(n - i) / 2];
    }
    T *medofmed = Select(temp, n5, n5/2);
    int part = Partition2(base, n, *medofmed);
    delete[] temp;
    if (inx < part)
        return SelectLinear(base, part, inx);
    return SelectLinear(base + part, n - part, inx - part);
}
```

Runtime

At least half of the elements found in Step 2 are greater than or equal to the median-of-medians x computed in Step 3. Thus, at least half of the $\lceil N/s \rceil$ contribute $\lceil s/2 \rceil$ elements that are greater than x except for two: the odd group containing $N \bmod s$ elements and the group containing x. Thus, the number of elements greater than x is at least

$$\left\lceil \frac{s}{2} \right\rceil \left(\left\lceil \frac{1}{2} \left\lceil \frac{N}{s} \right\rceil \right\rceil - 2 \right) \geq \frac{N}{4} - s$$

Similarly, the number of elements less than x is at least $(N/4) - s$. In the worst case, the function is recursively called on at most

$$N - \left(\frac{N}{4} - s \right) = \frac{3N}{4} + s$$

elements.

We can now develop a recurrence for the worst-case running time $T(N)$ of the algorithm. Steps 1, 2, and 4 take $O(N)$ time, so they can all be taken into account with a single $O(N)$ term. Step 3 takes time $T(\lceil N/s \rceil)$, and Step 5 takes time at most $T((3N/4) + s)$. The recurrence is therefore:

$$T(N) = T\left(\left\lceil \frac{N}{s} \right\rceil \right) + T\left(\frac{3N}{4} + s \right) + O(N)$$

The $O(N)$ bound on $T(N)$ can be proven by induction by substituting $T(N) = cN$. See the references for details.

SelectLinear runs about four times slower than the randomized Select routine given in Section 14.2, but its runtime cannot degrade to $O(N^2)$. Also, the SelectLinear routine given here probably could be optimized to reduce the difference in the constant factors.

Order Statistics Trees

The order statistics tree is a variant of the red-black tree designed especially to compute order statistics. It retains the $\Theta(\lg N)$ runtimes for all fundamental red-black tree operations such as `Insert`, `Delete`, and `Query`, yet it also supports `Select` (selection of the data set in the tree) in $\Theta(\lg N)$ time and `Rank` (rank of an element in the data set) in constant time.

Order statistics trees are an augmentation of red-black trees that work as follows: Each node contains a variable *size*, the number of nodes in the subtree rooted by the node (not including the node itself, so the minimum value of *size* is 0). As we shall see, the *size* field in each node can be used to implement fast order statistics operations on the data set in the tree. Figure 15.1 depicts an order statistics tree.

15.1 Select

To find the *i*th smallest key in an order statistics tree, we call the following routine with a pointer to the root node of the tree.

```
1  Select(Root, i)
2      Rank←0
```

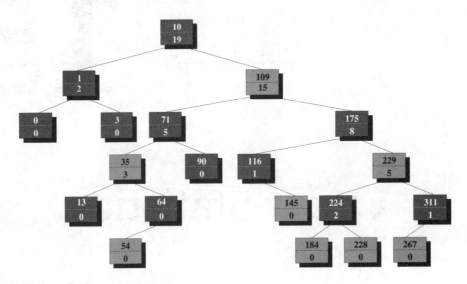

Figure 15.1.   Order statistics tree.

```
3     if Root.Left ≠ NULL then Rank←Root.Left.Size+1
4     if i = Rank then
5        return Root
6     else if i < Rank then
7        return Select(Root.Left, i)
8     else
9        return Select(Root.Right, i - Rank)
```

Rank is the rank of the root node. If the rank is the index desired, then the root node is returned. Otherwise Select can be called recursively on the left or right subtree, depending on where the desired key lies.

Select can easily be reformulated iteratively as follows.

```
1   Select(Root, i)
2       while Root ≠ 0 do
3            Rank←0
4            if Root.Left ≠ NULL then
5                 Rank←Root.Left.Size+1
6            if i = Rank then
7                 return Root
8            else if i < Rank then
9                 Root←Root.Left
```

```
10              else
11                      Root←Root.Right
12                      i←i-(Rank + 1)
```

Select examines one level of the red-black tree on each iteration, so it is $O(h) = O(\lg N)$ for a tree containing N nodes. Since the fastest possible selection algorithms on unordered data sets are $O(N)$, the runtime for Select on an order statistics tree is significantly faster. If the data set does not change or changes little between selections, an order statistics tree is far more efficient than performing selection from scratch on each data set.

15.2 Rotations

Rotations are a local modification to the tree, and the *size* elements can be maintained in constant time during a rotation. The child node being rotated receives the parent node's *size* field, since the child roots the subtree after the rotation. The parent node's *size* field can be computed from the *size* fields of its new children, with the proviso that NULL children have *size* = 0:

Parent.Size←Parent.Left.Size+Parent.Right.Size+2

Figure 15.2 depicts symmetric rotations in an order statistics tree with the *size* fields being updated.

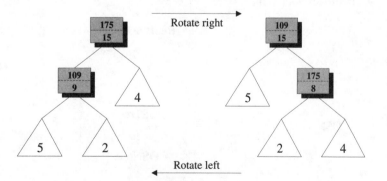

Figure 15.2.   Rotation in an order statistics tree.

15.3 Insertion

During the first phase of insertion, when the tree is being traversed to find the proper location to insert the node, the size of each node is incremented by 1 to reflect that a node is being added to the subtree rooted by the node. Once this is done, the only operations performed that affect the tree's layout are rotations. We have already discussed how the *size* fields can be maintained in constant time during rotations; insertion into an order statistics tree is $O(\lg N)$.

15.4 Deletion

For deletion, we first update the *size* fields after splicing a node out of the tree. This is done by traversing the tree toward the root

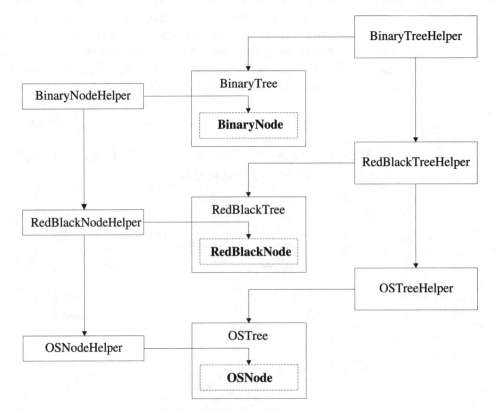

Figure 15.3. Order statistics tree class hierarchy.

from the spliced-out node, decrementing *size* as we go. During the second phase of deletion, when the red-black properties are being fixed, the only operations performed that affect the tree's layout are rotations (as with insertion), and *size* can be maintained in constant time during these operations. Therefore, deletion out of an order statistics tree is also $O(\lg N)$.

15.5 Implementation

OSTree, a family of class templates to implement order statistics trees, inherits from RedBlackTree as shown in Figure 15.3. The operations that need to be implemented are Select, RotateLeft and RotateRight, and Insert and Delete. Other operations, such as Query, can be inherited harmlessly from RedBlackTree and its parent class template, BinaryTree.

Listing 15.1 gives the class template definitions for OSTree and its helper class templates OSNodeHelper, OSNode, and OSTreeHelper. These class templates interact as described in Section 10.7 to share as much code as possible. In the source code included with the book, the order statistics tree implementation is given in <ostree.h>.

Listing 15.1.   OSTree class template definitions.

```
template<class T, class Node>
class OSTreeHelper : public RedBlackTreeHelper<T, Node> {
public:
    virtual T *Select(int i);
    virtual void PrintNodes();
    virtual void CheckNodes();
};


template<class T>
class OSTree : public OSTreeHelper<T, OSNode<T> > {
public:
    OSTree() { }
};


template<class T, class Node>
class OSNodeHelper : public RedBlackNodeHelper<T, Node> {
public:
```

(continued)

```
        OSNodeHelper() { }
        OSNodeHelper(const T& x, int Size = 0);
        OSNodeHelper(const T& x, Node *p);
        OSNodeHelper(const T& x, enum RedBlack clr,
                  Node *p, Node *l, Node *r):
            RedBlackNodeHelper<T, Node>(x, clr, p, l, r) { size = 0; }
        virtual ~OSNodeHelper() { }

        virtual Node *LeftRotate(Node *root);
        virtual Node *RightRotate(Node *root);
        Node *Delete(Node *z);
        Node *Insert(const T& AddMe);

        virtual T *Select(int i);
        virtual void PrintNodes();
        virtual int NumNodes();
        virtual int Rank();
        virtual void CheckNumNodes();
        virtual int Size() const;
private:
        int size;
};

template<class T>
class OSNode : public OSNodeHelper<T, OSNode<T> >
{
public:
        OSNode() { }
        OSNode(const T& x): OSNodeHelper<T, OSNode<T> >(x) { }
        OSNode(const T& x, OSNode<T> *p):
            OSNodeHelper<T, OSNode<T> >(x, p) { }
        OSNode(const T& x,
              RedBlackNodeHelper<T, OSNode<T> >::RedBlack clr,
              OSNode<T> *p = 0,
              OSNode<T> *l = 0,
              OSNode<T> *r = 0):
            OSNodeHelper<T, OSNode<T> >(x, clr, p, l, r) { }
        virtual ~OSNode() { }
};


// -----------------------------------------------------------
// Constructors for OSNodeHelper
// -----------------------------------------------------------
```

```
template<class T, class Node>
OSNodeHelper<T, Node>::OSNodeHelper(const T& x, int Size):
    RedBlackNodeHelper<T, Node>(x)
{
    size = Size;
}


template<class T, class Node>
OSNodeHelper<T, Node>::OSNodeHelper(const T& x, Node *p):
    RedBlackNodeHelper<T, Node>(x, p)
{
    size = 0;
}
```

Listing 15.2 gives the listing for Select, a member function of OSNodeHelper that implements Select as described in Section 15.1.

Listing 15.2. Select member function.

```
// ----------------------------------------------------------
// Select
//      When called on the root node of an order statistics
//      tree, select the index given (range of i is [0..N-1]
//      where N is the number of nodes in the tree.
// ----------------------------------------------------------
template<class T, class Node>
T *
OSNodeHelper<T, Node>::Select(int i)
{
    Node *trav = (Node *) this;
    while (trav) {
        int rank = (trav->left) ? trav->left->Size() + 1 : 0;
        if (i == rank)
            return &trav->contents;
        if (i < rank)
            trav = trav->left;
        else {
            trav = trav->right;
            i -= rank + 1;
        }
    }
    return 0;
}
```

Listing 15.3 gives the listings for LeftRotate and Right-Rotate, member functions of OSNodeHelper that implement rotation as described in Section 15.2.

Listing 15.4 gives the listing for Insert, a member function of OSNodeHelper that implements insertion. Note that because OSNode implements the needed functionality, Insert can borrow heavily from the red-black tree implementation of insertion; for example,

Listing 15.3.   LeftRotate and RightRotate member functions.

```
// ------------------------------------------------------------
// LeftRotate
//      Left-rotate the node with its parent.
// ------------------------------------------------------------
template<class T, class Node>
Node *
OSNodeHelper<T, Node>::LeftRotate(Node *root)
{
    Node *ret = RedBlackNodeHelper<T, Node>::LeftRotate(root);

    ((OSNodeHelper<T, Node> *) parent)->size = Size();
    size = (left) ? left->Size() + 1 : 0;
    size += (right) ? right->Size() + 1 : 0;

    return ret;
}


// ------------------------------------------------------------
// RightRotate
//      Right-rotate the node with its parent.
// ------------------------------------------------------------
template<class T, class Node>
Node *
OSNodeHelper<T, Node>::RightRotate(Node *root)
{
    Node *ret = RedBlackNodeHelper<T, Node>::RightRotate(root);

    ((OSNodeHelper<T, Node> *) parent)->size = size;
    size = (left) ? left->Size() + 1 : 0;
    size += (right) ? right->Size() + 1 : 0;
    return ret;
}
```

whenever the red-black tree implementation wishes to rotate nodes, the OSNode implementation of rotation is called, so the *size* fields get updated properly.

Listing 15.5 gives the listing for Delete, a member function of OSNodeHelper that implements deletion.

Listing 15.4. Insert member function.

```
// ----------------------------------------------------------
// Insert
//      Inserts the given item into the order statistics tree.
// ----------------------------------------------------------
template<class T, class Node>
Node *
OSNodeHelper<T, Node>::Insert(const T& AddMe)
{
    OSNodeHelper<T, Node> *x = this;
    while (x) {
        x->size += 1;
        x = (AddMe < x->contents) ? x->left : x->right;
    }
    return RedBlackNodeHelper<T, Node>::Insert(AddMe);
}
```

Listing 15.5. Delete member function.

```
// ----------------------------------------------------------
// Delete
//      When called on the root of the order statistics
//      tree, delete the given node from the tree.
// ----------------------------------------------------------
template<class T, class Node>
Node *
OSNodeHelper<T, Node>::Delete(Node *z)
{
    OSNodeHelper<T, Node> *trav;
    if (z && z->left && z->right)
        trav = (OSNodeHelper<T, Node> *) z->Successor();
    else
        trav = (OSNodeHelper<T, Node> *) z;

    while (trav) {
        trav->size--;
```
(continued)

```
        trav = trav->parent;
    }
    return RedBlackNodeHelper<T, Node>::Delete(z);
}
```

15.6 Conclusion and Applications

Any application where selection is performed on a data set that does not change, or changes very little, responds very well to order statistics trees. One obvious application for an order statistics tree is an order statistics-based neighborhood operation in image processing. Each pixel in the image is replaced by an order statistic of its neighbors. If the order statistic is the minimum or maximum, this operation is a building block for a family of image processing algorithms called *grayscale morphology*. If the order statistic is the median, the operation reduces noise in the image. The neighborhood varies in size from 3×3 on up. For large $M \times N$ neighborhoods, the order statistics tree is an efficient solution to the problem: The tree can contain neighborhood elements, and only M elements would have to be inserted into and deleted from the tree for each pixel. For example, for a 9×9 neighborhood, 9 elements would have to be deleted, then 9 elements inserted, to update the tree for each pixel. This contrasts sharply with the number of operations required to compute the median of 81 elements on each iteration.

Selection Wrapup and Future Work

16.1 Timing Results

All of the selection algorithms described run in expected or worst-case $O(N)$ time. The time to perform one selection, then, can be accurately modeled with a function $f = cN$. The only task is to determine the approximate values of c for the various implementations here. To time them, a program called TIMESEL.CPP is provided. TIMESEL takes two command-line parameters: a count of the number of elements to select on, and the number of iterations to perform. Using TIMESEL and the submicrosecond timer built into the Alpha, I found out the following.

Algorithm	Expected Runtime	Worst-case Runtime	Alpha Runtime (clock cycles)
Hoare (recursive)	$O(N)$	$O(N^2)$	196N
Hoare (iterative)	$O(N)$	$O(N^2)$	22N
Floyd-Rivest	$O(N)$	$O(N^2)$	189N
Blum et al.	$O(N)$	$O(N)$	94N

As expected, the iterative version of Hoare's selection algorithm crushes the recursive version; it is almost ten times as fast.

The scheme advocated by Floyd and Rivest does not appear to offer any advantage as implemented; it is only marginally faster than the recursive version of Hoare's algorithm. Perhaps an iterative implementation would be more competitive.

The most interesting result is that Blum et al.'s scheme, which is guaranteed linear, is about four times as slow as the iterative version of Hoare's algorithm. We have encountered this tradeoff before: Red-black trees take more time to organize data than naive binary trees, but they are not subject to the degenerate worst-case runtimes if sorted data is inserted. Similarly, while randomizing the partition makes the worst case of Hoare's selection algorithm extremely unlikely, you can pay a price in the form of a four fold performance degradation to guarantee a linear runtime.

16.2 Special Cases

Several special cases of order statistics are worth examining.

16.2.1 Median for Small *N*

Paeth [PAET90] describes an application for taking the median of small datasets: a filtering operation in image processing for noise reduction. Each pixel is replaced by the median of itself and its eight neighbors. Thus, a "median-of-nine" operation must be performed on each pixel in the image. Since images typically contain at least 300K pixels, performing this median operation should be as fast as possible.

The median of any dataset can be computed by repeatedly discarding the minimum and maximum elements. If the minimum and maximum are discarded until there is only one element left, the remaining element must be the median (since an equal number of elements less than and greater than the median have been discarded). The minimum and maximum are computed using the technique outlined in Chapter 14.

As an example, Listing 16.1 gives `Median5`, a function that computes the median of five elements given. This function is used by `SelectLinear` to compute the median of each five-element subarray in the input array.

Listing 16.1. Median5 function template.

```
// -----------------------------------------------------------------
// Median5 function template
//
//      Computes the median of a five-element array using
//      at most 7 comparisons.
//
// Parameters:
//      T *base         Base of the array to be sorted.
//
// Return value: None.
//
// Requires:
//      operator< must be defined for class T.
//
// Runtime:
//      O(1).
//
// -----------------------------------------------------------------
template<class T>
T
Median5(T *base)
{
    // Winner of base[0] and base[4] in 0.
    if (base[0] < base[4]) Swap(base[0], base[4]);

    // Winner of base[1] and base[3] in 1.
    if (base[1] < base[3]) Swap(base[1], base[3]);

    // Now base[0..2] contains winners and base[3..4]
    // contains losers.
    // Winner of base[0] and base[2] in 0.
    if (base[0] < base[2]) Swap(base[0], base[2]);
    if (base[0] < base[1]) Swap(base[0], base[1]);

    // Loser of base[3] and base[4] in 4.
    if (base[3] < base[4]) Swap(base[3], base[4]);

    // Median is now median of base[1..3].

    // Winner of base[1] and base[2] in 1.
    if (base[1] < base[2]) Swap(base[1], base[2]);
    // Loser of base[2] and base[3] in 2.
```

(continued)

```
        if (base[3] < base[2]) Swap(base[2], base[3]);
        return base[2];
}
```

This algorithm is an asymptotically inefficient $O(N^2)$, but has a small constant factor. It is nearly ideal for the nine elements called for by the median-of-nine smoothing operation for image processing; it requires 20 comparisons to perform the median, while the optimal decision tree requires 19 comparisons. Paeth includes C source code not only for the median-of-nine operation, but for the optimal decision tree of the more stable median-of-125 operation (5×5 neighborhood around each pixel).

16.2.2 Selection with Histograms

Grayscale images are often described in terms of rectangular arrays of *k-bit* elements, where $k \le 16$. The histogram of such an image is an array with 2^k elements; each element contains the number of pixels in the image that have that value. The histogram can be used to compute any order statistic, as follows.

```
1   ComputeHistogram(Pixels, Width, Height, Histogram)
2       Initialize the histogram elements to 0
3       for i←0 to k do
4           Histogram[i]←0
5       for i←0 to Width-1 do
6           for j←0 to Height-1 do
7               Histogram[Pixels[i][j]] += 1
```

ComputeHistogram computes the histogram for a *k-bit* image. Pixels is the two-dimensional array that contains the pixels; Width and Height are the width and height of the image, and Histogram is the array of 2^k elements that contains the histogram of the image. ComputeHistogram runs in $O(N)$ time for an image that contains N pixels, and, as you can imagine, the constant factor is extremely small.

```
1   HistSelect(Histogram, k, Index)
2       RunningSum←0
3       for←0 to 2^k - 1 do
```

```
4              RunningSum←RunningSum + Histogram[i]
5              if (RunningSum >= Index)
6                  return i
```

HistSelect performs selection using a histogram rather than the actual data. Histogram is an array of 2^k elements that contains the histogram of the image. Index is the index of the element that is to be selected. (For an image containing N pixels, you select the median by setting Index = $N/2$.) Since there are so few possible values in the input, scanning the histogram is more efficient than operating on the actual input.

HistSelect runs in $O(2^k)$ time, where k is the number of bits per pixel. When k is small, as when the input is image data, running ComputeHistogram followed by HistSelect is much faster than any of the selection algorithms presented in this book.

A P P E N D I X

A C++ Refresher

This appendix gives an overview of the C++ programming language, but it is by no means introductory; actually, it is targeted at C++ programmers with considerable experience. It serves several purposes. First, I don't feel comfortable with not presenting the material at all; I would rather provide readers with an appendix to refer to than force them to leaf through another reference book. Second, C++ embodies many schools of thought, and this appendix will give experienced C++ programmers a clear idea of where the author stands, when it comes to issues that are still being debated. Finally, some of the material, such as that on pointer arithmetic in Section A.2, just needs to be reviewed because it is used so frequently in the accompanying source code.

A.1 Overview

C++ is a general-purpose programming language well suited for implementing many different types of applications. It is a derivative of the popular C programming language. In fact, C++ compilers can compile well-written C code without modification. However, C++ is an infinitely more complex and expressive language than C. Its complexity is a two-edged sword; while it lets programmers write expressive, powerful code, C++ programmers must cultivate an eye for when to use which feature.

C++ is a *static* language, which means all the data types, function parameters, and other elements of the program must be described at compile time. In some languages, such as Smalltalk, new types can be defined at runtime; not so in C++. The C++ compiler requires you to describe everything so it can verify your code. For example, a C++ compiler will not compile code that calls a function for which the compiler hasn't seen a prototype.

C++ is a strongly typed language. "Strong" typing means only compatible types can be intermingled in expressions. Early versions of C treated integers and pointers identically; trying to do the same in C++ will cause the compiler to complain loudly. It knows enough to convert automatically between some types (for example, it will automatically promote an integer to a floating-point value), but it will refuse to compile code that mixes incompatible types.

C++'s static, strongly typed approach makes getting code to compile in the first place more difficult, but once it compiles, that code is more likely to be correct.

A.2 Pointers and Arrays in C and C++

The C programming language, which C++ is based on, is a very powerful procedural language. This book is not about C or even C++, but it makes heavy use of pointers and arrays, two concepts that elude even experienced C programmers. We'll start out with a brief discussion of pointers and arrays in C, since they are used heavily in the book. The discussion applies equally to C++, since it inherits all of the concepts about pointers and arrays from C.

A.2.1 Arrays

Arrays in C are declared by appending a size in square brackets [ ] to the declaration. For example:

```
int IntArray[10];        // Declare array of 10 ints
```

Elements in this array can be accessed using the subscripting [ ] operator:

```
// Write elements in IntArray to cout
for (i = 0; i < 10; i++)
    cout << IntArray[i] << ' ';
cout << '\n';
```

Arrays in C are indexed from 0. The **for** loop just given loops from 0 to 9 (inclusive), since the termination condition is met when i is equal to 10.

Some programmers, especially ones from languages that endorse 1-based arrays such as Pascal and FORTRAN, find 0-based arrays counterintuitive. This is unfortunate, since basing arrays from 0 is crucial to the close relationship between arrays and pointers that is fostered in C. The code in this book numbers array elements from 0. For those who are truly attached to numbering arrays from 1, Press et al. [PRES88] describe a way to use 0-based code: Pass the base of the 1-based array, *plus one*, into the function expecting a 0-based array. For example, to call the InsertionSort template function for a 1-based array:

```
InsertionSort(base+1, N);
```

A.2.2 Pointers

Pointers are data types that contain the location of a value. For every data type, a pointer can be defined to point at an instance of that type. Pointers are designated by appending a * to the type name, as follows:

```
int i;          // Integer
int *pi;        // Pointer to an integer
int **ppi;      // Pointer to a pointer to an integer
```

Pointers are as valid for user-defined types as they are for built-in types. For example:

```
// Define complex number class
#include <complex.h>

    complex c;      // Complex number
    complex *pc;    // Pointer to a complex number
```

The declarations we've shown so far are slightly dangerous. Pointers, like all other variables in C, are created uninitialized. In order to compute the location of an object, you can use the address-of operator &. The & operator is prepended to the object you want the location of, and the result of the expression is a pointer to that object. For example:

```
complex c;            // Complex number
complex *pc = &c;     // pc points at c.
```

Pointers can be manipulated in a number of ways. The most important is *dereferencing*, or examining the object pointed to. The dereferencing operator * is used to dereference a pointer. For example:

```
int i = 12;           // Here is an integer
int *pi = &i;         // pi points at i

i += 2;               // i now equals 14
*pi += 1;             // i now equals 15
```

The prefix * dereferencing operator nicely complements the prefix & address-of operator. For any type T, dereferencing a T * results in a T. In this way, pointer declarations are mnemonic. Writing

```
int *pi;
```

implies that *pi results in an int.

C does define *generic* pointers (void *), which cannot be dereferenced. Generic pointers can contain other types of pointer. They are useful when programmers want to treat memory as raw bytes, rather than the more regimented view imposed when a type is involved. For example, the memcpy library routine in the ANSI C language standard is defined as follows.

```
void memcpy(void *dest, const void *src, size_t n);
```

Since memcpy is intended to be called with a variety of data types, it takes generic pointers as input.

Generic pointers are more useful in C than C++, where parameterized data types (templates, as discussed in Section A.10) can elegantly solve many of the problems that void * is used to solve in C.

A.2.3 Pointers and Arrays

Pointers need not point at a single object. They can point at the base of an array of objects that are stored contiguously in memory. The members of that array can then be accessed using the subscripting [] operator. For example:

```
int array[5] = { 1, 2, 3, 4, 5 };
int *parray = array;

array[0] = 0;    // array now { 0, 2, 3, 4, 5 };
parray[1] = 1;   // array now { 0, 1, 3, 4, 5 };
```

When using a pointer as the base of an array, the number of elements in the array has to be tracked separately. Using pointer/count pairs to specify arrays is a common paradigm in the C programming language, and we've retained it for many of our algorithm implementations. For example, the QuickSort class template can be evaluated to create a template function with the following prototype:

```
void QuickSort(int *base, int N);
```

Calling this function sorts the N elements pointed to by base.

Pointer Arithmetic

Addition and subtraction can be performed on pointers. Adding an integer to a pointer makes it point at subsequent elements in the array of objects that it points to. As an example, let's write a function that prints out an array of integers. We'll start by using the subscripting operator []:

```
void
printarr(int *base, int N)
{
    for (int i = 0; i < N; i++)
        cout << base[i] << ' ';
    cout << '\n';
}
```

This function can be rewritten to use pointer arithmetic, as follows.

```
void
printarr(int *base, int N)
{
    for (int i = 0; i < N; i++) {
        int *pi = base + i;
        cout << *pi << ' ';
    }
    cout << '\n';
}
```

We can even modify the base parameter itself. Since C and C++ pass parameters by value by default, changing base in the function does not affect the caller.

```
void
printarr(int *base, int N)
{
    for (int i = 0; i < N; i++) {
        cout << *base << ' ';
        base += 1;
    }
    cout << '\n';
}
```

Finally, we can use the postincrement operator to write printarr in terms of another popular C paradigm, the *ptr++ paradigm where ptr is a pointer to some object. *ptr++ evaluates to the object pointed to by ptr, then increments ptr to point at the next element in the array. See Kernighan and Ritchie [KERN88].

```
void
printarr(int *base, int N)
{
    for (int i = 0; i < N; i++)
        cout << *base++ << ' ';
    cout << '\n';
}
```

Modern compilers generally will emit the same code for all of these implementations of printarr, so the emphasis in the source code should be on readability rather than efficiency. In my opinion, the first implementation using subscripting is the most readable. We won't often use *ptr++.

Subtracting from a pointer is the opposite of adding to it: It moves the pointer to point at elements that precede the element currently pointed to.

Note: The ANSI standard guarantees that pointer arithmetic will work only if there are elements to point to. That is, creating a pointer that goes out of array bounds is not guaranteed to work. The sole exception to this rule is that a pointer is allowed to point just beyond an array (the Nth element where the elements in the array are numbered from 0 to $N - 1$).

Pointers can be subtracted. The expression p2-p1 gives the number of elements from p1 to p2. Like other pointer arithmetic operations, the ANSI standard has strict guidelines that must be followed for pointer subtraction to be guaranteed to work. p1 and p2 must be of the same type; they must point into the same array; and p1 must point at an element that precedes p2. One consequence of these guidelines is that the result of the expression will be a positive integer.

We don't use many subtle pointer arithmetic operations in this book. However, we use pointer addition quite frequently, when called for. Algorithms such as Merge Sort and Quicksort operate on subarrays in the input data. Pointer addition is a natural way to create a description of a new array that is a subset of the input array.

A.3 Enhancements Over C

A number of enhancements were added to C++ strictly to improve on the C programming language. These include inline functions, overloaded functions, default function arguments, references, and the **const** storage qualifier.

A.3.1 Inline Functions

Inline functions cause the compiler to insert the equivalent code in-line wherever the function is called instead of generating a function call. Because inline functions can cause a formidable amount of object code to be generated, they usually are reserved for small tasks that take almost as little work as the call to the function itself. Efficiency is the sole motivation for inline functions: For small enough functions, avoiding the overhead of the function call is often a large performance win. To guarantee that the compiler knows what code to generate, inline functions are declared in headers rather than in implementation files.

The **inline** directive is a recommendation to the compiler, not an order. Compilers are free to impose restrictions on the generation of inline functions. Many compilers prefer to generate inline functions out-of-line when debugging information is being included in the object file, and most compilers cannot generate code inline for functions that include loop constructs such as **while** or **for**.

A.3.2 Function Overloading

Function names can be overloaded. More than one function can have the same name, on one condition: Each must take a different number of parameters, or the type of at least one of the parameters must differ. This restriction is intended to prevent programmers from writing ambiguous code. Also, it's not sufficient for the return type to differ, or for types to differ only by a storage qualifier.

Although it is legal, explicit function overloading should be avoided. There's no reason to give two functions the same name just for the sake of it. Instead, function overloading should be used implicitly when overloading operators, declaring more than one constructor for a class, or performing other C++-specific tasks that cause functions to be overloaded. For example, one easy way to use function overloading implicitly is to invoke two calls to the QuickSort function template, one to sort an array of **ints** and one to sort an array of **floats**. As discussed in Section A.10, this will result in two distinct QuickSort functions being created by the compiler:

```
void QuickSort(int *base, int N);
void QuickSort(float *base, int N);
```

Because the types of the function arguments vary, the compiler and linker can distinguish between the two.

A.3.3 Default Arguments

The arguments of a function can be declared with default values. This is done by giving an "= value" sequence after each argument that is to have a default value. Declaring

```
float Distance(float x = 0, float y = 0);
```

results in a function that can be called in any of three ways: Distance(x, y); Distance(x), which is equivalent to calling Distance(x, 0); and Distance(), which is equivalent to calling Distance(0, 0). Only the last arguments in the list can have default values. For example, the following declaration is illegal because the second argument does not have a default value:

```
float Distance(float x = 0, float y);
```

Like most C++ features, default arguments should be used with care. They can add greatly to the clarity of code, especially for constructors with a large number of arguments. However, they can make code much less readable if used improperly.

A.3.4 const Storage Qualifier

Objects can be declared **const**. Declaring an object **const** guarantees that it will not be modified after initialization. Besides letting you declare standalone constants, it allows functions to promise not to modify objects passed to them and allows member functions to promise not to modify the object they operate on.

The C++ compiler enforces the promises implied by **const**, so **const** must be used with care. C++ is willing to cast a non-**const** object to a **const** one, but never the other way around.

A few words about pointers and **const** are in order. In a pointer expression, **const** is written just before the object it is **const**-ifying. Thus,

```
const int *cpi;
```

declares a pointer to a **const** int. The pointer can be modified; the object it points to cannot. In contrast,

```
int const *pci;
```

declares a **const** pointer to an int. The int pointed to can be modified, but the pointer cannot.

const can be written more than once in the pointer expression, as follows:

```
const int const *cpci;   // Const pointer to a const
                         // int

// A pointer to a const pointer to a pointer to a
// pointer to a const int.
const int **const*cppcpi;
```

Fortunately, situations this complicated do not occur often in practice. Usually, we'll see **const** T * (pointer to a **const** object) and leave it at that.

A.3.5 References

A reference is a name for another object. References are most useful when used as function return values and function parameter types. Declaring a standalone reference variable is allowed but should be avoided; it is much too complicated to be worth the trouble.

Declaring a reference as a function parameter makes it possible to modify objects passed into the function. For example, the following function squares its parameter.

```
void
Square(double& x)
{
    x = x*x;
}
```

References are described here as an "improvement" over C, but they decrease the clarity of code when used as just shown. Because C++ passes arguments by value by default, using references to modify function arguments makes it less clear to function users that the function may modify the object passed to it.

Efficiency is the principal benefit that references offer. Like passing a pointer, passing a reference to an object often is more efficient than passing the whole object. Unlike passing a pointer, you do not need to take the address of the object when passing it. If you want the efficiency of passing a reference and want to retain the pass-by-value guarantee that the function won't modify the object passed in, use a **const** reference:

```
void SomeFunction(const BigObject& x);
```

Another benefit of references is that when declared as function return types, they allow the function return value to be used as an lvalue. For example, the function:

```
int&
SecondElement(int x[])
{
    return x[1];
}
```

can be used to modify the second element of the array passed to it:

```
int arr[5] = { 1, 2, 3, 4, 5 };
SecondElement(x) = 10;
// arr now contains {1, 10, 3, 4, 5}
```

As when using references as function parameters, this feature should be used with care. In C++, references as function return values usually are used when overloading operators. Operator overloading is described in Section A.9.

A.3.6 new and delete

The new and delete operators largely supplant the dynamic memory allocation facilities offered by C (malloc and free). Instead of writing

```
int *newint = (int *) malloc(sizeof(int));
```

you can write:

```
int *newint = new int;
```

You can also declare arrays with new, as follows.

```
// Allocate an array of 10 integers
int *newints = new int[10];
```

To deallocate memory that was allocated with new, use the delete operator:

```
// Delete the integer allocated above with new
delete newint;
```

To deallocate an array, make sure to put square brackets [ ] after
delete.

```
// Delete the array of integers allocated above
delete[] newints;
```

Technically, new[ ] and delete[ ] (allocation and deallocation
of arrays) are different operators from new and delete (allocation
and deallocation of single objects).

Besides offering type-safe dynamic memory allocation, the new
and delete operators invoke constructors and destructors when
used to allocate user-defined types. Constructors and destructors
will be discussed in detail in the next section.

Most C++ compilers let you use malloc and free, as before,
though the list of reasons to do so is very short. (Forward compat-
ibility when porting from C is one.) And although operators new
and delete usually are implemented in terms of malloc and free,
never mix the two paradigms.

A.4 Classes (Encapsulation)

A class in C++ is a data type defined by the user (as opposed to
primitive data types that are built into C++, such as int and long).
The class definition includes the following information.

Data in the Class (Class Members)

These are declared like other data declarations in C++. Every instance of the class will contain this data. These members can be
accessed using the . operator (for class member access) or the ->
operator (for access through a pointer), provided the client of the
class has the right to access the member. (See the discussion of scope
restriction that follows.)

Functions in the Class (Member Functions)

Member functions are designed to operate on instances of the class.
They take an implicit parameter called this that points to the class
instance that the member function is being called for. Explicit references to this are infrequent, however, because member functions

can refer to members of the class with the implicit knowledge that they are references to the members of that instance of the class.

Scope Restriction of Members (Private, Protected, or Public)

The scope of various members of the class can be restricted. Private members can only be accessed by member functions of the class. Public members can be accessed by anyone. Protected members are a benevolent combination of the two: They are freely accessible by classes that inherit from the class being declared. (Section A.6 discusses inheritance in detail.)

Grants of Access to the Class (Friends)

Friends of the class may access private and other members freely. The class must explicitly grant access to other classes or functions by declaring them friends, however. Friends are not inherited.

Once you have defined a class, you can declare instances of a class. This process is directly analogous to declaring instances of primitive data types. For example, after including the standard C++ header file <complex.h> you are free to write:

```
complex c;            // Create a complex number
complex points[10];   // Create an array of
                      // complex numbers
```

When an instance of a class is created, the compiler calls a special member function called a constructor. Constructors have the same name as the class. A constructor should be thought of as a special member function that takes parameters and uses them to transform raw, uninitialized memory into a valid instance of the class. You can declare as many of them as you like, and they will be overloaded just like other overloaded functions. (They are distinguished by the parameters.) Constructors are called not only when objects come into scope (as in the complex examples just given), but also when the new operator is used to allocate an object dynamically.

In C, you can declare (create) a local variable only at the beginning of a statement block. C++ eases this restriction for efficiency reasons: You don't want constructors and destructors to be called unless absolutely necessary. In C++, you can declare objects wherever you want; their scope extends from their declaration to the end of the statement block they were declared in. When they drop out of scope, they are automatically destroyed by calling their destructor.

Constructors cannot return a value. Exception handling provides a way for problems to be reported and for callers to respond to them appropriately. Section A.8 discusses exception handling in detail.

Several special constructors are always created by the compiler, even if the programmer does not define them in the class. When necessary, programmers should define them, but the compiler often can generate them correctly.

The first special constructor is called the *default constructor*, which takes no arguments. The default constructor is called when an object is created with no arguments.

```
BinaryTree<T> tree;    // BinaryTree<T>::BinaryTree()
                       // called on x.
```

The default constructor is also used when an array of objects is allocated with the new operator. In this case, the default constructor is called for every element in the array. Thus, if an object is going to be allocated in arrays frequently, it is best for default constructors to be as efficient as possible. If no default constructor is given by the programmer, the compiler generates one that calls the default constructors for the class contents and base classes. For concrete classes that contain built-in data types such as int, the compiler's default constructor does nothing. The uninitialized bits are left alone, and it is up to users of the class to ensure they are put into a stable state before use.

Another special constructor, the copy constructor, takes an instance of a class and makes a duplicate. The default copy constructor is a memberwise copy, which suffices for most classes. However, copy constructors must be implemented for classes that are deep, such as linked lists. The default copy constructor will merely copy the head of the linked list to the other linked list instance; once the first linked list is destroyed, the second will become invalid as well (since it pointed to nodes in the first linked list). To avoid this behavior, the copy constructor should create another linked list that contains copies of the nodes in the first. (For completeness, I should mention a more sophisticated and efficient technique available to copy constructors, a lazy evaluation technique called copy-on-write.)

Borrowed from the virtual memory managers of modern operating systems, copy-on-write means the new object that is a "copy" of the original merely contains a reference to the original object, until either object is modified. At that point, the object is actually copied and the modification is made. If neither object is modified over the course of their lifetimes, the copy is never made. Copy-on-write is not implemented in this book.)

The copy constructor takes a reference to the class as input. It then does what is necessary to make another instance of the class that is equivalent to the one given in the parameter list. Virtually all of the class templates implemented in this book, including `BinaryHeap`, `BinaryTree`, and `OSTree`, implement copy constructors.

Classes that need a copy constructor also need to overload the assignment operator. This operation is similar to that of the copy constructor, in that it must convert the class instance into a duplicate of the class instance given. The difference is that the assignment operator operates on a viable instance of the class rather than uninitialized memory. It must destroy the old instance before making a copy of the new instance.

These special member functions get called with impunity by the compiler, and it behooves C++ programmers to know which ones are called in what situations. The following function, which passes back the sine of a complex number and its conjugate, contains a number of implicit calls to special member functions.

```
void
sin2(const complex& x, complex *s, complex *cs)
{
    complex cx = conj(x);
    *s = sin(x);
    *cs = sin(cx);
}
```

Inserting comments where the implicit function calls occur, sin2 can be written as follows.

```
void
sin2(const complex& x, complex *s, complex *cs)
{
    // Copy constructor is used to construct a
```

```
// temporary copy of x, to call conj with.
// Default constructor is used to create the
// return value of conj.
// Copy constructor is used to copy the contents
// of the return value of conj into cx.
complex cx = conj(x);
// Destructor is called on temporary object.

// Copy constructor is used to construct a
// temporary copy of x to call sin with.
// Default constructor is used to create the
// return value of sin.
// Assignment operator is used to copy sin's
// return value to *s.
*s = sin(x);
// Destructor is called on temporary object.

// Default constructor is used to create the
// return value of sin.
// Assignment operator is used to copy sin's
// return value to *cs.
*cs = sin(cx);
// Destructor is called on cx.
}
```

The temporary copies of x created to call conj and sin are necessary because x is a **const** complex &, while conj and sin are both declared to take complex&. Because they are not declared **const**, the compiler creates a temporary to ensure that x is unaffected by the function call.

Contrast the compiler's usage of the copy constructor and the assignment operator. The copy constructor is used to construct cx from raw bits at the beginning of the function call. Later the assignment operator is used to copy function return values to other instances of complex (which presumably have already been constructed).

In fairness, modern C++ compilers can eliminate some of these steps, especially for simple, concrete classes such as complex. The code for the constructors or destructor is frequently declared inline, so the compiler can perform the inline substitution and optimize the resulting code. Also, many C++ compilers will issue warnings about function calls that elicit inefficient-looking calls to constructors.

A.5 Scope Restriction (Data Hiding)

Part of object-oriented programming is trying to treat objects as "black boxes." Allowing direct access to components of an object is inadvisable because it makes tracking the interactions between different parts of a program more difficult. C++ provides extensive facilities for scope restriction to help programmers enforce restricted access to class members. We have already seen some of those facilities in the **private**, **protected**, and **public** directives in the class definition. Declaring class members **public** means anyone can access those members. **Public** access should be reserved for members that are deliberately available to everyone. Declaring class members **private** means only member functions of the class can access them. Declaring class members **protected** is a combination of the two: Derived classes have direct access to the **protected** members of classes they inherit from.

A class can grant direct access to classes and nonmember functions by declaring them *friends*. This is a direct violation of the principal of scope restriction but is sometimes necessary in the face of other concerns.

Even public members of a class have restricted scope: They are restricted to the scope of the class. Class members can be accessed in only a few ways.

- With the . operator applied to an instance of the class (or a derived class).

- With the -> operator applied to a pointer to an instance of the class (or a derived class).

- With the scope resolution operator ::.

Restricting scope is important. Try to restrict the scope of class members to **private** when possible; use **public** only when necessary.

Try to define class relationships so that classes can treat each other as black boxes.

Restricting scope in other contexts is important too. Make variables local to blocks or functions whenever possible. If a variable must persist between function calls, make it **static** to restrict its scope to the file it is declared in. If a variable must be made global, place it in a class to restrict its scope to that class. Any program should contain only a handful of global variables, if any.

A.6 Inheritance

Inheritance is a way for classes to borrow functionality from other classes and refine that functionality to suit their particular needs.

The class that inherits is called the *derived class*; the class it inherits from is called the *base class*. When a class inherits from another, it inherits all of the members and member functions of the base class. In the jargon of object-oriented programming, the derived class bears an IS-A relationship to the base class. For example, the red-black tree, discussed in Chapter 11, is a specialized binary tree that balances itself. A red-black tree is everything that a binary tree is, plus it balances itself after inserting or deleting nodes. Inheritance is perfect for implementing this relationship.

When a class inherits from another, it becomes that class. A RedBlackTree is a BinaryTree. The C++ compiler knows that, so it will automatically convert instances of RedBlackTree to BinaryTree, if necessary. (For example, if you assign a RedBlack-Tree * to a BinaryTree *.) The converse does not hold: a BinaryTree is not necessarily a RedBlackTree, so you must explicitly cast a BinaryTree to RedBlackTree if you somehow know that it is a RedBlackTree and want to deal with it as such.

Of course, other classes can inherit from derived classes in turn. These classes include members that further distinguish them from their base classes. For example, the OSTree class template inherits from RedBlackTree, which inherits from BinaryTree. The principle that a derived class IS-A base class extends from OSTree through RedBlackTree to BinaryTree: An OSTree is a BinaryTree, even though it does not inherit from it directly.

A group of classes related by inheritance is called a *class hierarchy*. The class hierarchy is "rooted" at the class that all the classes in it ultimately inherit from. The BinaryTree class template is the root of a class hierarchy of dynamic data structures for searching.

Inheritance is a mechanism for code reuse, one of the hallmarks of object-oriented programming. Class libraries not only use inheritance internally, as with the BinaryTree class hierarchy; they also let you reuse its code by inheriting from their classes.

A.6.1 Inheritance and Function Overloading

Derived classes can overload functions implemented by their bases. The derived class's implementation will then be called instead of the base class's implementation. For example, RedBlackTree overloads BinaryTree's implementations of Insert and Delete, so it can balance the tree after inserting or deleting a node. If RedBlackTree wants to call BinaryTree's implementation of Insert, it can refer to BinaryTree explicitly using the scoping operator :: as follows.

```
BinaryTree<T>::Insert(x);
```

RedBlackTree does not overload any of the other functions implemented by BinaryTree, since the BinaryTree implementations are suitable. For example, finding the minimum node of a binary tree is the same whether it is a straightforward binary tree or a red-black tree. In this way, RedBlackTree reuses much of the functionality built into the BinaryTree class template.

A.6.2 private and protected Inheritance

The programmer can specify a base class as **public**, **protected**, or **private** when declaring a derived class. This storage restriction applies to the functionality of the base class as perceived by clients of the derived class.

The inheritance described so far is **public**. That is, the **public** facilities of the base class are available to clients of the derived class. The **protected** facilities of the base class are available to the derived class and classes that inherit from it. The **private** facilities of the base class are not accessible to anyone. **public** inheritance embodies the IS-A relationship detailed earlier.

protected inheritance allows the derived class and classes that inherit from it to access the non-**private** facilities of the base class, but hides the **public** interface of the base class from the rest of the world.

private inheritance forces the derived class to interact with its base through the base's **public** interface. The derived class has to behave like any other client of the base class. In effect, the inheritance causes the derived class to contain an instance of the base class without any of the usual effects of inheritance. Declaring an instance of the base class inside the class definition is cleaner than using inheritance. I've never found a case where it made more sense to use **private** inheritance.

A.6.3 Multiple Inheritance

Single inheritance, where the derived class inherits from exactly one base class, solves 99.9 percent of the problems that can be solved by inheritance. But for the other 0.1 percent of the time, the C++ programming language does allow classes to inherit from more than one base class. You can specify as many base classes as you want, each with its own storage restriction.

Multiple inheritance can have strange side effects. Imagine a class D that inherits from classes B and C, both of which inherit from A. Quiz: Are there two instances of A in D? Designs where that question has to be answered should be reconsidered.

When multiple inheritance seems to be called for, think twice. And if you decide to use it, make sure there aren't any ambiguities to make programmers reading the code scratch their heads.

(In case you don't believe me, here's the answer to the quiz: It depends on whether B and C inherited virtually from A. Virtual inheritance means that classes derived from the class being defined will contain only one instance of the base class that is being inherited from virtually. Of course, even if B and C inherit virtually from A, if another class E inherits from A nonvirtually and D inherits from B, C, and E, then D will contain two instances of A anyway. Those of you who enjoy this kind of thing should go read the ARM [ELLI92] and the rest of us will go on to polymorphism. Now that you know why I have a love-hate relationship with C++, take my advice and use single inheritance.)

A.7 Polymorphism

Polymorphism is a way for classes to be treated generically. Imagine creating a class that describes a geometric figure generically, so that when a user clicks the mouse the closest geometric figure can be lit up. Note that we haven't decided yet whether the geometric figure is a circle, a rectangle, or a Bézier spline. All we know is that we want a distance function to decide which is closest.

C++ offers language support for this concept, called *polymorphism*. Let's implement a class called `GeometricFigure` that implements the idea of a generic geometric figure.

```
class GeometricFigure {
public:
    ~GeometricFigure() { }
    double Distance(const Point2D&) = 0;
};
```

Appending "= 0" to the `Distance` member function designates it a pure virtual member function. Pure virtual functions are not actually implemented; they only describe the shape of the class, without giving any specifics. In the case of `GeometricFigure`, `Distance` returns the smallest distance from the given point to the figure.

Any class that contains a pure virtual function is called an *abstract class*. You cannot declare instances of an abstract class; you can only declare pointers and references to one. This is because the definition of the abstract class is deliberately ambiguous—the `GeometricFigure` class not only doesn't know how to compare two instances, it doesn't want to know. Now, when classes inherit from `GeometricFigure`, they are required either to implement all the pure virtual functions declared by `GeometricFigure`, or to leave the pure virtual function unimplemented.

If a derived class leaves any pure virtual function unimplemented, it is an abstract class just like its parent. This "passes the buck" to classes that inherit further down the line.

The former option, implementing all the pure virtual functions declared by the base class, results in a nonabstract class that can be declared just like any other class. Let's declare a class that inherits from `GeometricFigure` and defines the `Distance` member function.

```
class StraightLine : public GeometricFigure {
public:
   // ... Constructors and destructor
   double Distance(const Point2D&);
private:
   double a, b, c; // Normalized equation of the line
};

double
StraightLine::Distance(const Point2D& p)
{
   return fabs(a*p.x + b*p.y + c);
}
```

StraightLine inherits from GeometricFigure, inheriting all of the members of GeometricFigure, including the Distance member function. StraightLine implements Distance, however; now, whenever Distance is called on this object, StraightLine::-Distance will be called whether we know it is a StraightLine or not. Declaring GeometricFigure::Distance **virtual** instructs the compiler to generate the necessary infrastructure for this transparency. The caller does not need to know the type of object that is pointed to; it can call Distance and be confident that the comparison will be performed correctly. Thus, we can write a function that scans through an array of GeometricFigures and returns the closest one to a point.

```
GeometricFigure *
ClosestOne(const Point2D& p,
           GeometricFigure **figures, int N)
{
    double mindist = figures[0]->Distance(p);
    GeometricFigure *ret = figures[0];
    for (int i = 1; i < N; i++) {
        double dist = figures[i]->Distance(p);
        if (dist < mindist) {
            mindist = dist;
            ret = figures[i];
        }
    }

}
```

Virtual functions do not need to be pure. If this is the case, the virtual function implements a default behavior. This default implementation will be called unless it is overloaded by the derived class. The `BinaryNodeHelper` class template (described in Chapter 10) implements many nonpure virtual functions, and the class templates that inherit from it sometimes take advantage of their ability to overload the implementation. The `RedBlackTreeHelper` class template (described in Chapter 11), for example, overloads the `Insert` and `Delete` member functions of `BinaryNodeHelper` so it can balance the tree after inserting or deleting a node.

A.8 Exception Handling

Exception handling is a recent addition to the C++ programming language. Like the object-oriented extensions of the language, exception handling is intended to make large projects easier to implement and maintain. Exception handling allows programs to gracefully report and recover from error conditions that do not occur often in practice (such as "out of memory").

When an error condition is encountered that warrants generating an exception, a program executes a *throw expression*, similar to the following.

```
throw OutOfRange;
```

The expression thrown can be of any type. Usually it is of a type designed to be thrown as an exception, however; then it can contain as much information about the exception as desired.

Once an exception is thrown, the program unwinds the machine stack, calling destructors for objects as it goes, until it encounters an *exception handler* that can handle an exception of the type thrown. The code that caused the exception must have been enclosed in a *try block* to get handled. The syntax for a try block and exception handler is as follows:

```
try {
    // Code that may generate an exception goes here
}
catch (expression) {
    // Code that handles an exception goes here
}
```

Here is a short example program to illustrate how exception handling works.

```cpp
#include <math.h>
#include <stdlib.h>
#include <iostream.h>

class FloatException {
    enum Exception { NegativeSqrt, Overflow } why;
public:
    FloatException(enum Exception _why) { why = _why; }
    enum Exception Why() const { return why; }
    const char *WhyStr() const {
      if (why == NegativeSqrt)
          return "Negative value passed to sqrt";
      else if (why == Overflow) return "Overflow";
    };
    friend double sqrt2(double d);
};

double
sqrt2(double d)
{
  if (d < 0)
    throw FloatException(FloatException::NegativeSqrt);
  return sqrt(d);
}

int
main()
{
    try {
        double sqrt2m = sqrt2(-2);
    }
    catch (const FloatException& exc) {
        cerr << "FloatException detected: ";
        cerr << exc.WhyStr() << ".\n";
        exit(1);
    }
}
```

When executed, calling `sqrt2` with a negative number causes it to throw an exception. The exception handler in `main` then catches the exception and prints an error message ("`FloatException detected: Negative value passed to sqrt.`") before exiting.

You can specify as many `catch` clauses as desired, one after another, to catch different types of exception. The exception-handling mechanism will try to match each one in the order listed. Note that you can't specify a `catch` clause of a base class before that of a derived class, since that would guarantee that the derived class's exception handler would never be called.

`catch (...)` specifies an exception handler that will handle any exception. If present, this handler must be listed last.

If no appropriate handler is found at one level, the program will continue unwinding the stack. If it never finds an appropriate exception handler, a function named `terminate()` is called. By default, `terminate()` prints an error message and terminates the program.

The rules for matching exception handlers to the type of the exception thrown are very similar to those used when matching function calls. According to the *ARM* [ELLI90]:

A handler with type T, `const` T, $T\&$, or `const` $T\&$ is a match for a throw-expression with a type E if:

- T and E are the same type,

- T is a public base class of E, or,

- T is a pointer type and E is a pointer type that can be converted to T by a standard pointer conversion.

In an exception handler, the exception can be rethrown by writing `throw` with no parameters:

```
throw;  // Rethrow exception
```

A function can declare which exceptions it may throw by appending an exception specification to the function declaration, as follows.

```
void A();
void B() throw(X);
void C() throw(X, Y);
void D() throw ();
```

Function A, which lacks an exception specification, could throw any type of exception. Functions B and C declare which types they can throw; it is an error for these functions to attempt to throw exceptions of another type. Function D has declared that it will not throw any exceptions.

Note: A function's exception specification does not affect its type. That is,

```
void A(int a, double d);
```

is indistinguishable from

```
void B(int a, double d) throw(X);
```

The promises made by exception specifications are difficult or impossible for compilers to enforce. Accordingly, there is a runtime mechanism for detecting when a function tries to throw an exception not listed in its exception specification. If this happens, a function called `unexpected()` is called. Since `unexpected()` is called only when something is grievously wrong with the program, by default it simply terminates the program.

Another special function can be invoked by the exception-handling mechanism. If the stack is corrupted, a destructor tries to throw an exception while the exception-handling mechanism is unwinding the stack, or some other unrecoverable tragedy occurs, then `terminate()` is called. Like `unexpected()`, `terminate()` aborts the program immediately by default.

This book does not use exception handling heavily. We restrict its use to classes that are prone to misuse, such as iterators and manipulators. While it may be useful to have a sorting function throw an exception if it is called with a negative count, we haven't taken exception handling to that extreme.

Because many compilers do not yet support exception handling, the source code brackets exception-handling syntax with `#ifdef EXCEPTIONS` preprocessor statements. If your compiler does not support exception handling, just refrain from defining `EXCEPTIONS` and your code will run fine (if a little less robustly).

A.9 Operator Overloading

Operator overloading is a C++ feature that lets you give your own definitions of uses of C++ operators. We use operator overloading to declare pointerlike iterators that operate on binary trees, for example. The overloaded operators allow users of the class to interact with it more intuitively. For example, the contents of a binary tree can be traversed as follows.

```
for (BinaryTree<int>::Iterator iter(bintree);
     iter;
     iter++)
     cout << *iter << '\n';
```

This code prints the contents of the binary tree in order. The second expression in the **for** loop evaluates iter as if it were an integer; in this case, the integer is nonzero unless the iterator no longer points at a binary tree node. The loop terminates when the iterator has touched each element in the binary tree. The postincrement operator moves the iterator to the next element in the binary tree. Finally, the dereferencing operator returns the contents of the element currently pointed to by the iterator. All of these uses are arguably more intuitive than equivalent member functions with names such as Done, GotoNext, or Contents.

The most difficult aspect of operator overloading is the syntax. The overloaded operator is implemented by a function called operator*op* (e.g., operator+, operator<<). Unary operators, such as ~ and the unary + and - operators, are defined either by global functions (typically declared **friends** of the class they operate on) that take a parameter (the object that is being operated on), or by member functions that take no parameters (in which case the object being operated on is the implicit parameter to the member function). The most important difference between declaring the operator function as a member function and declaring it as a global function is that the member function can be overloaded by derived classes. Other than that, it is a matter of taste.

The type of the operator's result is given by the return type of the operator*op* function.

Overloading binary operators such as += and && is more complex. They too can be implemented either by member functions or global friend functions. If the operator is implemented as a member function, that function points to the left-hand operand (it is the implicit first parameter to the function) and the right-hand operand is given by the second parameter. If the operator is implemented as a global function, the function must take two parameters: The first and second correspond to the left- and right-hand operands.

In either case, as with unary operators, the return value gives the result type of the function.

The complex class, declared in the standard header <complex.h>, overloads a multitude of binary operators. They happen to be implemented as global functions (friends of complex). For example, the complex class definition includes a declaration to overload the binary + operator for complex.

```
friend complex operator+(const complex &,
    const complex &);
```

complex.h contains the inline implementation of operator+ later in the file.

It often makes sense to implement overloaded operators as inline functions, as most of the operators for complex are. If the operations being performed are as simple as those performed by the complex operators, then there's not only a significant time savings (because no parameters are pushed and no function is called), but a space savings as well, because calling the function frequently takes as much code as generating code for the function inline.

A.9.1 Limitations and Caveats

You cannot define new operators using the operator overloading mechanism. Nor can you change the precedence or associativity of the existing operators in C++.

Be tasteful when overloading operators. Don't overload operators whose precedence is wrong; for example, don't overload the ^ operator for exponentiation because the multiplication operator has higher precedence.

Model your operators' behavior after the behavior they exhibit during normal code development. The addition operator should take two objects, perform some operation akin to addition, and return another object of the same type.

Don't invent new meanings for operators without good reason. Readers of your code shouldn't have to look in your header to figure out what the operator is doing.

Have some sympathy for the people who read your code. Resist the temptation to sacrifice readability for conciseness.

A.10 Parameterized Data Types

Templates and parameterized data types are a recent addition to the C++ programming language. They complement the mechanisms for code reuse provided by inheritance. A template describes the shape of a related family of functions or classes. After the template has been defined, functions or classes can be instantiated that make use of the template.

Templates are fantasically useful. Almost every function and class in this book is declared as a template so the algorithms can work with *any* data type. Understanding templates is critical to getting the most out of the source code in this book.

Here is a function template that takes the minimum of two values.

```
template<class T>
T
Min(T x, T y)
{
      return (x < y) ? x : y;
}
```

This function template does not declare a function; rather, it declares a family of functions that all take two instances of a class, compares them with the < operator, and returns the smaller one. If you call it with two **ints**, the compiler will declare a function int Min(int, int) that returns the minimum of two integers. If you call it with two floats, the compiler will declare a function float Min(float, float) that returns the minimum of two floating-point numbers. And if you call it with UserDefinedClass, the compiler will use operator<(UserDefinedClass, UserDefinedClass) to compare the two instances of UserDefinedClass and return the first if operator< returns a nonzero value. In the latter case, the programmer is under no obligation to guarantee intuitive operation of the < operator. Since the programmer overloads the operator for the user-defined class (or the compiler will be unable to generate the Min instance of the function template), he or she can define operator< to compare the two instances of the class in any way that is desired.

One disadvantage of function templates is that every time the function is called with a different parameter for the template, another instance of the function is generated. As far as the object code of the program is concerned, the programmer might as well have written separate functions. Function templates are just a way to conserve source code without sacrificing efficiency.

Templates can be used to declare families of classes too. The most obvious application for class templates, and initially the most useful, is in implementing container classes. The `BinaryTree`, `RedBlackTree`, `SplayTree`, and `SkipList` class templates are all container classes. The parameter to the class template is the type that the list will contain.

An *instance* of the class template is a *template class*. Instances are declared using the same angle brackets that were used to declare the template: `BinaryTree<int>` is a binary tree of integers; `BinaryTree<float>` is a binary tree of `float`s. Both of these classes have a lot in common. They both contain root node pointers and have member functions with the same names.

Template classes are just like other classes. They can be inherited from and their **virtual** functions can be overloaded. In fact, inheriting from an instance of a class template often is a good idea. The `BinaryNode` class template inherits from the `BinaryNodeHelper` class template. (See Chapter 10 for a description of this hierarchy of class templates.)

The biggest disadvantage to class templates is the same as the disadvantage to function templates: object code duplication. Although the source code does not contain multiple implementations of `BinaryTree` classes for different types, it might as well from the standpoint of the resulting object code.

A.10.1 Usage Notes

One of the first things people want to do is declare a template class that utilizes a template class as a parameter. For example, a binary tree of linked lists of integers might be declared as follows:

```
BinaryTree<LinkedList<int> > ListTree;
```

Note carefully the space between `<int>` and the closing angle bracket `>`. Without the space, the compiler will parse `>>` as the right-shift operator. The more intelligent compilers will tell you exactly what is wrong, but other compilers will generate a mile-high pile of errors.

Another thing that people want to do, especially when implementing container classes, is declare embedded classes in templates. Iterators and manipulators seem like ready-made applications for embedding a class in a template. `BinaryTree<T>::Iterator` would be the iterator class for the binary tree class template; `SkipList<T>::Iterator` would be the iterator class for the skip list class template.

Unfortunately, classes are difficult for compilers to parse when embedded in class templates. Member functions of such classes are frequently required to be implemented inline, making them much less readable. Until better compiler technology arrives, it may be best to avoid embedding iterator and manipulator classes in template declarations. Instead, you can implement them as separate classes with **private** constructors and declare the classes they iterate on as **friends**.

A.11 Design Issues

C++ has features and limitations that encourage similar solutions to common problems. This section describes some of these design issues and the approaches taken to resolve each in this book.

A.11.1 #define

The #define preprocessor construct is largely obsolete in C++. Macros that declare constants can be replaced by const objects; functionlike macros can be replaced by inline functions. These constructs enforce type safety and allow the compiler to perform automatic type conversions, whereas preprocessor macros do not.

A.11.2 Iterators and Manipulators

Container classes are marvelous examples of the object-oriented paradigm in action. You declare a `SimpleList` class that keeps track of a list of objects in no particular order. You declare member functions for `SimpleList` with such names as `Insert` and `Query`; these functions have well-defined interfaces, and they perform well-defined tasks on instances of the `SimpleList` class. The `SimpleList` class is a "black box." However, this paradigm falls apart once you want to examine the list or insert nodes in a particular order. You are faced with a difficult choice: Should you make the elements of `SimpleList` **public** so users of the class can manipulate a `SimpleList` more effectively?

To avoid having to make the members of `SimpleList` **public**, obviating many of the benefits of an object-oriented approach, people typically define classes called *iterators* and *manipulators* that serve to examine and modify an instance of a `SimpleList`, respectively. Every instance of the `SimpleList` class template contains a class called `Iterator` (which, since it is declared within the scope of the `SimpleList` template, has the name `SimpleList<T>::Iterator`) that can be used to examine the objects in the list. An instance of `SimpleList<T>::Iterator` has a pointer to one of the elements in the linked list.

Another class called `SimpleList<T>::Manipulator` lets you modify the list by adding and deleting elements at the location of the current pointer.

The `SimpleList` class has to cooperate with its iterators and manipulators. For the sake of safety, for example, it is illegal to add or delete items from a linked list when an iterator is attached. To ensure that this does not happen, every `SimpleList` has a count of `Iterators` and `Manipulators` attached to it.

A.11.3 Read-only Access to Class Members

Often it is necessary for users of a class to access members of that class. The principle of scope restriction holds that providing this access is a violation of the class's integrity. A good compromise is to declare the class member **private** and provide a **public** access function that returns the member without allowing users of the class to modify it.

A.11.4 The static Keyword

static is a storage qualifier that means different things in different places. Many of its meanings are inherited from C, and C++ adds a few of its own.

When applied to a variable that is outside the scope of a function (a global variable), **static** restricts the scope of that variable to the file it is declared in. Similarly, when applied to a global function,

static restricts the scope of the function to the file. If a variable must be persistent, try to make it **static** so functions in other files cannot access it.

When applied to a data member of a class, **static** makes it persistent within the class; that is, not every instance of a class contains the member. Static data members of a class should be thought of as global variables belonging to that class. Static member functions do not take an implicit parameter; they must access members of class instances with . or ->.

APPENDIX **B**

The Disk

This appendix briefly describes the sample programs supplied with the book. After a brief overview of the environments and compilers supported and the directory structure that the source code is contained in, Section B.3 describes how to build the HIRES library, which must be built before building any of the sample programs. Section B.4 describes the sample programs for sorting and how to build them. Sections B.5 and B.6 describe the sample programs for searching and selection, respectively. Finally, Section B.7 describes various problems that you may encounter when trying to build for UNIX.

B.1 Environments and Compilers

The source code included with this book implements all of the algorithms described, plus numerous sample programs to test out the various algorithms and data structures and illustrate their use. The source code has been run under MS-DOS, Windows 3.1, Windows NT, and UNIX (actually IRIX, the Silicon Graphics flavor of UNIX). For MS-DOS and Windows 3.1, the environment used was Borland C++ 4.0. For Windows NT, either Borland C++ 4.0 or Microsoft Visual C++ 2.0 can be used.

When invoking Borland C++ 4.0 in an MS-DOS shell under Windows 3.1, the compiler will behave erratically if it runs out of memory. To make sure it will have enough memory, use the .PIF editor to edit DOSPRMPT.PIF (or whichever .PIF file you are going to use to execute BCC). Toward the bottom and on the right, just above the "Execution" checkboxes, the limit on the XMS memory available to the DOS shell is given (usually 1024K, or 1 megabyte). You probably need to increase this limit to at least 4096K. To remove any limit, enter −1. This will ensure that the command-line compiler will have enough memory to run.

Use caution when building for MS-DOS or 16-bit Windows. Because these programs are built in the Large model, they can handle arrays only up to 64K in length. It is easy to type a command line that attempts to allocate larger-than-64K arrays if you aren't careful. The programs don't check for this because it is so environment-specific. (Besides, they are intended to be illustrative, not production-quality.)

When executing recursive functions on large data sets, you may run out of stack space. For example, the SelectRecursive function template is run by the TIMESEL sample program. If you are going to be running these algorithms on large data sets, you will want to stick to the iterative implementations. Otherwise, consult your compiler's documentation to see how to increase the stack size of your program; the default stack size will not be enough to run on very large data sets.

B.2 Directory Structure

The default installation creates a directory structure like the one that follows.

Directory	Contents
\SSSCODE	All source code.
\INCLUDE	Include directory where all the headers are.
\HIRES	Source code for the high-resolution timer library.
\SORT	Source code for the sorting sample programs.
\SEARCH	Source code for the searching sample programs.
\SELECT	Source code for the selection sample programs.

B.3 Building the HIRES Library

Some of the sample code does performance analysis of the various algorithms and data structures. For the most accurate possible timing, a library called HIRES ("high-resolution") is provided. When available, HIRES is designed to use the clock-cycle counters on modern microprocessors such as the Pentium, PowerPC, and Alpha. (Only the Alpha is currently supported, but implementing support for other processors should be easy.) If no cycle counter is available, HIRES uses standard APIs such as Windows' GetTickCount to do reasonably accurate timing. The sample programs stay the same no matter which HIRES implementation is running.

The HIRES library lets the sample programs use a uniform API to time operations. Listing B.1 gives <hires.h>, the header file for all HIRES implementations. This header is included by sample programs that perform timing.

Listing B.1. <hires.h> header file.

```
/* ===========================================================
 * hires.h
 *    Header file for high-resolution timer library.
 * Copyright (C) 1995 by Nicholas Wilt.  All rights reserved.
 * =========================================================== */

#ifdef __cplusplus
extern "C" {
#endif

typedef struct _hires_t {
    /* Enough space for any of the schemes implemented so far. */
unsigned long lo, hi;
} hires_t;

/* Get the current high-resolution time. */
void hires_gettime(hires_t *now);

/* Compute the difference between the ending time and the
 * beginning time. This number is in seconds, if possible;
 * for cycle-counting resolution, it should be in cycles.
 */
double hires_difftime(hires_t *beg, hires_t *end);
```

```
/* Return the resolution (in Hz) of the timer, or -1 if the
 * resolution is effectively infinite (e.g. clock cycle counter).
 */
long hires_resolution(void);

#ifdef __cplusplus
};
#endif
```

hires_gettime is called before and after the event being timed. hires_gettime writes to a hires_t structure that records an absolute measure of the time (e.g., milliseconds since the computer was turned on). hires_difftime can then be called to compute the difference between these two times. Normally hires_difftime returns the number of seconds that elapsed. When the HIRES implementation is using a cycle counter, hires_difftime returns the number of cycles. (There is no portable way to determine the clock rate to convert to seconds.)

The function hires_resolution returns the resolution of the timer in Hz (e.g., the millisecond timer in Windows returns 1000). In the case of the effectively infinite resolution presented by cycle counters, hires_resolution should return $-1L$.

The hires_t type is large enough that it can contain any count that might be used by any of the HIRES implementations. It's 64 bits long, so it can even contain the cycle count for a Pentium without overflowing. For the convenience of lower-resolution timing methods, the 64-bit structure is split into high and low halves.

HIRES.LIB must be built for the platform you choose *before* any of the sample programs. Look in the following chart for your environment, and follow the instructions to build HIRES.LIB.

Environment	Command Line to Build
MS-DOS (Borland C++ only)	`make -fmakefile.dos`
Windows 3.1 (Borland C++ only)	`make -fmakefile.win`
Windows NT (Borland C++)	`make -fmakefile.bnt`
Windows NT (Visual C++)	`nmake -fmakefile.nt`
Windows NT for the Alpha (Visual C++ only)	`nmake -fmakefile.axp`

The Alpha version uses the process cycle counter for high-resolution timing. If you prefer to use the standard Windows NT API (which has millisecond resolution), just use the NT makefile.

The HIRES directory contains many files because it has every implementation of the HIRES library (MS-DOS, Windows NT, Alpha). For each environment, the files that participate in the build are listed.

Environment	Source Files
MS-DOS (Borland C++ only)	`makefile.dos`, `hires.dos`
Windows 3.1 (Borland C++ only)	`makefile.win`, `hires.dos`
Windows NT (Borland C++)	`makefile.bnt`, `hires.nt`
Windows NT (Visual C++)	`makefile.nt`, `hires.nt`
Windows NT for the Alpha (Visual C++ only)	`makefile.axp`, `hires.axp`, `rpcc.asm`
UNIX	`makefile.unx`, `hires.unx`

B.4 Sorting

If you are using Visual C++ for NT, each sample program has a .MAK file that can be used to build it. The existing files can build for the Intel and Alpha platforms; if you are targeting MIPS or the PowerPC, you will get a warning that you have to create a new target to build on the new platform. This can be done from the "Project/Targets..." dialog.

Also if you are using VC++, add the INCLUDE directory (e.g., `C:\SSSCODE\INCLUDE`) to the list of Include directories in the "Tools/Options.../Directories" dialog. (Directories is a file tab in the Options dialog.)

If you would rather just invoke a `makefile` from the command line and have it build all the sample programs, check the following chart and type the corresponding command line.

Environment	Command Line to Build
MS-DOS (Borland C++ only)	`make -fmakefile.dos`
Windows 3.1 (Borland C++ only)	`make -fmakefile.win`

Windows NT (Borland C++)   `make -fmakefile.bnt`

Windows NT (Visual C++)   `nmake -fmakefile.nt`

Note: There is no separate version of the Visual C++ makefile for the Alpha. Only HIRES has an Alpha-specific version; all the other Windows NT code is portable between different platforms.

The following list gives each program in the directory, its command-line arguments, and a brief description of what it does.

`TESTHEAP <numints> [seed]` This program serves as an example use of the `BinaryHeap` class template. It also does a sanity check to verify that the heap implementation is working correctly. `<numints>` is the number of integers to insert into the heap; if desired, the user also can specify a seed for the random number generator. If a problem arises during the test, the seed can be used to ensure that the problem can be reproduced.

`TESTSORT <cnt of items to sort>` This program tests the various sorting algorithms on an array. The length of the array is given by the user.

`TIMESORT <iterations> <cnt of items to sort> <algorithm>` This program uses the HIRES library to time a number of runs of the sorting algorithm given by the user. A `<cnt of items to sort>`-long array is randomized and sorted `<iterations>` times. The program reports the time it took to sort each array.

`<algorithm>` This is an integer in the range 0 to 8, as follows:

    0 Insertion Sort
    1 Selection Sort
    2 Shell Sort
    3 Recursive Merge Sort
    4 Iterative Merge Sort
    5 Recursive Quicksort
    6 Quicksort (median-of-three)
    7 Quicksort (full-blown)
    8 Heapsort

B.5 Searching

Building the sample programs for searching is the same as building the ones for sorting. You can use a project file (.MAK) under Visual C++ for Windows NT, or invoke a make from the command line.

The following list gives each program in the SEARCH directory, its command-line arguments (if any) and a brief description of what it does.

`BINTREE <number of items> [seed]` This program beats up the various dictionary classes by inserting and deleting items, invoking the copy constructor and assignment operator for each, and calling the `CheckInvariant` member function constantly to ensure that the data structure's integrity is always intact. The `<number of items>` parameter tells how many items to insert into each dictionary. The optional seed is used if a problem arises: By specifying the same seed, you can reproduce the same behavior whenever you want. Once you find a seed value that elicits a problem, you can rerun the program under the debugger over and over until you find and fix the problem.

`QUEUE` This program inserts ten random numbers into a queue, then removes them and prints them out. They should be printed in the same order they were inserted. (The first line of numbers printed by the program shows the order of insertion.) Besides illustrating how to use a queue, it tests the copy constructor and assignment operator for the `QueueLList` class template.

`STACK` This program inserts ten random numbers into a stack, then removes them and prints them out. They should be printed in the reverse order of insertion. (The first line of numbers printed by the program shows the order of insertion.) Besides illustrating how to use a stack, it tests the copy constructor and assignment operator for the `StackLList` class template.

`TIMING <numelms>` This program tests the performance of the various dictionary data structures by inserting elements in sorted order, reverse-sorted order, and random order.

B.6 Selection

Building the sample programs for selection is the same as building the ones for sorting and searching. You can use a project file (.MAK) under Visual C++ for Windows NT, or invoke a make from the command line.

The following list gives each program in the directory, its command line arguments (if any) and a brief description of what it does.

OS This program is a brutal test of the OSTree class template and, since OSTree is derived from RedBlackTree, the RedBlackTree class template is thoroughly tested as well. The program works by inserting 1,000 items into the order-statistics tree, checking invariants all the way. Then it performs selection on each item inserted into the tree, making sure each one can be found properly. It then deletes one item from the order-statistics tree and selects all the items in the tree again. Once the tree is empty, it goes back and starts inserting random items again. The insert/select/delete process is repeated 1,000 times. This program smoked out many bugs in the red-black and order statistics tree implementations.

SELECT This program illustrates how to use the selection function templates. The version shipped on the disk uses the Select function template. If desired, you can change the calls to Select to SelectRecursive, SelectFR, or SelectLinear. The behavior of the program should not change.

TIMESEL <number of elements> <number of repetitions> This program uses the HIRES library to time the various selection algorithms (SelectRecursive, Select, SelectFR, and SelectLinear). The timing results obtained by this program are summarized in Chapter 16.

B.7 Building for UNIX

I have provided some code that will help you build under UNIX, but you should be aware that UNIX is a family of environments, not a unified, well-defined environment. The makefiles and source code should work, but they may require minor modifications.

The quality of C++ compilers for UNIX varies. I could not test some of my sample programs on my Indy because the SGI compiler does not support embedded classes in templates. (This makes several of the class templates provided with the book unavailable.) Also, I ran into an interesting preprocessing problem: The comment in line 4 of `select.C` that could only be solved by removing an apostrophe after "Point2D." I could not have anticipated these problems before I attempted the port, nor can I anticipate the problems you may encounter, so please be tolerant while you are trying to get the code to work.

B.7.1 Filename Conventions

Before you can build for UNIX, you have to copy the source code from a PC to your workstation. Keep the same directory structure, except name the files and directories using lowercase. (This is standard UNIX.) You can do the transfer using FTP or rcp over the network. Once the files are copied, you need to make sure all the filenames are in lowercase (`ORDER.H` gets renamed to `order.h`, etc.). In addition, C++ source files have an extension of `.C` (capital C) rather than `.cpp`; thus, `SELECT.CPP` should be renamed to `select.C`.

Note: Text files in MS-DOS have two major differences from ones in UNIX. First, MS-DOS has two line terminators, while UNIX only has one. Second, MS-DOS terminates the file with a ctrl-Z (ASCII 26) character, while UNIX uses a ctrl-D character. Unless it knows better, your file transfer program will happily append the UNIX terminator character after the MS-DOS terminator. If left in, the ctrl-Z character will cause some compilers to fail, so be sure to check for this problem if the compiler generates "illegal character" errors. It's easy to remove the character with a text editor such as `vi`, if necessary.

B.7.2 Building HIRES

You are now ready to use the file `makefile.unx` to build the HIRES library, as follows.

```
make -f makefile.unx
```

The implementation included with the book uses the `gettime-ofday()` library function. If you're not sure whether your UNIX environment has this library function, you can type man gettime-ofday at the command prompt to check. If not, you have to reimplement HIRES using another high-resolution timer available in your environment. Of course, not all of the sample programs depend on HIRES, so you can live without it too.

B.7.3 Building the Samples

Once you have built HIRES, you should wind up with a library named hires.a in your hires directory. You can then invoke make in the sort, search, and select subdirectories that are parallel to the hires directory.

```
make -f makefile.unx
```

(Make sure there is a space after the -f parameter.)

These makefiles will build the equivalent executables to the ones that you can build on your PC. Because of the problem I mentioned about my UNIX compiler not supporting embedded classes in class templates, the commands to build some of the executables that depend on this feature have been commented out. If your UNIX compiler supports this C++ feature, you can uncomment those lines and build those samples as well.

Glossary

amortized runtime   Runtime averaged over a number of operations.

asymptotic runtime   Description of how the runtime of an algorithm is affected as the number of inputs increases toward infinity.

binary tree   Dynamic data structure made up of nodes that each contain up to two children. Binary trees form the basis for many other data structures.

circular linked list   Linked list where the "last" node's Next pointer points to the first node.

compare   Examine two elements to determine which should precede the other in the sorted order.

constant factor   A difference in performance that does not affect the asymptotic runtime. For example, implementing a certain algorithm in assembler may make it run faster than if it is implemented in a high-level language, but the runtimes of both implementations will grow similarly as the number of inputs grows.

diminishing increment sort   A sorting algorithm that works by sorting interleaved subarrays whose elements are a fixed increment h apart. The array is sorted by repeatedly sorting interleaved subarrays with smaller increments with a final pass at $h = 1$. Shell Sort is a diminishing increment sort. (See Chapter 3.)

doubly-linked list   A linked list that contains two pointers, one to the predecessor node and one to the successor node.

dynamic data structure   A data structure that is designed to easily grow and shrink in size, as required.

expected runtime   Runtime that is prohibitively likely to occur but that may degrade under special circumstances.

external sorting   A sorting technique designed to sort more elements than can fit in the computer's memory.

finger   A pointer into a data structure for searching usually intended to make queries faster.

internal sorting   A sorting technique designed to work with elements that are all in the computer's memory.

iterator   An object designed to traverse a data structure nondestructively.

key   The part of a data structure that is used to compare two elements.

lazy evaluation   A technique that puts off computation until absolutely necessary. The idea is that some or most computations never will become necessary, so putting them off is a good idea. Copy-on-write, where objects aren't actually copied until one of the two objects is modified, is a good example of lazy evaluation. If neither object is modified before one of the objects is no longer needed, the copy operation never occurs and lazy evaluation pays off.

linear algorithm   An algorithm whose runtime is $O(N)$.

manipulator   An object designed to traverse a data structure. Manipulators are like iterators but may modify the object they traverse.

operating system   Software that renders hardware abstract and provides services to use it effectively.

order statistic   The ith item in the sorted order. For example, the median is the $(N/2)$th element in the sorted order.

order statistics tree   A dynamic data structure that can quickly compute order statistics on its contents. Order statistics trees are described in Chapter 15.

priority queue   A dynamic data structure that supports `Insert` and `ExtractMin` operations.

probabilistic   In the context of computer algorithms, an adjective that means using random number generators to make worst-case scenarios unlikely. For example, a Quicksort implementation that partitions about a random element takes a probabilistic approach to avoiding its $O(N^2)$ worst-case runtime.

quadratic algorithm   An algorithm whose runtime is $O(N^2)$.

red-black tree   Balanced binary tree that guarantees $O(\lg N)$ performance for most operations. Chapter 11 describes red-black trees.

satellite data   The "non-key" data that accompanies an element that is to be sorted, searched on, or selected.

searching   Finding a query element in a data structure. Part II is on searching.

selection   Determining the ith element in the sorted order. Part III is on selection.

singly-linked list   A linked list whose nodes each contain a pointer to the succeeding node.

skip list   A probabilistic data structure that augments linked lists.

sorting   Reordering elements so they are in sorted order. Part I is on sorting.

splay tree   An adaptive binary tree that moves frequently accessed elements toward the root to optimize access time.

stable   In the context of sorting, a stable sort does not reorder elements with equal keys.

symmetric   In the context of binary tree operations, a pair of operations whose only difference is that references to the left and right children are swapped. For example, left and right rotation are symmetric.

translation lookaside buffer (TLB)   A construct in the memory management unit of a processor that quickly resolves virtual memory references into physical addresses.

virtual memory   In the context of sorting, searching, and selection, virtual memory lets the computer use its hard disk to pretend it has more physical memory.

Bibliography

ABRA83   Abramson, N. *Information Theory and Coding*. McGraw-Hill, New York, 1983. As cited by Sleator and Tarjan [SLEA85].

BAYE72   Bayer, R. and E. M. McCreight. Organization and maintenance of large ordered indexes. *Acta Informatica*, 1 (3): 173–189, 1972.

BENT86   Bentley, Jon. *Programming Pearls*. Reading, MA: Addison-Wesley, 1986.

BENT88   Bentley, Jon. *More Programming Pearls*. Reading, MA: Addison-Wesley, 1988.

BLUM73   Blum, Manuel, Robert W. Floyd, Vaughan Pratt, Ronald L. Rivest, and Robert E. Tarjan. Time bounds for selection. *Journal of Computer and System Sciences*, 7 (4): 448–461, 1973.

BOTT62   Bottenbruch, H. Optimized binary search. *Journal of the ACM 9* (1962), 214.

BROW77   Brown, Mark R. *The Analysis of a Practical and Nearly Optimal Priority Queue*. Ph.D. thesis, Computer Science Department, Stanford University, 1977. Technical Report STAN-CS-77-600.

CORB68   Corbato, F. J. *A Paging Experiment with the Multics System*. MIT Project MAC Report MAC-M-384, May 1968.

CORM90 Cormen, T., C. Leiserson, and R. Rivest. *Introduction to Algorithms*. Cambridge: MIT Press, 1990.

ELLI90 Ellis, Margaret and Bjarne Stroustrup. *The Annotated C++ Reference Manual*. Reading, MA: Addison-Wesley, 1990.

FLOY75 Floyd, Robert W. and Ronald L. Rivest. Expected time bounds for selection. *Communications of the ACM*, 18 (3): 165–172, 1975.

FRED87 Fredman, Michael L. and Robert E. Tarjan. Fibonacci heaps and their uses in improved network optimization algorithms. *Journal of the ACM*, 34 (3): 596–615, 1987.

HOAR62 Hoare, C. A .R. Quicksort. *Computer Journal*, 5 (1): 10–15, 1962.

KERN88 Kernighan, B. and D. Ritchie. *The C Programming Language*, 2nd ed. Reading, MA: Addison-Wesley, 1988.

KNUT73 Knuth, Donald E. *The Art of Computer Programming: Sorting And Searching*. Reading, MA: Addison-Wesley, 1973.

MAGU93 Maguire, Steve. *Writing Solid Code*. Redmond, WA: Microsoft Press, 1993.

PAETO Paeth, Alan W. Median-finding on a 3x3 grid. In *Graphics Gems*, Andrew Glassner ed. Boston: Academic Press, 1990, 171–175.

PETE57 Peterson, W. W. Interpolation search. *IBM Journal of Research and Development* 1 (1957), 131–132.

PRES88 Press, William H., Brian P. Flannery, Saul A. Teukolsky, and William T. Vetterling. *Numerical Recipes in C*. Cambridge: Cambridge University Press, 1988.

PUGH90 Pugh, William. *A skip list cookbook*. Tech Report CS-TR-2286.1. University of Maryland, July 1989.

PUGH92 Pugh, William. *Concurrent maintenance of skip lists*. Tech Report CS-TR-2222.1. University of Maryland, July 1992.

RIVE72 Rivest, Ronald L. and Donald E. Knuth. Bibliography 26: Computing Sorting. *Computing Reviews* 13 (6), June, 1972.

SEDG78 Sedgewick, Robert. *Quicksort*. New York: Garland, 1978.

SEDG92 Sedgewick, Robert. *Algorithms in C++*. Reading, MA: Addison-Wesley, 1992.

SHEL59 Shell, Donald L. A high-speed sorting procedure. *Communications of the ACM* 2 (July, 1959): 30–32, 1959.

SLEA85   Sleator, D. D. and R. E. Tarjan. Self-adjusting binary search trees. *Journal of the ACM* 32 (July 1985), 652–686.

VUIL78   Vuillemin, Jean. A data structure for manipulating priority queues. *Communications of the ACM*, 21 (4): 309–315, 1978.

WILL64   Williams, J. W. J. Algorithm 232 (heapsort). *Communications of the ACM*, 7: 347–348, 1964.

Using the Disk

Making a Backup Copy

Before you start to use the enclosed disk, we strongly recommend that you make a backup copy of the original. Remember, however, that a backup disk is for your own personal use only. Any other use of the backup disk violates copyright law. Please take the time now to make the backup, using the instructions below:

1. Insert your DOS disk into drive A of your computer (assuming your floppy drive is "A").
2. At the A:>, type DISKCOPY A: A: and press Return. You will be prompted by DOS to place the disk to be copied into drive A.
3. Place the master disk into drive A.

Follow the directions on the screen to complete the copy. When you are through, remove the new copy of the disk and label it immediately. Remove the original disk and store it in a safe place.

User Assistance and Information

John Wiley & Sons, Inc. is pleased to provide assistance to users of this package. Should you have questions regarding the installation of this package, please call our technical support number at (212) 850-6194 weekdays between 9 A.M. and 4 P.M. Eastern Standard Time.

To place additional orders or to request information about other Wiley products, please call (800) 879-4639.

Index